SUPERYOUNG

Superyoung

The Proven Way
to Stay Young Forever

Dr David Weeks and Jamie James

CORONET BOOKS
Hodder & Stoughton

Copyright © 1998 by Dr David Weeks and Jamie James

The right of Dr David Weeks and Jamie James to be identified as
the Authors of the Work has been asserted by them in accordance
with the Copyright, Designs and Patents Act 1988.

First published in Great Britain in 1998
by Hodder and Stoughton
A division of Hodder Headline PLC

A Coronet paperback

10 9 8 7 6 5 4 3 2 1

A CIP catalogue record for this title
is available from the British Library.

ISBN 0 340 68234 5

Typeset by Hewer Text Ltd, Edinburgh
Printed and bound in Great Britain by
Clays Ltd, St Ives PLC

Hodder and Stoughton
A division of Hodder Headline PLC
338 Euston Road
London NW1 3BH

CONTENTS

AUTHORS' NOTE

The research contained in this book was directed by Dr David Weeks; the book was written jointly by Dr Weeks and Jamie James. However, we use 'I' in the text in order to tell the story of the research as clearly and directly as possible. Where 'I' is used, it refers to Dr Weeks' thinking and research. Jamie James conducted all the interviews with the designated celebrities, and Dr Weeks and members of his research team carried out all the other interviews, tests and assessments.

ACKNOWLEDGEMENTS

It is impossible to do any long-term research study, such as the one upon which this book is based, without being obliged to a great number of people. These friends and colleagues generously provided good advice, encouragement, practical help and support, inspiration, and honest feedback. We would like to express our gratitude to all of the following people:

In America, Dr Patch Adams, the late and great Dr Isaac Asimov, John Brockman, Jordan Elgrably, Kevin J. Fleming, Valerie Harper, Harvey Horton, Dr Cecilia Hurwich, Bart Matheny, Katinka Matson, Dorothy Munro, Missy Peterson, Adam Rothberg, Marysue Ricci, the late Dr B. F. Skinner, Diana Stoneberg, Chief Tantaquidgeon, Professor Henry L. Tischler, and David's brothers, Bill and Chris Weeks.

In England and Wales, Dawn Bates, Rachel Bond, the late Dr Donald Broadbent, Richard Carr-Gomm, Professor Anthony Clare, Dr John Clark, Steve Commer, Rodney Elgie, Dr David Fontana, Dr Chris Gilleard, John Graham-White, Professor Mark Griffiths, Anna Hodson, Annabel Huxley, Linda Jackson, Dr Ron Lyle, John McCrone, Dr Kevin Morgan, Professor Elaine Murphy, Dr Richard Smith, Tammy Spencer, Dr Paul Spicker, Dr Simon B. N. Thompson, Professor Anthea Tinker, Rowena Webb, and Sarah, Duchess of York.

In Scotland, Dr Kirsty Anderson, Dr Simon Backett, Dr Halla Beloff, Dr John Beloff, the late Jill Birrell, Dr Douglas Blackwood, Dr Bill Boyd, Professor Emeritus Eric Burke, Dr Jonathan Chick, Professor Jack Cohen, Professor Richard DeMarco, Dr Rathi Ann Guldberg, Dr Mike Hepworth, Drummond Hunter, Dr Alan Jacques, Professor Robert E. Kendell, Dr Stephen King, Dr John Loudon, Ralph McGuire, Dr Angus McKay, Kathryn McKay, Karen McKenzie, Professor Robert McLennan, Ray Milne, Stanley Mitchell, Professor Robert Morris, Donna Morrison, Dr Paul Morrison, Dave

Peck, Dr André Phanjoo, Dr Alistair Philip, Professor Steve Platt, Dr David Player, all the staff of Project Ability Glasgow, Margaret Reid, Dr Sam Robinson, Dr Hilary Roxborough, Dr David St Clair, Dr Rhea Shedden, Dr Alec Stuart, Dorothy Walster, Kate Ward, Tom Ward, Glenda Watt, Dr Lawrence Whalley, Janice Whittick, Professor Jimmy Williamson, and Jacqueline Wilson.

In Belgium, Dr Herman Le Compte.

In Germany, Dr Gunter Ammon and Christian Franz.

In Australia, Dr Elsie Harwood.

In Japan, Zenya Hamada.

Our project is also greatly indebted to numerous professionals throughout the world who work in mass media broadcast, documentary work and print journalism. They have greatly helped us to reach out to many of the subjects of our study, and, in the process of being interviewed by many of them, helped us to better conceptualize our thoughts and observations. We especially would like to thank the following individuals, who have invariably treated our endeavours with much courtesy and understanding: Allison Alan-Booth, Clive Anderson, Dominic Arkright, Andrew Baker, Richard Baker, Simon Bates, Geraldine Bedell, Peta Bee, Anna Bergman, Alexandra Black, Fiona Black, Sharon Black, Jessica Bondy, Martin Bisker, Amelia Bowman, Jackie Brown, Inke Burke, Beverly Campbell, Rob Carey, John Carson, Julia Clark, Mary Conder, Emma Cook, Glenda Cooper, Virginia Crompton, Lorraine Dakers, John Darnton, Kate Devine, Aileen Docherty, Ian Dovaston, Andrew Duncan, John Dunn, John Evans, Liz Feely, Ronald Faux, Annabel Ferriman, Dan Fields, Jessica Fowler, Lorna Frame, Louise France, Dave Freeman, Bridget Freier, Ron Geraci, Bill Gibb, Gillian Glover, Richard Glover, Johanna Hall, Lee Hamblin, David Hamilton, Joyce Hannah, David Harron, Andrew Harvey, Nathalie Haughton, Brian Hayes, Stephanie Hazeldean, John Heriott, Roger Highfield, Charlie Hoff, Sally Holloway, Carl Honore, Nikki Hope, Mary Hopkins, Brenda

Acknowledgements

Houghton, Gloria Hunniford, Diana Hutchinson, John Illman, Richard Ingrams, Linda Jackson, David Jacobs, Cathy James, Derek Jamieson, Jackie Kemp, Richard Kilroy-Silk, Christine Kinnear, Hans-Hermann Klase, Tom Knight, Maggy Lennon, Magnus Linklater, Tom Little, Eleanor Logan, Elsa McAlonan, Gavin McCarthy, Neil MacKay, Victoria McKee, Fiona McKinnon, Ron McManus, Jill Manley, Daniel Mason, Marie Claire Mason, Sharon Maxwell-Magnus, Corinne Meyer, Meg Milne, Joanna Morgan, Rachel Munro, Sarah Naylor, Angela Neustadter, Victor Olliver, Joe O'Shea, Mike Parr, Roland Peece, Rebecca Penrose, Nikki Phillips, Sue Phillips, Henry Porter, Christopher Price, Gian Quaglieni, Elizabeth Quigley, Joanne Rae, Gareth Roberts, Liz Roberts, Kitty Robinson, Helen Rogers, Sybil Ruscoe, Michael Ryan, Marilyn Smith, Julie Smythe, Helena St James, John Stapleton, Hannah Stephenson, Anastasia Stevens, Corinne Streich, Gill Swain, Niall Sweeney, John Taylor, Sue Tranter, Edna Tromans, Francesca Turbey-Green, William Underhill, Jon Ungoed-Thomas, Penny Walk, Johnny Walker, Sue Walker, Mike Walsh, Geoff Watts, Michael Watts, Cath Wiener, Andrew Wilson, Nigel Wrench, Agnes Wright, Colin Wright, and Jimmy Young.

We reserve especial acknowledgement and warmest gratitude for all our research participants, without whom this work could never have been done. They fulfilled our hopes and expectations, but often surprised us too. Throughout, they gave us as much help and information as was needed, and usually did much more besides. We greatly value their patience, delightful humour and tolerance in doing so.

Jamie James wishes to thank Lindsley Cameron and Teri Noel Towe for their advice and support in writing this book.

PART ONE

The Superyoung Project

CHAPTER ONE

THE RESEARCH

Grow old along with me!
The best is yet to be.
Robert Browning

When Antonia Barber made the mistake of mentioning her age at a dinner party, her host grabbed her by the arm, pulled her over to a lamp, and studied her face under the strong light. 'I don't believe it,' he declared. 'There's no way you can possibly be forty-six.'

That was sixteen years ago: since then, Antonia, a successful author of children's books, has avoided mentioning her age, because it invariably elicits that incredulous response. At five feet six inches and weighing less than nine stone, her healthy figure radiates vitality, and her steel-blue eyes glint vivaciously; even under a strong light, the faint laugh lines around her eyes are scarcely visible. 'If you're not careful, it can become the most interesting thing about you,' she says. 'At sixty-two, I look and feel fifty' – trained, impartial observers would later guess her to be in her forties – 'so I think of myself as having a 20 per cent discount on age. Why should people who are born in the same year all be thought of as the same age?'

At thirty, Philip Grady is a fully qualified doctor, but when he sees patients at his suburban clinic, they nearly always think that this slim, practically beardless young man with fine blond hair, guileless blue eyes and a boyish smile can't be old enough to be a doctor, despite his identification badge and the stethoscope

3

draped around his neck. 'I got so tired of hearing that I didn't look old enough to be a doctor that I chopped off all my hair in a military cut, and started wearing glasses I didn't really need. Yet they still don't believe I'm a doctor.' Smiling ruefully, Philip says, 'My friends, especially older friends, keep telling me how lucky I am. But I get pretty tired of hearing the baby face jokes.'

Sally Grant, at forty, is often taken to be in her late twenties, but, she says, 'I only feel about twenty. A couple of years ago, a pollster in the street stopped me and asked me if I was over eighteen. I thought *that* was pushing it a bit.' Sally wears her glossy, sandy-blond hair long, sometimes on top of her head, to set off her freckled, smiling face, and at other times down, to flatter her slim figure. She says that she spends a lot of time watching the other mothers waiting for their children at the school gates, and has come to the conclusion that 'wrinkles don't have that much to do with the apparent age projected by people. A lot of women who are less wrinkly than me nevertheless, at a slight distance, look at least ten years older. They have sensible, easy-to-manage hair, sensible below-the-knee skirts, and sensible shoes.' She herself prefers flowing skirts or faded blue jeans.

Sally says that although she and her husband are the same age, he has aged much more than she has. 'We met in the sixties, when we were both long-haired hippies and had many things in common. Now he leads a sedentary life with pipe and slippers and paunch, which makes me very twitchy.' Sally loves to go surfing and snorkelling; her husband usually watches her from the beach or a shady seat on the boat. Her mother tells her that she's just like her father, who, when he was in his forties, Sally says, 'shocked the neighbours by leaping out of the bushes wearing only a loincloth, a feather, and war paint from my paintbox. Could this be hereditary?'

Antonia, Philip and Sally are among the superyoung – the fortunate few who look, act, think and feel years, sometimes decades, younger than the age on their driving licences. We all know them: those irritating people who show up at their twenty-fifth school reunion looking exactly like their last school photographs; mothers who go out with their daughters and are taken for their sisters; old geezers who can whip men half their age at tennis and then swim twenty lengths before they hit the showers. It's a familiar truism that you're as old as you feel; ten years ago, in my position as principal clinical neuropsychologist at the Royal Edinburgh Hospital, I decided to see whether there was a scientific basis for that old saw. Then I took it a step further: is it possible that you also *look* as young as you feel, perhaps even *think* as young as you feel?

To answer these questions, I launched an extensive, first-ever study of the superyoung phenomenon. It all began eighteen years ago, when I was working in a large, urban general practice, and I realized how misleading appearances can be. By the late eighties, researchers throughout the world had begun pointing out how young and vigorous some people were late in life, while others of the same age were frail and listless. My interest in the subject was further piqued when I saw two doctors having a heated argument over this issue, which nearly came to blows. The difference of opinion concerned the question of whether ageing was somehow related to certain diseases, such as high blood pressure and mature-onset diabetes, or purely coinciden- tal. Meanwhile, in my own practice, I was seeing hundreds of elderly people afflicted with senile and pre-senile dementia, who looked much older than their years, which raised the question whether Alzheimer's disease might not actually be nothing more than accelerated cognitive ageing of the brain.

Obviously, ageing isn't entirely a subjective matter of how you feel, as any man who has lost his hair, or any woman who has experienced the menopause, can attest. Undeniable proofs of the ravages of time make themselves evident even to those in deep denial. As a clinical psychopathologist, I had studied medical conditions that define the extremes of the physical manifestations of the ageing process. At one end of the spectrum is a rare disease, known as hypogonadism, in which males can remain, physically, forever young – with tragic results. In hypogonadism, a boy's glands don't develop properly and thus fail to give him the testosterone he needs in order to make the passage to physical manhood. Someone afflicted with hypogonadism can remain a 'boy', at least in body, forever – or until hormone therapy is administered, allowing him to develop male secondary sexual characteristics. At the opposite end of the spectrum is progeria, which causes people to age at a rapidly accelerated rate, so that a girl of nineteen may have the physical features of a 70-year-old woman.

Given this extreme flexibility in the outward manifestations of ageing, I began to wonder: is Antonia right? Is it downright unscientific to think that everyone born in the same year must be the same age? It occurred to me that it might be good science to look upon hypogonadism and progeria as the extremes of a continuum, ranging from extraordinary prolongation of biological childhood to a disastrously accelerated ageing process, with normal people, as usual, occupying the middle range. I am accustomed in my research to studying normal processes by looking at abnormal states; one of the principal lessons any psychologist learns early on is that there are no reliable, absolute standards that apply to everyone, that there's no such thing as 'normal'. Most mental and physical processes are like shoe sizes: how big is a big foot – a size ten? eleven? In a family of thirteens, a size ten is petite.

Lady Astor was propounding an unwholesome view of life when she said that you can never be too rich or too thin, but no one would have disagreed with her if she had said that you can never be too youthful: money and inches on the waistline come and go, but youth and all that it can bring – good health, energy, resilience, optimism, a world of opportunity – can never be recaptured once it has been lost. Yet what if youth really were a quality that could be nurtured and maintained throughout maturity and even beyond, into chronological old age?

Ten years ago, when the phenomenon of the superyoung began to take definite shape in my mind, I decided to set about studying it scientifically, to see what the rest of us could learn from the extraordinarily youthful men and women who live all around us. Is there some way to learn from them, to emulate their successful strategies for coping with the inevitable process of ageing? After an exhaustive study of people endowed with prolonged youth, I found that, compared with the rest of us, the superyoung:

- have more, and more satisfying, romantic relationships over the course of a lifetime – and lots of great sex in the context of mature, mutually shared erotic unions,
- frequently form friendships and love affairs with people ten years, or more, younger than themselves,
- are very confident about their sexual orientation and gender roles,
- are more likely to be childless, and, if they are parents, have smaller families,
- are extremely vigorous and athletic, tending to prefer strenuous outdoor activities, such as mountain walking and swimming, to team sports, and never want to sit on the sidelines and watch,
- have good posture,
- tend to travel more widely and more often,
- have low to normal blood pressure,
- sleep deeply and well, and wake up refreshed and ready to go,
- are more likely to tell the truth,
- read more and watch television less, and generally prefer any challenging mental activity over passive pastimes, and
- have parents who live to a healthy old age, and who fit many of these criteria themselves.

I was half expecting a clear pattern in the diet and personal habits of the superyoung – the typical 'Don't smoke, don't drink, early to bed and early to rise' mantra of the spry old codger whose hundredth birthday is reported in the local news. It was true that a significant percentage of the superyoung, 10–15 per cent, were vegetarians, but there were also plenty of happily unrepentant aficionados of red meat, red wine and dark chocolate. There were a large number of teetotallers but also a substantial cadre of regular consumers of wine, beer and spirits – and not always in moderate quantities. Non-smokers outnumbered smokers by about twenty to one; the science on that subject is incontrovertible, for in addition to the mortality statistics, the ageing effect on the skin of constant smoking is even stronger than that of time itself. Moreover, the superyoung are mostly well-educated, middle-class people, amongst whom smoking is no longer such a familiar habit. As for their spiritual life, I encountered a number of avid yoga practitioners, but as a group the superyoung are neither more nor less religious than the rest of us.

When I decided to make a study of this topic, the first question was, how could I make such a subjective issue objective? Of course, as a psychologist, that's meat and drink to me, exactly what I do every day. If a friend comes to you and tells you she's feeling blue, you may think you know what she means by that, but unless you've been discussing the subject with her intimately over a long period of time, you may be completely wrong. I've learned that when patients come to me and say that they are feeling sad or depressed, I have no way of judging such general comments until I spend some time with them, asking standardized, open-ended questions about their lives, temperament and mood, and compare their replies with those of other people.

In just the same way, it's difficult to know what people mean when they say they feel young, or old. Such judgments are based upon their life experiences, which vary widely from one person to the next. I decided that the place to begin was with those who looked younger than their age — that's something objective, which can be measured scientifically. My research into the superyoung began with a study of people who claimed to look younger than their age. I devised a test to see if they were right.

How the Study was Done

The first, crucial step in any psychological study is to find your subjects, for the results will never be valid unless you start with a good, representative group. The method I used for finding my superyoung sample, called *multimedia survey sampling*, was the same one I had used previously for studying eccentric people, a research project described in *Eccentrics* (Weidenfeld and Nicolson, London, 1995). Multimedia survey sampling simply means using the print and electronic media to get out the message about one's research, and encouraging readers and viewers who think they might qualify to get in touch. Thus, at least in the beginning, it is a self-selecting group, but as the research progresses, additional subjects are brought in by third-party recommendations. The technique might seem at first sight not to be terribly scientific, but in fact over the years it has become more widely accepted. A team of clinical psychologists working in the British Midlands, who were studying people addicted to computers, used my method. Statistical analysis of these and other studies has strongly supported the validity of samples created in this way.

Multimedia survey sampling relies on what has been called the snowballing factor — the tendency of research topics such as the ones I have studied to capture the public's interest and garner ever greater publicity. The Superyoung Project began with a small notice in *New Scientist*, a leading popular science magazine published in London but also widely read in America, which simply asked people over the age of thirty who believed that they looked and felt younger than their chronological age to write to me, describing in their own words how and why this had happened. Soon, newspapers throughout Britain picked it up, and after every story appeared there would be another great batch of letters in the mailbag. Radio and television inevitably followed, just as it had done in the study of eccentrics, and this time it reached an even broader audience, ensuring that the group would be both comprehensive and representative. News of our research found its way across the Atlantic to the great youth-obsessed society of the New World, through newspapers, magazines and nationally syndicated television programmes.

Journalistic accounts of my superyoung research have reached at least 120 million people in America and 35 million people in Great Britain, and a smaller but important sampling in continental Europe, Australia and further abroad, through the BBC World Service. It was vital to have as large a sample as possible, for the incidence of the superyoung in the population is widespread.

The snowballing effect – which is basically electronically amplified word of mouth – has gained respectability as a research tool in the social sciences. If someone sees an interview with me on television, talking about my superyoung research, it may prompt him to think of friends who fit the criteria, whom he will call on the telephone and tell to tune in, or to write.

Multimedia survey sampling worked brilliantly in the eccentricity project, for there was a built-in failsafe: why would non-eccentrics offer themselves for such a study? There would be something a bit eccentric about anyone who decided to answer the call. It might seem that multimedia survey sampling would be less reliable as a way of gathering subjects for a study of the superyoung phenomenon. Eccentricity is a quality that society regards with ambivalence – if not actual hostility, in some cases – whereas looking young is widely considered to be a positive trait.

Yet there was also a failsafe built into the multimedia survey sampling method in the superyoung research: if a person claimed to be youthful in appearance and then showed up for the interview looking ancient and withered, he would immediately be unmasked as a fraud, or at least as suffering from wishful thinking. Moreover, by a process similar to that at work in the eccentricity project, there proved to be a self-validating aspect to the sample: if a person says that he feels younger than his age, it's very likely, indeed almost certain, that there's some truth in his claim. It simply doesn't occur to a person who feels old to say that he feels young. Just saying you feel young is an essentially youthful – and, therefore, a potentially superyoung – thing to do.

In the beginning, we winnowed out the respondents who revealed themselves to be inconclusive or irrelevant to our study, but the great majority of them appeared to all the members of the research team to be serious, intelligent individuals who belonged in the study. That intuitive reaction was strongly reinforced by the scientific results of the study, as we shall see.

For the most part, we only recruited people who sent photographs of themselves or who said that they looked younger, but we also opened the gates to some of those who said that they felt younger. It cannot be overemphasized that the superyoung phenomenon is as much a matter of *feeling* young as of *looking* young. The two usually go together, but certain genetic predispositions, such as that for early male-pattern baldness, or for osteoporosis in women, might prevent some superyoung people from looking as young as they feel.

Our study of the superyoung had two major components: the large-scale study, based upon everyone who responded to the multimedia survey sampling appeals, and a smaller, more intensive group, chosen from the superyoung in the south-east region of Scotland surrounding Edinburgh, where my research group is based. The local study had ninety-five subjects, drawn from respondents in this area, and an equivalent number of control subjects, ordinary people selected at random from the same neighbourhoods as the experimental subjects, whose responses represented the norm against which to measure the superyoung.

In science, randomness is not as easy to come by as it sounds: if we stood in front of Edinburgh Castle and stopped the first ninety-five people who walked by, we would most likely end up with an equal number of American, Japanese and Italian tourists, with a smattering of Scottish barmaids on their way to work and local businessmen on their way home. In order to find a group of people whose backgrounds and experiences would be similar to the superyoung – and thus to isolate the qualities of the experimental group – we developed a system that matched each of the superyoung subjects with someone who shared his or her age, marital status and socio-economic circumstances.

The first two factors were easy enough; the third requirement was satisfied by looking in the rolls of each superyoung subject's electoral district until we found someone who might be a match in the first two categories. In several cases, the control subject resided in the same or an adjoining street as the superyoung person. We had a back-up for each match, in case the first control candidate refused to be a part of the study, but fewer than ten per cent said no to the researcher on their doorsteps when they were personally invited to join in the study.

Once we had identified the two groups in south-east Scotland – the superyoung subjects and their matching controls – we set to work. We employed three principal methods to study them: a double-blind test that used photographs to evaluate the participant's apparent age; an intensive examination of the subject, with questionnaires that assessed the personality of the subject and his attitudes towards ageing; and, finally, a detailed face-to-face interview.

The photographic analysis was done by mixing together pictures of the superyoung and the control subjects, and presenting them to a randomly selected group of graduate students who were not associated with any of the courses that I was teaching. A separate experimenter told them that they were participating in an experiment on person perception, and asked them to answer a number of questions about the people in the photographs. Although the principal purpose of this exercise was to determine as objectively as possible the apparent age of the superyoung subjects, we made every effort to conceal that fact until after the exercise was completed.

In other words, we adopted a classic double-blind experimental design; the purpose of this was to reduce to zero any possible bias or influence, however inadvertent. To begin with, no one connected with the study was ever told the real reason he was examining the photographs. The experimental raters were asked to answer a wide range of questions about the subjects' personalities; the age question was tossed in casually, almost like an afterthought, at the end of the interview. Furthermore, since it is a well-known phenomenon that the experimenter can influence the outcome of a project such as this, the experimenters (i.e., the people who posed the questions to the raters, as well as those who were answering the questions about the photographs) were also unaware of the real purpose of the research. Like the raters themselves, they were in the dark as to which of the photographs belonged to the experimental group and which to the control group. Hence the term 'double-blind': it was, literally, a case of the blind leading the blind.

I was the 'mastermind' of the exercise, supervising it at two removes – the only one who, at this stage, knew the real purpose of the experiment. Given the double-blind method of the project and the way it was presented, there is no reason to think that the participants were anything but candid and as objective as humanly possible in their evaluations of the ages of the subjects.

From the beginning, the results were exciting: the overwhelming majority of the superyoung participants appeared to the objective raters to be much, much younger than their chronological age. This initial photographic analysis revealed that the objective raters thought that the women in the superyoung group looked on average 9.7 years younger than their age, while the women in the control group appeared to be 4.8 years younger – a factor of more than two. (If it seems contradictory to state that the control subjects appeared to be younger than normal, bear in mind that they were carefully matched in many ways to the superyoung, and tended also to be well-educated, prosperous middle-class people, who were thus likely to be healthier and better nourished than the norm.)

The results were even more dramatic for the men. The raters misjudged the true age of the superyoung men by an astonishing average of 12.1 years, while they were almost right on target with the control group, believing them to be on average just one year younger than their actual age. The much more marked difference between the observed ages of the men, as compared with the women, is probably attributable to prevalent social attitudes: as much as social mores have evolved over the past twenty years, there is still far greater pressure on women to maintain a youthful appearance than there is on men of the same age. The vast majority of beauty products are produced for and consumed by women; women are also much more likely to dye their hair, have cosmetic surgery, and take other measures to make themselves look younger. By the mid-nineties, Americans were spending annually more than $4 billion on cosmetic surgery and $1 billion on skin moisturizers. Women accounted for about 75 per cent of the former and 80 per cent of the latter, though the male share has been growing continually. However, the much greater gap between the perceived and the actual ages of the men in my study, as opposed to the women subjects, might be interpreted as an indictment of the efficacy of all these remedies. In any case, very few of the superyoung subjects of either sex had resorted to any extreme measures to restore the appearance of youth – they didn't need to!

The results of the photographic study wiped out any lingering doubts we might have had about the validity of our sample. We subjected the data to a frequency test, a type of statistical probability analysis often used by psychologists, and found that the difference between the perceived and real ages was so great that the odds that such a result could have arisen between the two groups by chance were one in 500. The minimum meaningful result in such a probability test is one in twenty; our results factored out to twenty-five times that.

I then began a systematic study of the superyoung group, by subjecting them to a barrage of established psychological questions and tests. The first of these was the Eysenck Personality Questionnaire. This widely used research tool consists of ninety yes-or-no questions, such as:

Were you ever greedy by helping yourself to more than your share of something?

Are your feelings easily hurt?

Do you lock up your house carefully at night?

Do you like telling jokes and funny stories to your friends?

Do you have enemies who want to harm you?

Do people tell you a lot of lies?

Would you feel very sorry for an animal caught in a trap?

The Eysenck questionnaire has been shown to be accurate at measuring four aspects of the human personality: proneness to psychoticism, extroversion, neuroticism, and what is known as social desirability, a euphemism for dissimulation, the degree to which people deceive others – and sometimes themselves – in order to be more acceptable socially. Overall, the superyoung group's response fell well within an essentially normal pattern.

The test for psychoticism is the more ambiguous aspect of the questionnaire. For people who are more or less normal, it's fairly accurate, and the superyoung sample scored at the healthy end of the scale. Two factors contribute towards extroversion: sociability and impulsiveness. Both the superyoung and the control group tended to be above average, particularly with respect to sociability. On both the neuroticism and social desirability scale, the superyoung scored below the norm, a backwards way of saying that they're measurably more stable and more truthful than most people. The Eysenck Personality Questionnaire confirmed what we had already observed informally, that from a psychological perspective, the superyoung have a healthy outlook on life.

The second questionnaire, devised by my research team, was the foundation of our database about the superyoung. In addition to standard questions about age, occupation and marital status, there were forty questions relating to age and perceptions about ageing. Here's the test in its entirety:

1. How many years younger than your age do you feel?
   To what do you attribute this?
   Do other people comment that you act younger than your years?
   VERY OFTEN   MODERATELY OFTEN   RARELY   NEVER

   Who is likely to make such comments?

2. How would you describe your personality?
   Would you describe yourself as
   - a realist
   - an optimist
   - a pessimist
   - an extrovert
   - an introvert
   - even-tempered
   - sociable
   - impulsive

3. What age did your father live to?
   If still alive, how old is he?
   What illnesses did/does he suffer from?

4. What age did your mother live to?
   If still alive, how old is she?
   What illnesses did/does she suffer from?

5. How many years younger than your age do you look?
   To what do you attribute this?
   Do other people comment that you look younger than your years?

   VERY OFTEN   MODERATELY OFTEN   RARELY   NEVER

   Who is likely to make such comments?

6. How active are you mentally? Please specify in detail what you actually do of an intellectual nature that requires active thinking.

7. How active are you physically?
   What forms of physical activity do you participate in, and for how long have you taken part in them?

8. How often, in a typical week, do you interact meaningfully with another person?

9. How lonely are you?

   A LOT   SOMEWHAT   A LITTLE   NOT AT ALL

10. How many friends do you have?
    How often do you see them?

    A GREAT DEAL   MODERATELY OFTEN   RARELY   NEVER

11. Are you an outgoing person?

12. How often do you socialize with people outside your immediate family?

    A LOT   MODERATELY OFTEN   RARELY   NEVER

13. Do you attend any form of social club or gathering on a regular basis? If yes, what are they and for how long have you attended them?

14. What hobbies do you have, if any?

15. How many times have you been married?

16. How many significant other relationships have you had?

17. How many children do you have?

18. How many grandchildren do you have?

19. Does anyone else in your family look younger than their years? If yes, what relation are they to you?

20. Does anyone else in your family feel younger than their years? If yes, what relation are they to you?

21. How would you describe your sex life?

22. How feminine are you?

23. How masculine are you?

24. Do you have any regular contact with younger people? If yes, describe how regular it is.

25. Are you a religious believer?
    What form of religion do you practise?
    Do you gain comfort or strength from your faith?

26. Do you approach life on a 'day-to-day' basis, or are you rather more forward-planning?

27. Are you, in general, a happy and contented person?

28. How often do you manage to travel (in one year)?

29. How would you describe your diet?

30. Do you take any vitamin or mineral supplements? If so, what are they?

31. How often do you see a doctor?

32. What illnesses have you had?

33. Are you a good sleeper?

34. How many hours of sleep do you have at night?

35. How many minutes or hours of sleep do you have during the daytime?

36. What do you think are the chances of someone being killed by:
    (a) a road accident?
    (b) heart disease?
    (c) cancer?

37. What do you think are the chances that you will be killed by:
    (a) a road accident?
    (b) heart disease?
    (c) cancer?

38. To what age do you think you will live?

39. To what age would you like to live?

40. Is there anything else you would add concerning the subject of ageing?

At the conclusion of the interview, the researcher would estimate the age of the participant. The face-to-face interview lasted from one to two hours, which meant that many factors other than physical appearance were taken into account. A lively manner and a quick mind can do as much as a trim jawline or a full head of hair to create the impression of youthfulness. We asked the same questions of the control group and the superyoung subjects, and a similar double-blind structure was built into the way the research was carried out as had been the case with the photographic experiment.

After we had administered the questionnaire to both the superyoung and the control group, we began to analyse all these disparate strands of data. Some raw numbers were immediately revelatory, right off the top. For example, we found that the superyoung had fewer children than the control group, averaging 1.4 children, as opposed to 1.8 for their 'normal' counterparts. They were also more likely to be childless – 15 per cent, well above average, had no offspring. Also, as you would expect, they therefore had fewer grandchildren, 1.4 as against 2.8 for the control group.

For convenience, the data were broken down by gender, which ultimately resulted in some intriguing revelations about the differences between the sexes – with applications far beyond the confines of the superyoung group. For example, among the superyoung women the factor most often mentioned as contributing towards looking young was physical appearance – beauty, stature, good posture. Second on the list was having a positive disposition. The men in the study, to an overwhelming extent, attributed their youthful appearance to regular physical activity and strenuous exercise: 50 per cent of the men mentioned it first. The second most frequently cited factor among the men was having an active sex life; 40 per cent of the men cited sex as an important factor, twice as often as the women. (Why is that not surprising?)

Yet virtually all the participants – particularly the men – emphasized the central importance of their life partners to their emotional lives, more so even than the physical aspect of their relationships. The superyoung had richer, or at least more eventful, love lives than did the control group, averaging 2.6 major romantic relationships over the course of a lifetime, while the control group had had 1.5 life partners. Only a handful of the superyoung, no more than 5 per cent, were confirmed in a single lifestyle. Those who were alone when we met them were mostly widowed or recently divorced, and actively looking for a new mate. It seemed not to be age-related; those who had lost their partners late in life were just as keen as the younger participants to find someone new to cherish and love.

The higher number of lifetime relationships reflects the heightened desire of the superyoung for a life partner. Most people, if they are widowed in their late fifties or sixties, having recovered from the loss, will simply shrug and resign themselves to their new condition of life, perhaps dismayed by the perceived difficulty of dating at such an awkward age, and overwhelmed by fears of rejection. Significantly, the superyoung see mating as a necessity, and look upon the search for a new partner as a challenge to be met and surmounted. The phenomenal rate at which they succeed in this quest is also a tribute to their high level of self-confidence – not to mention the advantages of a youthful appearance in dating!

In all my years as a clinical psychologist, I've never encountered a group of men and women in which there was such a healthy, robust romantic life – and I see many normal, well-adjusted people in my research. By any standard, the superyoung have a remarkably well-developed ability to communicate with their partners and to empathize with one another with great delight, which accounts for the greater stability and rich rewards of their long-term relationships.

Ultimately, I found that by almost every standard of life, the superyoung are fortunate, well-endowed people. While they are by no means immune to the problems that beset ordinary people, they cope with them better. I learned a lot from the superyoung – and so can you.

Michael DeBakey

One of the most spectacular examples of the superyoung is Michael DeBakey, the pioneering heart surgeon. He has been a leader in his field for nearly fifty years, and shows no sign of letting up. In 1997, at the age of eighty-eight, he supervised open-heart surgery on Boris Yeltsin, the President of Russia; at present he is in the final stages of perfecting a new artificial heart, working in collaboration with engineers at NASA. In an interview at his offices in the Baylor College of Medicine, in Houston, the great physician shared the secrets of his dynamic life.

At an age when most men would be hobbling around on a cane and concerned about some muddling of the mental faculties, DeBakey has an erect carriage, a firm handshake, and a piercing gaze. His face is lined and fleshy, of course, but he could easily pass for a man twenty years younger. When asked to explain his vitality and longevity, he answered succinctly: 'I don't know. I don't think anyone knows for certain. It's a combination of genetics and lifestyle, but that's true of most health issues.' He certainly has genetics on his side: his father lived to be ninety-two.

DeBakey's lifestyle is a simple one. He rises at five a.m., eats a light breakfast of fruit, reads the newspapers, and then he goes to work – and stays at it until midnight, performing operations, consulting, reading and writing. He explained that while it may not be possible to extend life beyond a finite, genetically predetermined limit, by reducing the risk of the life-threatening diseases of late middle age, it is possible to prevent being robbed of what years one is allotted. 'Cells replicate fifty times, then they can't replicate anymore. They just die. In life we have the same cycle; we can't predict how much we might be able to extend life by reducing vulnerability to disease.'

The three controllable factors he singled out as most important are familiar to most of us – in large measure because of his own writings and influence on public-health policy. The most important steps you can take to prolong life are:

- to control hypertension, which can now be done effectively in most cases through the use of medications;
- to stop smoking, which is directly responsible for at least 20 per cent of all deaths from heart disease, and for at least 30 per cent of all cancer deaths; and
- to eat a diet that's low in fat, to reduce the risk of arteriosclerosis and heart disease.

DeBakey favours a diet that is low in fat but not by any means severe or restricted. In clinical studies 'rats and mice that have been on a near-starvation diet have been shown to live longer, but that's not the end in itself. You may live longer, but you won't function that well.' He advocates a broad spectrum of foods in the diet, and for that reason advises against vegetarianism. 'Haemoglobin, in order to be replenished, needs certain nutrients, and vegetarians don't get it.'

But it isn't simply good health that keeps Michael DeBakey and other superyoung people going strong in advanced age, it is drive and stamina. When asked how he has been able to maintain the mental energy of a young man, he replied, 'We say of muscles, "Use it or lose it." Well, the same thing applies to the mind: the more you use it, the better it functions. It's better to be mentally active than to be a couch potato.' DeBakey believes that the greatest threat to preserving mental vigour is television. 'It's the worst thing of all. It seems to me such a waste of time, when there are so many better ways to stimulate the mind. Television has become an addiction in our society.'

Unlike some physicians, DeBakey doesn't see his mission as the prolongation of life *per se*. 'The important thing isn't the actual number of years but to function well, both mentally and physically. That's what constitutes life. These people who linger on for years, unable to enjoy life – I call that the prolongation of death.' His father, he believes, made the perfect exit: 'He dropped dead while he was working in his garden. He died instantly, undoubtedly of a myocardial infarction. That's the way to go, while you're still doing something you love.'

J. J.

CHAPTER TWO

FEELING YOUNGER

*Give me a young man in whom there is something of the old, and
an old man with something of the young: guided so, a man may
grow old in body, but never in mind.*

Cicero

As we met and talked with the superyoung in depth, we probed
into the complex question of exactly *why* people feel younger than
their years. It's a mysterious subjectivity, similar to what used to be
called sex appeal: it's closer to defining how many lumps of sugar it
takes to sweeten a cup of tea than to anything that can be measured
with a scientific yardstick. If one person says he feels older than his
age, and the next person says she feels younger, how can we know
what they mean? Perhaps they feel the same, and the young-
feeling person simply has a more positive outlook, her standards
not quite as demanding as the person who says that he feels older
than his age. If we took the young-feeling person out of her
environment and found her a job as a school teacher, and then
placed the old-feeling person in a retirement home, at the end of a
week their responses might very well be reversed.

Another difficulty is that while the young may imagine what
it means to feel old, they don't really know until they actually
arrive there. Conversely, old people sentimentalize youth, as
their memories of the emotional stress and strife associated with
that period of their lives conveniently fade away, and they
construct a golden age when they never had to go to the doctor
and they could stay out all night partying, without feeling the
high cost of low living.

If two people say that they feel young, they probably mean very different things by it. It's not a matter of chronological age: someone turning thirty, who worriedly examines his face in the mirror for minute wrinkles and barely perceptible thinning of the hair, may feel older than an 80-year-old who has accepted the outward manifestations of the ageing process. (Besides, once your eyesight starts going, you can't see the wrinkles so well!)

Young people don't feel young – they feel normal. As far as they're concerned, they feel just the way a person ought to feel. The young may notice that they don't have any of the problems of old people, that they spring up the stairs faster and can go full steam for hours without feeling exhausted, but they take it for granted. It's only when a person realizes that he's getting tired a bit sooner while performing a familiar task, or notices the first visible signs of ageing, that it becomes an issue. As Einstein used to say in jest, it's all relative. In this case, the relativity is that between present reality and memories of the younger self, and while the sensation of feeling younger is based mostly on one's self-image and self-perception, we may also feel younger (or older) by noticing the manifestations of age – or the lack of them – in our contemporaries. After all, the superyoung only seem so by comparison with other people their own age.

An unexpected finding of the superyoung study was that, nowadays, a vast majority of people feel younger than their age. All the participants in our research, in the control group as well as in the superyoung group, responded positively to the question. However, the control participants mostly said that they felt a few years younger than their age, whereas among the superyoung it was at least ten years, and sometimes a great deal more.

Another factor I had to take into account was whether the study might not have subtly encouraged the members of the control group to wish to be perceived as young – even if it was not really a major concern for them. Some people who might never have seriously pondered the question of whether or not they looked or felt young, once the question was asked, could well have said that they felt younger simply out of a desire to please (and to be pleasing to) the interviewers, who were generally younger than the interviewees. None the less, there can be little doubt that the overwhelming response of the superyoung arose from a strongly held belief about themselves – the same belief that attracted them to the study in the first place.

In my study of the superyoung, three criteria emerged as the reasons why most people, superyoung or not, felt younger: **energy**, **resilience** and **adaptability**.

Energy

Everybody's energy level declines with age: that's one of the most basic physiological aspects of the process. As we shall see in greater detail in a later chapter, the body component parts lose their power and effectiveness after years of continuous use. By the age of thirty-five, we begin to lose cells in our brain – perhaps as many as 7,000 a day – as well as other vital organs including the heart and skin, while those that remain must work harder and use ever greater amounts of energy to replace the remaining components as they wear out. The more energy required for maintaining the whole organism, the less there is for 'optional' use, such as for sex, mountain-climbing, or reading for hours at a stretch.

The superyoung keep those abilities for far longer in life because they are able, for a variety of reasons, to maintain more of that finite amount of energy 'for themselves', to be used for optional goals. The principal reason is probably genetic; their cells are simply programmed to live longer. Yet that's only a part of the story. Maintaining high energy levels as we age is also associated with being a good sleeper. That doesn't necessarily mean sleeping a great deal; all his life, Michael DeBakey (see page 22) has got by very well on four or five hours of sleep a night. A good sleeper is someone who has no trouble falling asleep and doesn't wake up before he has had all the rest he needs. While sleep remains one of the most mysterious of human functions, one of the few things scientists are certain about is that sleeptime is when the body repairs the brain, restoring some of the substances depleted during waking hours, and doing repair work on vital proteins and amino acids.

The superyoung tend to be good sleepers, which has a highly beneficial effect not only on their physical well–being – and thus their high levels of energy – but also on their mood. Subjectively measured, the outlook of the superyoung is at the brighter end of the mood spectrum, a fact which can be partly explained by their good sleeping habits. Everybody knows that sleep depriva- tion makes us grumpy and muddled; similarly, clinical studies have shown that one way of treating depression is simply to help the sufferer to sleep better. In third–world countries, such as Egypt, where resources for public health are limited, therapists sometimes treat depressive illnesses simply by providing physical exercise programmes, which can bring a measure of immediate relief, because of its own salutary effects and because it induces better, deeper sleep, which in turn helps to brighten the patient's mood.

Resilience

The second factor in feeling younger is resilience, the ability to bounce back from what psychologists euphemistically refer to as stressful adverse life events. These can be physical, environ- mental or psychological. The former are self-evident: if a mixed group is stranded on the open sea for two weeks in a lifeboat, the younger people will obviously recover from the trauma more quickly than the elderly.

Psychological stresses and strains, however, are harder to evaluate. One study, conducted by the American psychologists

T. H. Holmes and R. H. Rahe, attempted to establish a scale ranking stressful experiences according to their severity. Not all stressful episodes are necessarily perceived to be adverse, especially at the mild end of the scale. Moving house or getting married, for example, are minor traumas that require some resilience. Yet further up the scale (or down, depending on how you look at it), the traumas become progressively more distressing, with woeful calamities such as the death of a young child at the extreme end of the spectrum.

The superyoung tend to bounce back from these disasters more quickly than most people do. Probably the most common adverse life event encountered by the subjects in the study was the death of a partner, a supremely demanding challenge to a person's resilience, since it usually comes at a time of life when most of us are becoming more set in our ways. Yet in almost every case the superyoung coped admirably well with this terrible experience.

One superyoung participant, Barbara, lost her husband at the age of sixty-four, after a long illness. She went through a normal process of grieving, but, she said, she was 'determined not to lapse into obscurity'. Although she had worked all her life, she gave up her job two years before her husband died in order to take better care of him. After a period of mourning, she gave herself a complete make-over: 'I had my white hair dyed, I lost a few pounds, and bought new clothes. Then I set out to find a job – not easy at my age.' This decision was made even more difficult by the fact that she and her husband had moved to a new town just before he became ill. Yet she finally got a part-time job, and successfully trained to use computers. Now Barbara works full-time as the manager of a new branch of the company, where, she says, she is 'considered to be something of a whiz-kid'. Now seventy, she's retiring from her job. No one at her office knew her age, and when she told them, they were astounded, all of them saying that they thought she was in her fifties. She has two lovers, she says, and 'I still find sex very delightful.' As if all that were not enough, she took up the study of Latin at an adult extension course, where, she says, she was considered the star pupil.

Resilience among the superyoung may also be measured negatively: that is, by the relative rarity of depressive responses. One out of three people in the control group had reacted in the past to extremely adverse life events with episodes of depression, though not all of them were severe. These ranged from a generally depressed mood and affect, to pathological guilt (particularly in the case of the tragic death of a family member or lover), to, at the outer extreme, seriously contemplating suicide. Other typical effects were persistent lethargy and an inability to perform well at work long after the tragic event occurred. However, many fewer among the superyoung reported such responses to catastrophic life episodes.

From a scientific point of view, happiness has been poorly defined. It's not necessarily a youthful emotion, of course: adolescence and young adulthood are the most trying periods of life for many people; more suicides and attempted suicides occur in the late teens and in the twenties than in any other age group. Yet happiness certainly contributes towards the sensation of being contented and satisfied with one's life, and that in turn allows a person to concentrate on positive pursuits, and contributes to overall resiliency.

The reason that brightness of mood – habitual happiness, as it were – has never been studied thoroughly is because, as is so often the case in clinical psychology, the healthy state is simply taken for granted. Yet in the superyoung project we found that the subjects were happier than the control group and had a better quality of life. Based upon their own self-descriptions and our observations, the rarity of depressive incidents in the superyoung group was coupled with a palpable, positive sense of well-being and happiness.

Most people feel that they know what it means to be happy, and therefore don't bother to analyse such feelings any further.

However, there is a substantial body of objective evidence that happy people are more constructive, more creative, more generous, and healthier than their gloomy counterparts. For a eudologist – eudology being the science of happiness – the ideal life is one that allows a person to steer a path between anxiety and boredom for as long a time as possible. One of the best ways to do this is by pursuing an achievable challenge that demands increasingly complex skills and rewards them at regular intervals. Such life projects should evolve progressively, so that the more you do them, the more rewarding it becomes. If it's a cooperative enterprise that can be done in a sociable context, so much the better – the social setting provides opportunities for other people to congratulate you when you succeed. It also provides another kind of back-up – when your faith in yourself begins to flag, there will be someone around to encourage you, someone to act as a sounding board to bounce ideas off.

Many of the subjects in the superyoung project stressed that humour was high on their list of things that contributed towards a sense of well-being. It's a way for people to make light of their foibles and frailties – an ability that becomes increasingly valuable in later life. So while happiness, that great desideratum of human existence, is not exactly a criterion for feeling young, it does seem to be a common characteristic, and perhaps a means to that end.

Adaptability

The third principal criterion for feeling young is adaptability, the capacity to adjust to new situations or new people – indeed, anything that is unfamiliar. This trait is associated with people who travel widely, an activity pursued by many of the superyoung in the study. When young people travel to exotic places, they tend to accept the outlandish ways of foreigners quite readily, and often take them up – hence the subculture of backpacking world travellers, young drifters who often dress in native garb and make friends and lovers with the local people they meet with in their peregrinations.

Most older people who travel to faraway destinations go on group tours with others their own age, and stay at hotels and eat at restaurants that closely resemble what they are accustomed to at home – the Holiday Inn in Tahiti, and McDonald's on the Champs-Elysées. The superyoung, by contrast, frequently prefer to travel in the more free-wheeling style of the young, independent and unprogrammed. A retired swimming teacher of seventy-seven, who claimed to have 'the mentality of a 10-year-old', told us that she and her husband had travelled to Australia, Kenya, Russia and Singapore since they had retired. A 73-year-old lady from Somerset likes to travel in cargo ships; she has cruised around the world twice that way. A retired airline pilot of seventy-five is planning to fly to Easter Island for his holiday next year. A 77-year-old Scottish lady (who has climbed Mount Vesuvius) also displays this mental adaptability; she says, 'Every year I try to learn something new. I've taken adult-education classes during the day. Since they began I have studied Scottish history, learned to play a keyboard, and now I'm attending lectures in psychology.'

The Test Results

The following conclusions are based upon our interpretations of the data amassed by the study. Such statistical analysis of experimental test results is at the heart of psychology: it's an imperfect science, if it's a science at all, but it's the only way we have of objectifying and quantifying the elusive enigmas of the human mind and personality.

To sort through the data from the superyoung study, we began by creating what are known as matrices of correlations, to match the perceptions of the study's participants against the forty categories of data in the questionnaire. Despite its somewhat surrealistic name, a matrix of correlations is a straightforward tool that allowed me, in the first place, to make comparisons between the superyoung subjects and the control group, and then to determine which factors were most fundamentally characteristic of the superyoung. This analysis, which was carried out using a standard technique called the Pearson Product–Moment Correlation, revealed that the correlations were very robust – in other words, our superyoung sample was *significantly distinguishable from the control group.*

This system of measuring the relationships between answers, the most reliable method under a variety of circumstances, and the one most commonly in use now, can cope simultaneously with both binary (yes or no) answers to questions and with ones giving a range of scores (in numbers on a scale). This gave us the opportunity to combine those sorts of more precisely scored answers with the more subjective (or qualitative) responses from more open-ended questions. We could do this by assigning numerical values to these responses. It goes without saying that there's no such thing as a wrong answer on the questionnaire; we stated so explicitly at the top of the form. However, one of the points of the questionnaire was to gauge the positive values associated with being superyoung, and it was to that end that we conducted the statistical analysis. For multiple-choice questions, we set up a numerical scale. Thus, for a question such as

Do other people comment that you look younger than your years?

VERY OFTEN   MODERATELY OFTEN   RARELY   NEVER

we assigned a numerical value of +3 to 'very often', +2 to 'moderately often', +1 to 'rarely', and 0 to 'never'. With the very subjective essay questions, such as 'How active are you physically?' and 'How would you describe your sex life?', another group of double-blind raters acted as umpires and assigned numerical values to the various responses as methodically as they could.

Next, we used a technique known as Factor Analysis, which allowed us (with the help of a computer) to find simple structures, to reduce the complex maze of data we had gathered, consisting of both subjective and objective information, to as few factors as possible, in order to elucidate the most important ones, to work out what they meant and graph them. In this way, we could make graspable what is essentially multidimensional. Some might say that such a statistical investigation oversimplifies the information, but when we do an analysis of this sort, we always keep firmly in mind that human beings are basically mysterious, unknowable creatures.

Psychology alone, at this point in its evolution, can do little more than to suggest the broad outlines. As the data going into an analysis like this one become more and more subjective, the more sceptical we must be – in other words, we must allow for a wider margin of error – so that really significant differences must make themselves evident before we give them credence.

For convenience's sake, I divided the superyoung study by gender. We ranked the participants' responses by weighting the various factors they raised in order of emphasis, rather like the balloting for a 'top ten' list. If someone laid the most stress upon the fact that her ancestors had lived to a ripe old age, embellishing it with stories about her grandmother and auntie who both lived to be 101, and then mentioned in passing that she led a very active life and had always been healthy, then we gave a much higher numerical value to her long-lived family than to her activity and good health.

The factor analysis of why the women in the superyoung group felt younger broke down like this:

Feeling Younger (Women)

1. Secure lifestyle   17%
2. Positive disposition/Empathic approach   13%
3. Long-lived family   12%
4. Activity, physical and mental   11%
5. Good health   5%
6. Sociability   4%

These factors add up to 62 per cent, leaving 38 per cent unexplained, which may seem surprisingly high. That doesn't mean that we don't know anything about why that 38 per cent feel so much younger than their chronological age, only that the factors which contribute towards that feeling could not be precisely ascertained, or that it was a combination of different factors.

The results for the superyoung men were a bit more susceptible to this type of correlational analysis, with 86 per cent of their responses explained. Here's the factor analysis of why they felt younger:

Feeling Younger (Men)

1. Insatiable interests/Preference for novelty   23%
2. Mental stimulation and curiosity   18%
3. Enthusiasm and positive motivation   15%
4. Creativity/Playful sense of humour   12%
5. Stress avoidance/Challenge-seeking   11%
6. Minor to mild non-conformity   7%

The first two factors might seem to be very similar: it might have been more accurate to call the first one, insatiable interests and a preference for novelty, the boredom factor, a deep restlessness of the imagination, whereas the second means that the subject is deeply engrossed by doing things that he finds mentally stimulating.

After evaluating hundreds of superyoung people, I was struck above all by their diversity: very few traits emerged that could be applied to all of the participants in the project. Whenever a pattern did emerge, it immediately took on a heightened importance. In addition to objective characteristics, such as the high degree of athleticism and pronounced mental activity of the superyoung, I soon began to discern a subtler mental quality in these remarkable people.

The superyoung have evolved a unique strategy for coping with one of the greatest health hazards of life at the end of the twentieth century: stress. Stress isn't necessarily a bad thing – falling in love and winning the lottery are both stressful events in a person's life. Yet the way many people react to stress, with anger and frustration, can be terribly harmful: chronically angry people suffer a range of psychosomatic symptoms, from elevated blood pressure to a heightened risk of heart attack or stroke.

The superyoung have developed a healthy, three-fold response to stress: when they realize they're in an insoluble situation, rather than allowing themselves to be defeated – or, worse, dithering indecisively – they immediately confront it and deal with it constructively. The second step is that they convert the initial event that caused the stress into a positive challenge. The third step is straightforward: they avoid defeating situations. Whereas for most people the act of avoiding difficult predicaments has a negative connotation, suggesting inadequacy or even cowardice, for the superyoung it's a healthy, positive choice. If a person or a professional situation becomes intolerable, it's better simply to walk away, for continuing to endure it will result in chronic anger, unhappiness, perhaps even an ongoing state of depression.

A good case in point is Alison Tessier, who, after fourteen years at a job she loved, chucked it away. 'I worked in education at a psychiatric hospital,' she explained, 'and there were so many cutbacks, it just wasn't fun anymore. That was very hard to deal with.' When the hospital moved her job forty miles away, rather than muddling by in a deteriorating situation, she resigned, enrolled in a computing course, and started a new career. 'You need to be prepared to market yourself,' she explained. 'Nobody's going to come and knock at your door, are they? You have to go out and find what you want.'

Even at forty, Alison, a pretty, lissome blonde, says that she always carries identification with her, for she is so youthful-looking that bars and restaurants sometimes refuse to serve her the occasional pint of beer. Like many of the superyoung, she has a hobby she is passionate about, writing poetry. 'One of them was published in a book,' she says proudly.

Alison's way of coping with the stress she encountered at her job is a quintessentially superyoung strategy. Most people would experience great anxiety and trepidation at the prospect of embarking on a new career in mid-life, but Alison regarded it as a challenge – an opportunity to succeed rather than a risk of failure.

Maria Shaw, a 42-year-old flying instructor, has developed a characteristically practical approach to problem-solving in her life: 'When I feel down, I'll give it time to get better, but if it doesn't, then I approach the problem quite systematically by laying down a time period. I'll say to myself, "If this problem hasn't improved by December 31, then I'll take such-and-such an action." And I always do.'

The superyoung pursue an analogous approach to stress in their personal relations. Whereas many people will stay in a bad marriage for years before they find the courage to deal with the problem, the superyoung are quick to communicate candidly with their partners, even when it means conveying bad news. We all know that negative feelings must be dealt with sooner or later, but while most people have the natural tendency to procrastinate, hoping to avoid an embarrassing scene, the superyoung prefer to avoid the bad situation itself. The clarity and quality of communications in their relationships enhances the superyoung's sense of fulfilment and enjoyment.

Another key factor cited by many of the subjects as contributing towards feeling young was their life-long association with people considerably younger than themselves. A great many of the superyoung participants, nearly a majority, volunteered the information that they preferred the company of young people, and that most of their friends were anywhere from seven to twenty years younger than themselves. Sometimes that created tension at home: adolescent and young adult children of the superyoung, like everyone at those ages, were embarrassed by their parents – and what is more excruciating for a sensitive teenager than a mother who thinks she's young, and makes friends with people near her own age?

A 38-year-old woman told us that she tried to go with her 14-year-old daughter to a school dance. 'I know I would have enjoyed myself, but Stephanie didn't agree. Stuffy, isn't she?' The mother's friends often tell her to grow up and act her age, to which she replies, 'Why should I, when I'm young at heart? How does one act at thirty-eight, anyway? If I'm breaking any rules – good. At least I won't be bored old.'

There was a lower incidence of superyoung–superyoung marriages and romantic liaisons than I expected; more often, the superyoung prefer the company of the 'real thing' and form relationships with people who are several years younger than themselves. Nearly 20 per cent of the superyoung subjects had been involved in a significant romantic relationship with someone at least ten years younger than themselves.

Maria Shaw, after having been married and divorced twice (in both cases, following her philosophy of not letting a bad situation get worse), is now living with a man ten years younger than she is. She found a felicitous way of expressing the rejuvenating effect of life with a younger person: 'I don't think a relationship with a younger man necessarily makes me feel younger, but I think it reinforces a younger outlook – we both have so much life ahead of us.' Maria would most likely have had a young outlook in any case; she reported that her mother, at seventy-four, was desolate when her doctor made her give up alpine skiing on account of her arthritis.

Often, the in-laws on both sides are disapproving of super-young–young relationships, whether the older partner is a man or a woman. Typically, the friends and relatives of the older of the pair make comments such as 'He's making a fool of himself,' or 'At her age, she should know better,' while those of the younger point out that when the older partner grows old, the younger will have to become a care-provider. Meanwhile, the couple usually defy everyone's rancorous predictions by being very happy together. Indeed, the fact that others disapprove sometimes brings them closer.

Wendy Hamelin was first married at nineteen, and twenty-five years later divorced her husband to marry a man ten years younger than herself. After separating from her second husband, at the age of fifty, she fell in love with a 22-year-old man. He was amazed when she revealed her age to him, telling her that she neither looked nor acted anything close to fifty. Although the affair was very passionate and sexually exciting, the young man ultimately left her because he couldn't face the social oppro-brium attached to living openly with a woman of his mother's age.

Wendy's case notwithstanding, most of the age-gap relation-ships of the superyoung succeed, providing strong proof that the date on a person's birth certificate may not be the best measure of his age.

The superyoung love to give advice: it's one of their most characteristic traits. The single bit of advice we heard most often in the study was exactly what we had expected to hear: the key to feeling young is staying active. The degree of physical activity of the superyoung is pronounced, occasionally even extreme, in every age category. It frequently takes the form of athleticism: we had a great many indefatigable walkers and mountain climbers, long-distance swimmers, marathon runners and tennis players in their seventies, and golfers in their eighties. A 68-year-old man teaches judo to teenagers two nights a week; another man regularly plays doubles tennis with three men whose combined ages are less than his own eighty-one years.

There were other, more surprising, manifestations of physical activity as well. A high proportion of the superyoung subjects enjoyed dancing of all kinds. An 87-year-old man and his wife have gone ballroom dancing regularly since 1936. Many of the superyoung participants from the Edinburgh area took up Scottish folk dancing in their retirement; one 70-year-old lady reported that in addition to ballroom and Irish and Scottish folk dancing, 'I can still rock 'n' roll like I did back in the fifties. I'm still quite nimble on my feet — two years ago I took up *t'ai chi.*'

The most extreme case of someone dancing into old age is that of Eve Schwimmer, now sixty-six, who took up tap-dancing a few years ago, when her husband died. Originally from New Jersey and now an Israeli citizen, Eve studied tap with a class of ten- to 16-year-olds, and now performs a routine to the tune of 'Tea for Two' several times a month.

There was a natural tendency among the older subjects to go into extensive detail about their physical activities, for it's a source of great pride to them. There's nothing very unusual about people in their thirties and forties playing tennis regularly or going out dancing of an evening. People in the prime of life often simply told us that they were very active; it was only when we started asking questions that we realized just how active they were.

In some cases, we learned about the vigorous activities of the young superyoung from the accounts of their exploits they told later in life. A life-long vegetarian from Edinburgh told us that he was a wrestler and weight-lifter into his thirties; a cyclist, footballer and badminton player into his sixties; and still, at seventy-six, swam regularly, taught handicapped children as a volunteer at a local hospital, and went dancing two or three nights a week. When he was in his thirties, he said, he used to play football every Saturday. 'I would cycle eighteen miles down the coast to meet a crowd of lads to play football for at least two hours.' At the end of the game he went for a dip in the sea – the North Sea, that is, in the middle of a Scottish winter! – and then drank a few pints with his friends before cycling the eighteen miles back home. 'This went on for years,' he said, 'but I won't pretend I wasn't tired at the end of the day.'

Not all the superyoung were so astonishingly robust. There was a high proportion of people who focused to a great degree on their work. William Dasheff is still active in his nineties, showing up every day at his club in midtown Manhattan for a lunch that invariably begins with a Bloody Mary. In his prime, he said, he was a heavy drinker and smoker, consuming a bottle of whiskey and a cigar every day. Dasheff was a legend in the New York advertising world, famous for having invented Reynolds Wrap aluminium foil, for which he coined the slogan 'A Hundred and One Uses'.

Dasheff attributes his long life to the fact that he never stopped working. 'The most important thing was to get up and out of the goddamned house and into the office before anyone else. By the time everyone else showed up, I had already done a couple of hours' work.'

Questionnaire: How Young Do You Feel?

This questionnaire, based upon the one we administered to the subjects in the superyoung project, is designed to find out what attitudes, preferences and interests you have. There are no right or wrong answers, because everyone has a unique way of coping and looking at the world. Answer the questions accurately and truthfully, but don't ponder over them too much: give the first, spontaneous answer that comes to you. There are no trick questions or hidden meanings. Choose the answer that reflects how you actually feel at the moment, not how you think you ought to feel, or what other people might want you to feel. Answer all the questions, or your score will not be valid.

1. I make time in my life for activities that will boost my self-esteem.

   True (2) Sometimes (1) False (0)

2. I can be comfortable in solitude, in my own company.

   True (2) Unsure (1) False (0)

3. I never agonize over past failures.

   True (2) Sometimes (1) False (0)

4. My lifestyle usually feels relaxed and well balanced.

   True (2) Unsure (1) False (0)

5. I can express my needs whenever they are not being met.

   True (2) Unsure (1) False (0)

6. I tend to welcome constructive criticism.

   True (2) Unsure (1) False (0)

7. It is important to nurture your positive emotional feelings.

   True (2) Unsure (1) False (0)

8. I can initiate behaviour that leads to fun for me or for others.

   True (2) Sometimes (1) False (0)

9. I would never wish to be overly self-absorbed.

   True (2) Unsure (1 False (0)

10. I keep on trying to realize my own potential.

    True (2) Sometimes (1) False (0)

11. It is good for my character to stand up for my rights.

    True (2) Unsure (1) False (0)

12. I can empathize with people who are suffering.

> True (2) Unsure (1) False (0)

13. I look for support and help from others when I really need it.

> True (2) Sometimes (1) False (0)

14. Even unhappy circumstances can be made enriching in some ways.

> True (2) Unsure (1) False (0)

15. I never feel controlled by past events in my life.

> True (2) Unsure (1) False (0)

Interpreting Your Responses

Add up your total score. The interpretations that follow are based upon data comparisons between the superyoung subjects and the control group in my study. The average adult score on this questionnaire is fifteen, the median for a scale with a top mark of thirty. For adolescents it may be closer to thirteen, and for seniors over sixty years of age, eleven.

More than 26 You are exceptionally healthy emotionally, clearly a superyoung candidate. The word 'can't' isn't in your vocabulary. Your attitude towards life is one of continual exploration, supported by powerful self-affirmation.

19–25 Some may think you selfish, but you are actually involved in self-awareness and personal fulfilment. You are variously perceived as fun-loving, warm and empathic, and never allow yourself to be abstracted from deeply felt emotions and intuitions. Success in many fields has propelled you to a heightened self-confidence.

12–18 You're not entirely placid but mostly unruffled in your day-to-day activities. You seldom allow your emotional needs to permit you to ignore practical realities. None the less, you recognize the existence of inner longings, and sense that there's something missing from your life so far.

5–11 You swing between wanting to maintain control and finding some impetuous release. You are searching for new ideas, but feel incapable of committing yourself to any central, sustaining ideal. You might consider relaxation techniques and/ or meditation to isolate your areas of resistance and help yourself to relax and unwind better.

4 or less You struggle to keep pace with people your age, and are increasingly aware of stifling feelings of envy. If you could let yourself be less censorious – of yourself and of others – you might begin to see the way forward, emotionally. Some of the newer forms of humanistic, person-centred psychotherapy might help you to break this self-thwarting cycle.

Angela Lansbury

In 1940, when the German *Luftwaffe* launched its massive bombing raids on London, a 15-year-old girl named Angela Lansbury was evacuated to Los Angeles. Four years later, she was nominated for an Academy Award for her performance as a frisky maid in her first film, George Cukor's classic thriller *Gaslight*. This quickly led to a contract with MGM and many juicy parts in such films as *The Picture of Dorian Gray, The Harvey Girls* and *Samson and Delilah*. She was skilled at playing roles much older than her actual age; in *The Manchurian Candidate* she was cast as the mother of Laurence Harvey, a man three years younger than her – a stunning performance that earned her another Oscar nomination. In the sixties and seventies, Lansbury became one of Broadway's great leading ladies, winning four Tonys (for *Mame, Dear World, Gypsy* and *Sweeney Todd*) – setting a record for the category of best actress in a musical. Yet despite her distinguished and honourable career on screen and stage, Lansbury is probably best known for the role of Jessica Fletcher, the novel-writing sleuth in *Murder, She Wrote*, one of the most popular dramatic series on television.

Angela Lansbury lives in an airy, Spanish-style house in the Brentwood section of Los Angeles with Peter Shaw, whom she married in 1949. Tall and shapely, she sweeps into the living room with her shoulders squared and a warm smile on her lips. Wearing a plum-coloured silk shirt and elegant white trousers and sandals, she looks more athletic and trim in person than she does on the small screen: after playing all those matronly roles when she was young, now she's having her revenge by looking a good deal younger than her age. A moment later her husband ambles in, carrying a tray with a pot of tea and gingernut biscuits. As she pours the tea, Lansbury says, 'I have simply never thought about my age – never did. When I was young, about thirteen, I was studying with youngsters who were seventeen, eighteen years old. Now that I'm seventy-two, I still think of myself as being . . . forty.'

Lansbury was seventy-one when *Murder, She Wrote* was cancelled, in 1996, but she wasn't about to retire: she says that she will star in a series of feature-length Jessica Fletcher television films, at the rate of two a year. 'The tragedy of so many people is that when they are sixty-five, they find the zest has gone out of their lives. They don't have the resources to fill all that time. Of course some people can't wait to retire, to be able to do all those things they've wanted to do, to pursue their hobbies, to travel. It's mostly a question of emotional mindset.'

She believes that the disposition to this 'mindset' is genetic. 'I'm pretty sure it is in my case. I have a family history of activism, particularly on my father's side. But so many people just give up. *I* understand that, too: it's easy to give up. I don't play tennis any more, I don't swim as much as I used to. But I garden – I garden enormously.' She gestures towards the patio, beyond which a wide green lawn glints invitingly in the California sun. 'It keeps me outside, and it lets me take charge. The gardener comes every Monday and Thursday, but on the other days, if something's going to get done, it's up to me.' Befitting her English heritage, Lansbury concentrates on roses, but she also has a vegetable garden, and now she's taking up orchids. Proudly, she points to an exquisite white orchid she grew, in a vase on the grand piano.

Eloquently articulating a basic superyoung principle, she says, 'I've found that being interested in a lot of different things at the same time helps me to maintain a useful, healthy outlook.' The living room where she entertains guests reflects that catholicity of taste; it is furnished in a relaxed mixture of comfortable modern furniture and antiques, and is everywhere piled with books – novels, gardening guides and art books.

Although she earned her daily bread for twelve years as an actress on television, Lansbury says that she has 'one fixed rule – I never turn on the TV in the daytime.' However, this week, she admits, she has made an exception: this interview took place just days after the death of Diana, Princess of Wales, and Lansbury, like many people in the world, watched the extraordinary events unfold on television. Yet she says that this exception has only validated her rule: 'I've found that it dulls my spirits. It has precluded me from making any sense of anything that matters in my own life. I hate to say it, but people who sit at home and watch the soaps all day are literally wasting hours of their lives. They are planning the diminution of their own existence. It's very sad.'

Lansbury watches her diet very carefully, following a regimen that Michael DeBakey (see page 22) would approve of, concentrating on fresh fruits and vegetables, whole grains, and preferring fish to meat. Laughing, she says, 'The adage "You are what you eat" is certainly true. We just came back from spending two months at our house in Ireland. While we're there, it's hard to avoid eating lots of butter and rich food. But now that we're home, it's back to the straight and narrow.' She and her husband both stopped drinking alcohol in any form in 1974. 'It didn't agree with me,' she says with a frank smile, 'just as it doesn't agree with a lot of people.'

'I've been lucky,' she declares. 'I was always a strong, muscular woman, and I've had no hint of osteoporosis.' She pauses to touch the wooden arm of her chair. 'Of course, like anyone my age, I have the occasional headache, or a pain in my shoulder. I have osteoarthritis in my hip, and had to replace one hip, but I'm trying to deal with the pain without resorting to the use of anti-inflammatory drugs.' She says that she's trying out alternative treatments, such as homeopathic drugs, herbs and vitamins. 'I'm trying to sort out the good supplements from the not-so-good, which isn't easy nowadays – there are so many products out there now. I'm very encouraged to see that doctors now are recommending the use of vitamins and minerals more and more in recent years.'

Like many superyoung women, Lansbury tried hormone replacement therapy when she came to the menopause. 'I told Peter, I'm going to do everything in my power to fight this. I had oestrogen implants when the time came – a little pellet under the skin, right here,' she says, pointing to her hip. 'They did it in London – I think we're a little bit behind on this one, here in America.'

She graciously offers another gingernut biscuit, and then, straightening her already perfect posture just a tiny bit more, declares firmly, 'There's one thing I want to say. It's very easy for me to sit here and say that life is interesting. I have been very fortunate: I've achieved a certain success in my career as an actress, and I get tremendous feedback, constantly. For people like me, it's much easier. But there are a lot of people out there who are tremendously active and creative, and we just never hear about them. They're doing it for themselves.'

J. J.

CHAPTER THREE

THINKING YOUNGER

The young man who has not wept is a savage, and the old man who will not laugh is a fool.

George Santayana

Perhaps the most unfortunate effect of the ageing process, even more distressing than the alteration in outward appearance, is the inevitable, creeping decline of certain mental functions. Forgetting the names of people one has just met (or, worse, an old acquaintance!), constantly mislaying eyeglasses or the latch key, a feeling of bafflement when confronted with an unfamiliar task or technology – these are unmistakable adumbrations of advancing age. Yet while a certain degree of forgetfulness and confusion may be inevitable, the most important functions of the mind – creativity, imagination, affection, the critical faculties – are often left untouched by the ageing process. Sophocles was hard at work in his nineties; so was George Bernard Shaw. Michael DeBakey, at eighty-nine, remains one of the most influential medical innovators in the world (see page 22).

Declines in mental function due to ageing don't usually become apparent until the middle years, beginning in the mid-forties. The expression 'the prime of life' is ordinarily applied to the forties and fifties – decades when the outward manifestations of ageing are sometimes cruelly apparent, but the mind is sharp and able to benefit from a lifetime of experience and learning. The reflexes and muscular strength of the young may be superior, but the mind continues improving, gaining knowledge and wisdom well into maturity. While many 70-

47

year-olds may wish they could recapture the mental faculties they enjoyed in their thirties, few people in their forties and fifties would want to exchange their adult brains for the excitable, naïve minds they had as teenagers – not even if they came festooned with the thick hair, hard bodies and keen eyesight associated with that age.

In the superyoung project, we isolated and described some of the essential attributes of the youthful mind. With regard to their mode of thinking, the superyoung:

- are highly **adaptable**, open to new ideas from within and from beyond their immediate environment;
- are **playful** in their mental attitudes, always willing to have fun with new ideas;
- like to **think for themselves**, rather than relying on received wisdom;
- frequently **explore new areas of learning** and acquire new skills, at any age, and pursue knowledge for its own sake, rather than necessarily to advance their professional careers;
- **don't censor themselves, or expect others to do so**;
- have **faster reaction times** than other people their age;
- frequently **continue working** constructively long after they have passed the official retirement age.

The Myth of the Dying Brain

The superyoung subjects in the study tended to retain intellectual vigour until much later in life than their contemporaries, so it was really only possible to ascertain what those mental qualities were by making comparisons between the young and the elderly. It was only when the elderly superyoung began to notice certain declines in their mental functions that they were able to describe what their unimpaired abilities were. None the less, declines in intellectual ability are by no means universal: many people in late middle age and well beyond retain almost precisely the same mental powers they possessed when they were young. Why do some people hold on to these abilities, while others slowly grow more forgetful and confused?

The explanation for declining brain functions in later life always used to be that we lose brain cells as we age. However, a recent study by neurobiologists at Boston University, Washington University and Harvard Medical School has shown that that venerable old chestnut just isn't true. In studies using both human and monkey brains, these researchers discovered that nearly all of the ten billion cells that constitute the neocortex, the part of the brain that we use for most of our thinking, survive well into our seventies.

The myth of the dying brain came about as the result of studies in the post-war years that included victims of Alzheimer's disease with normal people; in those days, Alzheimer's was not nearly as well diagnosed as it is today, and some of its early and mild symptoms were accepted as the inevitable aspects of old age. A close study of brain scans reveals that the normal brain does shrink slightly, but the shrinkage doesn't occur in the so-called grey matter, which contains many of the more important neurons. The new research has found that the decline in mental functions associated with ageing results from a breakdown in the myelin, the fatty sheath that surrounds axons, the core of a nerve-fibre which conducts the impulses out of the cell. Acting as an insulator, myelin enables messages to be transmitted quickly and efficiently throughout the cells that constitute the brain's network. This sheath is normally interrupted every few millimetres along the length of the axon by narrow gaps, called the nodes of Ranvier. When a nerve impulse travels down the axon, it must shoot across these gaps. Nerve impulses decrease in strength as they travel down the axon, but whenever they encounter a node, they are powered up to their former strength.

The nodes of Ranvier have aptly been likened to miniature booster stations or superchargers.

If for any reason the myelin sheath should break down, the nerve cells become exposed. Such a breakdown might occur, for example, if the sheath becomes swollen or inflamed. This process is known to occur in people afflicted with multiple sclerosis; now there is strong evidence that a similar process happens during the course of normal ageing. Those who retain keen mental powers into later age probably have a genetic predisposition that protects the myelin sheath from breaking down. The good news, for those who don't have such genetic good fortune, is that the new findings hold out hope that new medications and treatments may be developed which can halt the decline of mental functions by preventing the deterioration of myelin in the first place.

There may be some alternative solutions to this sort of neural deterioration. It has long been known that when one part of the brain is damaged, unaffected areas may take over for it – a mysterious process known as neuronal plasticity, which is more potent the younger you are. Usually, cells in adjacent, undamaged areas partly take over for those that were lost or damaged. A sufferer who is aware of what's going on can sometimes perceive the effects of this process as it occurs. What is happening within the brain is reflected by behaviour, and that behaviour can cause aspects of the brain to improve – or cause further problems.

The playwright and screenwriter Robert Bolt, the author of *A Man for All Seasons*, had a stroke after heart-bypass surgery. Previously the most articulate and eloquent of men, always engaged in writing and reading and conversation, the stroke paralysed his right side and left him nearly speechless, at least in the beginning. His problems included a loss of natural speech cadences and a new distractibility, which made it difficult for him to divide his attention as he once could. Even his enjoyment of music was impaired: pieces that had once been sources of great delight grated on his ear. His fluent knowledge of French, and his ability to perform simple mathematical computations were also lost. It seems that the actual brain cells that had contained that specialized information had been destroyed. However, his ability to appreciate music did eventually return, and the surviving parts of his brain reorganized. He ultimately found that even though he had lost the natural flow of words that had been his gift before the stroke, he gained a greater grasp of concepts – a superb example of plasticity in the brain.

Another remarkable example of plasticity is that of a French magazine editor named Jean-Dominique Bauby, who suffered a rare form of stroke, which left his body completely paralysed, while his mental capacity was left unimpaired. Bauby wrote a book about the experience by developing a system with a collaborator, which used eyeblinks to communicate: one blink for yes, two for no, and a complex, Morse-style code for the alphabet. The book he 'wrote' by this method was a huge bestseller in France, but Bauby didn't live to enjoy his success: sadly, he died two days after the book was published.

New clinical studies have shown that your lifestyle may have a much more powerful effect on your mental condition than body chemistry. Making the right choices in early adulthood and later life can retard the effects of ageing on the mind to a significant degree. This is admittedly not an easy phenomenon to study. One difficulty is that to examine human subjects in a rigorously scientific way, researchers must carry out what are known as prospective longitudinal studies: i.e., following the same subjects over a long period of time, as opposed to cross-sectional studies, which compare groups of different ages at the same time. Longitudinal studies are expensive to perform, and take many years to gather enough information to form meaningful con- clusions. Nowadays, most young academic researchers lack the time and patience – and the funds – for such protracted studies. Cecilia Hurwich's 10-year research into the lives of elderly women in the San Francisco area (see page 134) is an excellent example of a successful longitudinal study.

One longitudinal study of mental activity, tracing the mental functions of a group of elderly people over the course of nearly twenty years, was conducted by researchers at the University of Queensland, Australia. This investigation, known as Operation Retirement, began in 1966 with 389 participants ranging in age from sixty to ninety-three. However, as the principal researcher, Elsie Harwood (originally partnered in this project by the late George Naylor), drily noted, 'It is scarcely necessary to add that wastage in an ageing sample is an inevitable fact to be reckoned with when a study is planned.' The mental alertness of the group, based upon much more reliable criteria than those used in previous studies, was examined at 5-year intervals. After a 10-year review in 1976, the investigators found that people in their sixties and seventies suffered a decrease in mental capacity of less than 1 per cent annually. Those in their eighties and beyond experienced an annual decrease of 2 per cent or less.

The researchers' most interesting discovery was that the subjects who were the youngest at the beginning of the study scored significantly higher when they reached their seventies than the older group had done at that age. They had taken part in a learning experiment, receiving lessons either in playing the recorder or in reading and translating German, or both – new activities which they pursued in some cases for as long as ten years. The older subjects, who had not participated in the learning experiments, showed much greater decreases in their mental powers.

Harwood concluded that 'under the guise of learning experiments, we had inadvertently provided rehabilitation activities for people whose ages in the initial learning experiments ranged from sixty-three to ninety-one'. She found that on average these subjects had increased their brains' ability to accept new information at the rate of 5 per cent annually. The recorder players scored best of all on the mental-activity examinations. When a standard examination in German was administered to those who had chosen that path, two-thirds of them passed, including one 89-year-old man; seven of the fifty-five German-language students received A grades.

One factor that skewed some of the individual results was the temporary effect of traumatic experiences, such as the death of a partner, or a domestic upheaval of one sort or another, such as moving into a new house. Whenever such an event was noted, the test was repeated six months later. In every case the subject's performance had returned to its previous level. That's an essential point, for traumatic experiences can occur to a person of any age. This finding suggests that some elderly people who are diagnosed with psychological dysfunction or incipient dementia may in fact only be suffering from the normal reaction to a sad or stressful life event.

Harwood stressed that the statistical analysis masked the fact that some members of the group, even a few of the very old people, had suffered no measurable mental decline at all, and a handful, at the end of fifteen years, had even improved. 'Generalization about deterioration in the aged,' she concluded, 'is statistically reasonable but clinically dangerous.' That judgment was strongly bolstered by a French researcher named Suzanne Pacaud, who conducted a study of railway workers, which disclosed a similar pattern in ageing subjects performing a wide variety of mental tasks. However, like Harwood, Pacaud found that something like 20 per cent of the group appeared to be altogether immune to the process of mental deterioration. Most of those whose capacities were undiminished by age had held jobs that demanded constantly changing mental activity.

The fact that a constant percentage of the people studied were exempted from the effects of ageing on the mind tends to suggest that there may be one or more genetic indicators for declining brain functions – or, to put it positively, for maintaining the youthful vigour of the mind – just as there is for some of the physical symptoms of ageing. However, a third study provides more than a glimmer of good news. In the nineteen-sixties, the American psychologist K. Warner Schaie, now at Pennsylvania State University, carried out an investigation that combined longitudinal and cross-sectional techniques. He measured the intellectual abilities of people from several different age groups, known as cohorts (a term he borrowed from Roman military nomenclature). Each of these groups was re-examined periodically at seven-year intervals over the course of thirty-five years, in what amounted to a parallel series of longitudinal studies. This approach neutralized the effects of age differences arising from the distinct cultural and historical circumstances of the successive cohorts.

Schaie's innovative research disclosed a pattern quite different from conventional expectations: rather than a rise through youth and a gradual, symmetrical fall in old age, in every cohort he found a series of undulating parabolas, with many rises and falls throughout all ages of life. He concluded that 'while it does not follow that all old people have declined intellectually, some indeed have, but so too have some people at age thirty. Our longitudinal studies of individuals show that we have some remarkable individuals who *gained* in levels of performance from age seventy to age eighty-four; others have *declined* from age twenty to age thirty.'

Schaie and company believe that the best model for describing the relationship between chronological age and intellectual capacity is one of plasticity – a capacity for growth or loss throughout every period of life. The plasticity model offers two alternative explanations for why the elderly generally score lower than the young on tests that measure cognitive abilities. One is that disuse has resulted in a temporary – yet reversible – diminution in brainpower; and the other has already been suggested, that members of the generation now in its seventies were not able to benefit from the educational advances and social reforms of the post-war era.

Since Schaie published his study, there seems to have been an emerging consensus among scientists studying the brain that age *per se* is not the prime determinant for intellectual ability. Regardless of age, if a person's mental functions have inexplicably regressed, the chances are good that there may be a lack of intellectual stimulation – and that means that the process can be reversed by enriching the mental and sensory environment.

As Michael DeBakey pointed out, the same principle of 'Use it or lose it' that describes the development and atrophy of muscles may also be applied to the brain, mysterious organ that it is. Although this metaphor is oversimplified, it has much to commend it, particularly in so far as it helps us to visualize the relationship between use and strength. Like a muscle, the brain will wither away unless it is exerted. That doesn't necessarily mean learning to play the harpsichord or read ancient Greek: it is primarily a question of enriching the basic intellectual environment. Psychologist Mark Rosenzweig, of the University of California, carried out a series of neurological experiments which strongly bolstered this point of view. Rosenzweig and his team put a group of laboratory rats into a complex environment full of playthings, such as ladders, ramps and wheels, which gave them the opportunity to experiment and remain active. The control group was left in bland, boring boxes. At the conclusion of the experiment, the rats who had been given the opportunity to entertain themselves were found to have thicker, heavier cerebral cortices.

Just to make sure that it wasn't simply the visual interest of the enriched environment that made the difference, Rosenzweig repeated the experiment with three groups: in addition to those who were allowed to interact freely with the playthings and those who were confined to the dull environment, a third group was allowed to watch what happened in the enriched environment but not to enter into it. The second experiment confirmed the findings of the first: the cerebral cortices of the third group, allowed to look at but not take advantage of the stimulating environment, were scarcely larger than the group with the impoverished environment, while the active group was once again found to have a heightened brain capacity.

The logical conclusion: it isn't enough simply to live in a stimulating environment; you must actively engage the mind in order to reap the advantages. Thus someone living in isolation in the country or a dreary suburban neighbourhood may still have an exciting life of the mind, by reading, writing, and making contacts with other people through whatever media are available; whereas a person living in the midst of a culturally rich place, say central London or New York, who goes to a tedious job every day, rides home on the underground or subway, and watches junk television when he gets home, may lead a mental life as impoverished as the rats in those drab boxes.

The problem of diminished brainpower is more often the end result of years of diminished stimulation. For many people, this sensory deprivation may begin to worsen in later life, as a result of a traumatic change such as widowhood or a drastic reduction in income. In my research, I have encountered many stories resembling this one:

A woman in her sixties, call her Megan, is widowed and forced to live on a fixed income. Her children have moved far away, as have most of the friends and neighbours with whom she spent her youth and maturity. Strangers, young people with families and concerns of their own, now live in her neighbourhood. She takes a small apartment, where she is surrounded by other retired folk. One day at the supermarket, Megan bumps into the wife of a business associate of her deceased husband, and she can't remember her name. Try as hard as she can, the name won't come to her. She's flustered, embarrassed. Even when she is at home again she can't remember the woman's name.

Megan interprets this quite ordinary event as something abnormal, an omen of mental decline. She predicts that the next time she's in a similar situation, the same thing will happen, building up a store of anxiety for the future. And true to the pattern of self-defeat, the next time she's out and sees someone familiar coming towards her, she panics. Now Megan avoids going out, fearful of social failure. Gradually, by stages, she becomes effectively agoraphobic, needlessly housebound and desperately lonely.

Loneliness is one the most serious and widespread mental-health problems of modern society. Today something like a third of the men and a quarter of the women over sixty-five are severely isolated. We are paying a terrible price for this, in terms of human suffering. Lonely people lose their self-esteem and become demoralized and self-focused to a morbid degree. They have difficulty introducing themselves, participating in groups, asking questions, enjoying themselves at parties – any activity that requires asserting themselves or risking potential embarrassment. Eventually, such people approach all encounters with other people with cynicism and bitterness; they notice faults in everyone they meet, and perceive slights that aren't really there. They evaluate themselves in negative terms, shamefully, and expect that others will view them in a similar light. They expect to be rejected, and so they are.

Chronic loneliness leads to sensory and perceptual deprivation. In the information age, television and the published media are poor substitutes for the stimulation of live human contact. Only 39 per cent of elderly people see their friends weekly or more often – which means that the majority spend most of their time alone. People isolated to that extent develop peculiar strategies to cope, which poignantly reveal what has been lost. They talk to themselves, first while pottering around the house and then in public; they argue with the talking heads of politicians and newscasters on television. They become desperately attached to their pets, whose deaths plunge them into deep mourning; they weep at the problems of complete strangers baring their souls on confessional TV talk shows. The village green has been all but abandoned; now most of our senior citizens stay at home, alone, confined in separate box-like dwellings, staring at small boxes glowing with identical, unreal images. There is still a commonality, but it is purely passive: we watch the same programmes on television, living our lives vicariously, in the vapid, unreal worlds of Oprah, Geraldo Rivera, and Richard and Judy.

In addition to loneliness, the other common barrier to a healthy degree of active participation in life is involuntary reticence – shyness – which afflicts some people later in life who, in their youth, may have had healthy social skills. Shyness arises from over-attention to oneself in social situations, which results in fearful, inappropriate behaviour and mild internal distress. Too timid to say boo to a goose, the shy retreat reluctantly from almost every situation in life. They speak less; they start fewer conversations, intervene in them less often, and take longer to respond to others when they are spoken to. Whereas most people become uncomfortable with long silences, the shy learn to tolerate them. They have an air of aloofness and indifference which results from their expectation that others will not find them interesting. It's a self-fulfilling prophecy, of course: those who are overcome with the fear that they will be dull, are dull.

People who forfeit human interaction and sensory stimulation in these ways for any length of time suffer the same sort of mental shrivelling as the rats living in the impoverished environment in Mark Rosenzweig's experiments. When they are asked to describe this vicious decline in the life of the mind, they use phrases such as 'mental clouding', 'thoughts hopping around', 'thoughts drifting in a random sequence', and, perhaps most accurately, 'a difficulty to think coherently'. In the beginning, this lack of stimulation occasionally jumbles their thoughts; with time, it becomes increasingly difficult for them to organize their thoughts and regain the clarity they once had. Finally, the effort becomes too great, and they simply give up, which leads to depression and even greater problems in concentrating.

The situation seems irreparable only because the sufferers don't seek help: they accept their state as normal, what inevitably happens to everyone who reaches an arbitrary age, some say sixty-five, or seventy, or eighty. The medical establishment sometimes conspires in this insidious process, providing momentary reassurances to the patients by telling them, 'It's just old age creeping up on you', or by using high-falutin jargon such as 'benign senescent forgetfulness'. Benign? Hardly.

The superyoung are at the opposite end of the spectrum. While they must cope with many of the same pressures and disappointments that face other elderly people, that's just the point: they cope. They persevere. When their mate dies or leaves them, they grieve and then set about finding someone new. Yvonne, an 88-year-old lady from Lincolnshire, who told us, 'I look sixty and feel thirty', had been widowed five times – a remarkable achievement not only of hope triumphing over experience, as Dr Johnson put it, but also of self-confidence. Yvonne describes herself as having a 'very happy personality', adding that she was 'able to turn each unhappy page in my life and start again. I don't brood on the past.' Every day is an adventure, she says – 'even if it's only to meet someone out shopping for a chat'.

The elderly lonely can learn from superyoung people like Yvonne. In retirement, inertia propels us towards isolation; the solution is to fight back, to see that a chat in the supermarket can be an adventure rather than an ordeal. As the avenues of sociability are cut off, the lonely must open new ones. The Australian experiment with German language study and playing the recorder are slightly recondite choices for late-life elective study: Italian cooking, bible study, or a course in the films of Alfred Hitchcock will do just as nicely. A new organization for seniors that has gained great popularity in the United States is Elderhostel, a non-profit educational organization based in

Boston, which offers modestly priced, short-term programmes that frequently involve excursions and foreign travel. The participants visit colleges and universities throughout the world, where they attend lectures by academic professionals and go into the field to explore what they are learning in class.

The subjects offered by Elderhostel range from the traditional pursuits of retirement, such as watercolours, pottery, music appreciation and ballroom dancing, to scholarly studies of the African-American church and learning the basics of blacksmithing in a traditional forge. The international programme covers the globe, from a musical pilgrimage to Salzburg to trekking in the mountains of China. The service programme attracts the most physically active seniors with programmes that allow them to work as volunteers in academic research, usually alongside undergraduates, and in charitable service projects. Elders with an interest in marine biology can help scientists study the bottle-nose dolphins of Belize; those inclined towards archaeology can dig alongside the professionals at a Mayan ruin or help to conserve an Anasazi site in Colorado.

The key to the success of Elderhostel and similar programmes is that it allows the participants to aim high. One of the principal reasons that we have consistently miscalculated and underestimated the intellectual abilities of the elderly is because we insist on comparing them with adolescents and young adults. A retired person studying the culture of the Plains Indians or Italian Renaissance architecture does so for the sheer pleasure of it, whereas a college student undertakes a course of study out of necessity, to launch a career and a life.

The same distinction needs to be drawn in the nature of adult education. When curricula and teaching methods created for adolescents are applied to elders, the results can be disappointing and disheartening. Undergraduates at Harvard are expected to read 500-page novels and history books at the rate of two or three a week, with the underlying supposition that the course of instruction is designed to prepare them for graduate school, and ultimately to become literary scholars or political scientists. The purpose of elder education is to improve the quality of the students' lives by keeping their minds sharp. The point is not that the elderly student is incapable of reading *Tom Jones* and a biography of Abraham Lincoln in one week, but rather that when there's no compelling need to cram as much information as possible into the brain, there will be little motivation to do so. Indeed, there would be something almost unnatural about a retired person who pursued such an extreme course of study: far better to vary the intellectual regime with a mystery novel, an evening at the theatre, some time in the garden.

Elder education is just one way of accomplishing these aims. In some areas, particularly in rural communities, there may be no facilities for formal education (however informal), or the curriculum choices may be very limited. However, the brain is the most adaptable of organs, and there are really limitless ways of diverting and expanding it. The most obvious method is by reading; the most insidious is by watching television. Some members of the superyoung study were adamantly opposed to television-viewing; most seemed indifferent. The one thing that almost all of them shared was a passion for mental activity.

Oxygen is the key: although the brain has only two per cent of the body's weight, it accounts for a quarter of its oxygen intake. When you use a particular part of your brain, the flow of oxygenated blood to that region (and therefore of oxygen) increases by about 30 per cent. One of the most common physiological perils of old age, arteriosclerosis, affects the arteries leading to the brain as well as those leading to the heart; when fat clogs them up, the supply of oxygen to the brain is reduced, seriously diminishing its ability to function. In one study, elderly people who had their arteries cleaned out improved their scores on IQ tests markedly – by 4.6 points on verbal comprehension, and a whopping twelve points on perceptual organization. Moreover, their mental health was significantly better, with lower incidences of anxiety, suspicion, distress and disorientation.

The brain's oxygen supply, and thus its ability to function properly, can also be curtailed by atherosclerosis and high blood pressure. A ten-year longitudinal study at Duke University found that elderly people with high blood pressure experienced a steady rate of mental decline, while those with normal blood pressure had no decrease. Thus one of the major factors in mental deterioration in old age, declining oxygen supply, may be entirely physiological – and, therefore, often reversible. Furthermore, a therapeutic programme of oxygen-enrichment has been shown to repair damaged mental faculties. Even very brief periodic sessions in an oxygen chamber can sometimes work wonders in revitalizing the brainpower of elderly people.

Such remedies are usually only necessary in extreme cases: for most people, the oxygen enrichment provided by physical exercise is enough. Even in modest amounts, exercise possesses curative powers for both mind and body. The latest research proves beyond any doubt that those who exercise become less depressed, tend to be less hypochondriacal, develop more positive attitudes to life, and have an improved self-image.

An increased activity level is broadly conducive to a richer emotional life and better intellectual functioning, particularly in extreme old age. Up to a point, the more physiologically aroused a person remains, the better. Good levels of alertness and open-mindedness are associated with faster reaction times and better recognition memory. People with a younger attitude towards life have livelier brains, pure and simple.

In addition to physical exercises, therapeutic mental exercises can also greatly expand the powers of the brain. For the past twenty-five years, I have been developing a strategy for building a healthy brain and maintaining it in optimum condition – a programme I call the Brain Plan, which is described in the second part of this book. Some of these exercises for the brain are especially designed to enliven and restore the brains of elderly people who have fallen into patterns of mental inertia, boredom and atrophy, but most of them are intended for younger people, to help them keep their faculties sharp and prevent any mental degeneration from occurring in the first place.

Questionnaire:
You *Are* as Young as You Think You Are

This questionnaire, based upon our interviews with the subjects in the superyoung project, is designed to help you analyse your mental condition and attitudes. There are no right or wrong answers, because everyone has a unique way of coping with and looking at the world. Answer accurately and truthfully, but don't ponder over each statement too much: give the first, spontaneous answer that seems right to describe you best. There are no trick questions or hidden meanings. Choose the answer that reflects how you actually feel at the moment, not how you think you ought to feel, or what other people might wish you to feel. Be sure to answer all the questions, or your score will not be valid.

1. On first seeing someone I know, the person's name immediately springs to my mind.

    Always (2) Sometimes (1) Never (0)

2. My memory is as sharp now as it was when I was younger.

    Strongly agree (2) Sometimes (1) Strongly disagree (0)

3. My mind and thinking is very well-organized.

    All the time (2) Sometimes (1) Never (0)

4. I can concentrate on one detail of a single topic for as long as necessary.

    Always (2) Sometimes (1) Never (0)

5. When aroused, my curiosity is boundless.

    Always (2) Sometimes (1) Never (0)

---

6. I have a number of goals which I want to attain.

    True (2) Uncertain (1) False (0)

7. I like to analyse the causes underlying obstacles and difficulties.

    True (2) Uncertain (1) False (0)

8. I choose activities that may offer me learning experiences.

    Often (2) Sometimes (1) Never (0)

9. I am not afraid to learn from an error or mistake, whether it be mine or another's.

    True (2) Unsure (1) False (0)

10. It is my own responsibility to set realistic long-term goals for my future.

    Strongly agree (2) Unsure (1) Strongly disagree (0)

11. I never let my attention wander when I'm looking at something.

    True (2) Sometimes (1) False (0)

12. Images in my mind's eye are vivid, and as important to me as words are.

    Strongly agree (2) Unsure (1) Strongly disagree (0)

13. I am never distracted by stray, irrelevant thoughts.

    True (2) Sometimes (1) False (0)

14. I love to experiment with new ideas.

    True (2) Sometimes (1) False (0)

15. To solve a problem, I will try out several different approaches.

    True (2) Sometimes (1) False (0)

Interpreting Your Responses

Add up your total score. The interpretations that follow are based upon data comparisons between the superyoung subjects and the control group in my study. The average adult score on this questionnaire is 15, the median for a scale with a top mark of 30. For adolescents it may be closer to 13, and for seniors over sixty years of age, 11.

More than 25 You are quite likely to be among the superyoung, a bright, assured person always searching for bolder challenges to test your intellect. Your faculties are now razor-sharp.

18–25 Although you may not be totally satisfied with your mental skills, you are basically sharp and stable. You prefer to be, and are, in control of most aspects of your life.

11–17 You are in the middle of the field. You like to plan ahead, and do so successfully more often than not. You are sociable yet independent; you have some capabilities that may have been held back by your occasional lapses and inadvertent mistakes.

5–10 You have begun to discern some mildly discouraging changes in your concentration and learning abilities, but if you have a history of self-awareness, you may use this realization as a spur to further your personal growth.

4 or less You have significant mental difficulties, at least at present. You might consider examining more closely what is happening to your intellectual abilities, and take some steps to restore the vigour of your mind.

Ben Bradlee

At seventy-six, Ben Bradlee is still as powerful a presence today as he was during his years as executive editor of the *Washington Post*, when he broke the Watergate stories that ultimately brought down Richard Nixon's presidency, and defied the Federal government by publishing the secret documents known as the Pentagon Papers – ushering in a new era of investigative journalism. Bradlee still comes into his office at the *Post* five days a week, dressed in his signature Asser & Turnbull dress shirts, the sleeves rolled up to the elbows of his meaty arms. The walls are covered with memorabilia from his fifty-two years as a newspaperman, much of it pertaining to President John F. Kennedy, who was a close personal friend.

Bradlee greets his visitors with a firm handshake and a sparkle in his eyes. When asked about his experiences since retirement, he throws up his hands and says, 'I sometimes wonder what I'm doing. I was very concerned, when I left the post of executive editor here, that the phone would never ring.' Of course, the phone never stops ringing for a person of his vigour and dynamism. In the years since his retirement as top editor at the *Post*, at the age of seventy, he has headed up a \$40 million capital fund drive for Washington's Children's Hospital; assumed the presidency of a historic commission in southern Maryland (where he has painstakingly restored an eighteenth-century frame house); served as an active director for an international chain of small newspapers; written a 500-page, best-selling memoir (*A Good Life*); and taught a course at Georgetown University. He regularly plays golf and tennis, and works out twice a week, with weights, at the gym. With a dazzling smile, Bradlee adds, 'And every Saturday morning, at the house in Maryland, I go out into the woods with my toys, my tractor and chainsaw, and just go at it until I'm exhausted – usually three or four hours.' Some retirement.

Like many superyoung people, Bradlee relaunched his personal life in middle age: in 1973, at the age of fifty-two, he split up with his second wife to live with a younger woman, the journalist and broadcaster Sally Quinn. They married five years later, and in 1982 Quinn gave birth to a son. Describing his life with Quinn, he used exactly the same language we heard continually from the subjects in the superyoung clinical study: 'Having a wife twenty years younger than me has definitely helped keep me young. I prefer the company of younger people.

I still have some friends in their seventies and eighties, but the problem is, now they're starting to die off.'

Of all his professional pursuits in 'retirement', the one that has consumed him most has been the presidency of the Historic St Mary's City Commission, which administers the fourth oldest English settlement in America – and the country's first Catholic community. 'It was an experiment in religious freedom. St Mary's was the first place where women voted.' The Commission is now excavating and rebuilding the oldest Catholic church in America. 'I've been enormously energized by thinking small,' he says. 'Doing something like this for a huge institution like Harvard College wouldn't interest me at all.'

When Bradlee was an undergraduate at Harvard, he was enrolled in the Grant Study of Adult Development, a pioneering longitudinal study financed by W. T. Grant, the department store magnate. The study chose young men from among Harvard undergraduates, on the premise that they had already achieved some success in life, to determine what factors 'led to intelligent living'. The study has continued to follow Bradlee and the other 267 men throughout their lives. 'They're amazingly persistent,' he says. 'I just mailed in the last questionnaire a few weeks ago.' The study has found that the Harvard group has had about the same percentage of divorce, alcoholism and financial success or failure as the general population. 'The study's motivation was a little suspect,' Bradlee confides. 'Grant's idea, I think, was that we shouldn't waste our money on blacks, lepers and left-handed psychopaths, but instead figure out how to produce winners.'

What most interested the Grant Study scientists in Bradlee, after their first interviews with him, was the fact that he had recovered fully from a severe bout with polio. There had been an epidemic of the disease, then known as infantile paralysis, at his boarding school; young Bradlee was among those paralysed, but he never succumbed to despair at the prospect of life as a cripple. 'The shrinks in the Grant Study were stunned by the fact that "this person", as they always called me, didn't worry about being paralysed. Looking back, I can't believe it myself. Either it was a strong sense of fatalism, or else I was just too dumb to think about the future.'

Leaning back in his chair and musing, Bradlee says, 'Maybe that's the key to staying young, how each of us handles stress. My father was very stoical, accepting of his fate. I wonder if it's possible that stress management is genetic. My wife and I were discussing this last night. First we were saying "It can't be genetic," and then we said, "Why *can't* it be genetic?"'

J. J.

CHAPTER FOUR

LOOKING YOUNGER

'You are old, Father William,' the young man said,
  'And your hair has become very white;
And yet you incessantly stand on your head –
  Do you think, at your age, it is right?'
'In my youth,' Father William replied to his son,
  'I feared it might injure the brain;
But now that I'm perfectly sure I have none,
  Why I do it again and again.'
'You are old,' said the youth, 'as I mentioned before,
  And have grown most uncommonly fat;
Yet you turned a back-somersault in at the door –
  Pray, what was the reason of that?'
'In my youth,' said the sage, as he shook his grey locks,
  'I kept all my limbs very supple
By the use of this ointment – one shilling the box –
  Allow me to sell you a couple?'

                                    Lewis Carroll

The only objective quality of the superyoung is their appearance: the impartial observers in our study, remember, thought that the women in the study looked, on average, ten years younger than their true age, and the men got a discount of more than twelve years. Quite a sizeable number were judged to be a solid twenty years younger than they are.

Kyle Johnson, a criminal defence lawyer in Texas, is forty-five and looks to be in his early thirties. His black hair is so thick that it piles up in a forelock, and his athletic figure is exactly as trim as it was in his college days. It's only when you look closely that you notice some fine lines around his eyes. As the superyoung so often do, he married a woman twelve years younger than himself, but despite her youthful vivacity – and much to her chagrin – people who meet them invariably assume that they're the same age. Johnson says that while his youthful appearance is a social asset, it can cause problems for him professionally. 'People in Texas say everybody wants a young doctor and an old lawyer. I always casually drop my age into the first meeting with a client – I get a lot of clients in their early thirties, and they usually assume that I'm younger than they are, instead of ten years older.' Johnson's grandmother, now in her nineties and in excellent health, still keeps her own house and garden, a few doors down the street from her daughter, Kyle's mother.

Meg Barone is a lively, voluptuous woman with flowing blond hair and cobalt blue eyes that sparkle in an oval, unlined face: she's forty-three and could easily pass for thirty. She now works as a reporter for a newspaper in Connecticut, but for several years she was a model, and found that even in her late thirties she was invariably cast as an *ingénue*. She has mostly dated men much younger than herself, sometimes quite innocently, with no idea that they're as young as they are. When she was thirty-four, she began dating an 18-year-old boy: she thought he was in his mid-twenties – and that's what he thought about her! Like Kyle Johnson, Barone makes a habit of revealing her age to people she's interviewing, so they don't treat her like a cub reporter. 'The minute someone finds out my age, there's a bit of a prejudice,' says Barone. 'But I don't care. I'm proud of my experience.'

Almost everyone who meets Kyle Johnson or Meg Barone immediately assumes that they're much younger than they are. Why is that? What are the underlying factors that contribute towards that assumption? What exactly do we mean when we say that someone looks young? The answer begins, obviously, with the degree to which people in middle and advancing age retain the appearance they had in their youth. That absence of the changes wrought by ageing, a quality of unchangingness, constitutes the most powerful impression of youth.

One way of defining the qualities of youthfulness is to do so negatively, by searching out the factors that most frequently give visual evidence of ageing. The most obvious of all is grey hair, which is proverbially associated with old age: not only Father William but also Coleridge's Ancient Mariner, for example, were known to be old men by their long grey beards or hair. People whose hair grows grey or white in early middle age are often taken to be older than their years; the corollary is that those who keep a shock of jet-black hair into advanced age (whether natural or out of the bottle) will be likely to have a few years knocked off their apparent age. There's an advantage here for blond and especially red-headed people, for their hair tends to go gradually sandy rather than to turn grey.

Thinning hair or baldness contribute powerfully towards creating the impression of old age. Male-pattern baldness affects as much as 40 per cent of the adult male population, primarily among men of European descent, but advanced hair loss doesn't ordinarily make itself apparent in most men until they reach their fifties and sixties. Thus a man who has a polished cue-ball dome by the age of forty will be taken for someone much older than his years. The situation is even worse for women: there's nothing unusual about a bald man, but extremely thin hair on a woman may be regarded as an abnormal condition.

Another factor that contributes towards a youthful impression is small size, both in terms of height and weight. As illogical as it is, short people remind us of children and thus seem cute. Slender people also have a more youthful image because of their perceived similarity to adolescents and young adults, who are less likely to be overweight. The association of a slender body type with youth is greatly reinforced by the popular culture, especially advertising, which banishes images of obesity to the same Siberia reserved for old age.

Perhaps the most conspicuous clues to a person's age are to be found in the skin. Our visual perception of a person usually begins with the face; and if the eyes are the windows of the soul, as the poets say, then we form our first impression of a person, and hence his age, by the window dressing. Wrinkles and bags under the eyes can make one look prematurely aged just as decisively as can greying or thinning hair.

Wrinkles eventually come to everyone, and genetic predisposition plays a major role, but the onset and severity of facial wrinkles are affected by a number of factors, notably prolonged ultraviolet exposure, smoking, diet and sleeping habits. The most deleterious factor, undoubtedly, is continual exposure to strong sunlight. Outdoor labourers in tropical climates – or, for that matter, ski instructors and tennis pros in northern climes – often have the leathery, deeply lined skin of 70-year-olds while they are still in the prime of life.

However, for people who spend most of their lives indoors, smoking is undoubtedly the face's worst enemy. The destructive effects of smoking have been incontrovertibly proved by a detailed study of identical middle-aged twins carried out by doctors at St Thomas's Hospital, London. It was an elegant, nearly perfect case-study: in every pair of twins, one sibling had been a chronic smoker while the other had never smoked. Therefore, the comparisons were between people who had shared identical family and school environments throughout childhood and adolescence – and, of course, they possessed identical genes.

The smokers, on average, looked ten years older than their non-smoking twins. Fine-grained ultrasound measurements showed that the smokers' skin was 40 per cent thinner, more fragile and thus more heavily lined than that of their siblings. Some of the chemicals in cigarette smoke produce a harmful enzyme which breaks down collagen, thereby decreasing the skin's natural elasticity. Cigarette smoke also reduces blood flow throughout the skin, which damages the tissues that maintain its healthy tone. Finally, the skin of cigarette smokers is substantially drier than that of non-smokers, the result of the smoke's destructive influence on the skin's protective oils.

Many of the participants in the superyoung study, nearly as many men as women, were eager to contribute detailed accounts of the beauty regimens they followed in order to maintain the youthful tone of their skin. There can be little doubt that some form of moisturizing is essential for middle-aged skin to retain its suppleness and healthy glow: the skin's oil ducts slowly dry up as part of the ageing process, and unless those natural oils are replenished, the skin will become cracked and sere. However, many of the superyoung reported that inexpensive moisturizing lotions were just as efficacious at doing the job as exclusive products with famous names and flowery perfumes added to them.

Medical journalist Anne-Lise Gotzsche also believes that a lifetime of heavy make-up use may accelerate facial ageing – an ironic side-effect of overenthusiastic attempts at self-beautification. The late biochemist and nutritionist Adelle Davis, author of the bestseller *Let's Eat Right to Keep Fit*, showed that an entire generation of American women had aged their skin prematurely by using 'cold creams', as they were called, which contained a high concentration of mineral oil, which clogged the skin's pores and contributed towards wrinkling.

Yet we discovered in the superyoung project that the secret to looking young lies not in facial scrubs or ointments but rather is directly linked to feeling and thinking young. If you worry too much throughout your life, it will show on your face: why do you think they call them worry lines? Our study revealed the following profile of the superyoung people who looked much younger than their years (in descending order of importance). The most youthful looking subjects:

- **exercise regularly**, though there was a lower-than-expected threshold for the beneficial effects;

- enjoy a **robust sex life**, significantly higher than average for their age group both in terms of quantity and quality, usually in the context of a loving relationship;
- **work and socialize with younger people**;
- are significantly **more likely to marry people younger than themselves** (usually seven to fifteen years younger);
- are somewhat **more likely to be vegetarian**, though there was no pronounced tendency to adopt dietary fads;
- tend to put a great deal of **credence in legitimate scientific studies** pertaining to health and disease prevention.

We found that the first two elements are far and away the most important for maintaining a youthful appearance. Regular aerobic exercise for about forty minutes daily can add as much as twelve years to a person's life, but to look younger requires much less. The equivalent of three brisk one-mile walks a week, we found, is sufficient to help you look between five and eight years younger, in middle and later years. The major advantages arise from improved circulation, bone strength and immune-system functions, and a more favourable muscle-to-fat ratio in the body, caused by a small rise in the release of growth hormone. Some of the benefits of exercise can be lost, especially when it begins in mid-life, if it is time-pressurized or produces undue amounts of mental stress.

Improving the quality of your sex life and, less importantly, the frequency of intercourse, can help a person to look between four and seven years younger. This results from significant reductions in stress, greater contentment, better sleep, and, in men, a slight increase in testosterone output, caused by the natural bouncing motion of the testicles during intercourse.

Sexual intercourse, most people would agree, is one of the most pleasurable of human experiences. When it culminates in orgasm, the body feels good, setting in train further physical responses. Like a number of other stimulating sensations, sex releases a group of substances in the brain, among them the beta-endorphins, natural painkillers that also alleviate anxiety.

Any exercise as vigorous as sexual intercourse also acts to trigger a small release of human growth hormone. HGH is primarily secreted in short, sharp bursts, which occur approximately seven times a day. These bursts can arise spontaneously or after several different sorts of internal or external stimulation. Many of the effects of growth hormone act through another group of peptide hormone substances, called either the soma-tomedins or insulin-like growth factors, to reduce fatty tissue and increase lean muscle in various parts of the body, giving a more youthful appearance. Of course, these secretions are not only triggered by sex; sleeping dreams and waking fantasies may also cause the process to take place.

We also found that sex, and orgasm in particular, can help stimulate and tone the immune system. The American gynaecologist Dudley Chapman, for instance, studied twenty-four women with breast cancer, and found that those who had orgasms regularly recovered faster than those who didn't. It wasn't the presence of a loving partner that made the difference, necessarily; it was purely the physiological effects of the orgasm, which boosted the body's T3 and T4 lymphocyte cells, which are known to fight infection, by as much as twenty per cent.

The significance of the sex factor came as a surprise. As much as physical activity, sex is an important part of life for the superyoung from late adolescence to early adulthood. Their erotic interactions are characterized by a willingness to express themselves to each other as intimately and thoroughly as possible, and to be good listeners in return. Their emotional sanity relieves, or prevents, a build-up of harmful amounts of stress-related anxiety, and complements the physical benefits of sex and exercise.

Short stature, male-pattern baldness, greying hair – all these are hereditary traits, over which a person has no control. As far as these factors are concerned, the superyoung really are just lucky. Attempts to rectify these conditions are generally doomed to failure: lifts in the shoes can't make the limbs longer or the shoulders wider; wigs and toupees will go awry; even the best dye job eventually grows out. Still other visual factors, however, arise directly from a person's life style and personality. Posture probably has even more to do with a person's apparent age than does his height and weight: a young man with a stooped, round-shouldered posture adds decades to his perceived age. Good posture can actually help prevent some aspects of the ageing process, such as decreases in the mass and greater brittleness of the bones. A person's gait also makes a strong statement about age: young people have a spring in their step, while old folks not only move more slowly but also tend to shuffle their feet.

The most conspicuous statement people make about their self-image is the way they dress: as the French say, 'The hat makes the man.' As a group, the superyoung proved to be way above average in fashion-consciousness, and many of them made a point of trying to dress in the latest styles. Jo Ann Jacobsen is a successful fashion designer, now forty-four years old, though she appears to be scarcely thirty. And the reason isn't simply her girlish, curvy figure, or her fresh, unlined skin. In Jacobsen's profession, it's important to dress in hip fashions, and she carries this to an extreme, sporting witty, flamboyant styles to show off her figure, which many a woman in her late twenties would think twice about.

Jacobsen's passion in life is rock 'n' roll, which she follows avidly. Rock music is famously hostile to ageing; while most of her contemporaries have settled down to the early-to-bed habits of family life, Jo Ann rocks on. 'To me, it's not about being young,' she says, 'it's about being alive, it's about being open and continuing to grow. That's what I admire about youth and young people: they keep changing. They make things change.'

Jo Ann is currently dating a 22-year-old musician, and frequently goes out to rock clubs with him. Brash younger lads at the clubs sometimes approach her and flirt with her out-rageously, mistaking her for someone of their own age or younger. She has a lot of stories like this one: 'Last weekend I went out to a club, and a musician, a very talented kid who can't be much more than seventeen years old, asked me to kiss him. I didn't want to laugh – that can really hurt the pride of a guy that age – so I kissed him on the cheek. He said, "No, I mean a real kiss." So I told him, "Kid, if I really kissed you, I could be picked up for child molesting." He had no idea what I was talking about.'

Looking young isn't always a blessing. James Fairbanks, a journalist from Kent, is forty years old but looks like a lad in his twenties, with a round, cherubic face that is usually turned up in a smile. He is well known among his friends and colleagues for his youthfulness; at work his buddies call him 'Dorian', identify-ing him with the protagonist of Oscar Wilde's novel. He has found that while his boyish good looks have always given him great luck with the ladies, in his professional life it has been a palpable disadvantage (just as it has been for Meg Barone, see page 70). As a reporter, he must frequently deal with the public – often powerful figures in politics and business, whom he needs to impress as being trustworthy and professional. 'I'm constantly having to "prove" myself to people. A lot of times I will have spoken with them on the phone, and then when they meet me, they react by saying "I expected a much older man."'

James has been aware of the fact that he looks younger than his chronological age since adolescence, when the concept of ageing first begins to have a serious meaning for the growing child. His puberty was 'perfectly normal', he says; he matured at the same time as his contemporaries, but 'old school photo-graphs show that around the age of sixteen I got left behind'. When the other boys began to develop beards and hair on the chest, and other secondary sexual characteristics, James remained childish-looking.

Like many superyoung people, James believes that his super-young appearance is a major factor towards making him feel younger. He delights in it, admitting that he looks forward to the day when his daughter, now twelve, will be old enough for busybodies in public places to whisper 'Disgusting – he's old enough to be her father', so he can turn around and say, 'Madam, I am!'

There is a fuzzy grey line that separates the exceptionally youthful and the immature. There was a small but significant number of participants in the superyoung project, mostly male, who were unhappy on account of their extremely youthful physical and mental life. Bernard Parker, from London, told us that even at the age of forty-three, he feels juvenile and is unable to accept the responsibilities of an adult. He still suffers from acne, and his hobbies are those of a boy: building model aeroplanes and playing computer games.

When he told us about his adolescence, he explained himself with the awkwardness of a teenager: 'I had early difficulties "growing up",' he said, putting the quote marks around the phrase verbally. 'I was embarrassed at actually "becoming a man", if you understand my meaning.' Bernard's immaturity has prevented him from enjoying a normal romantic life; at the time we interviewed him, he and his wife were getting divorced. He told us sadly, 'She's fed up with living with a little boy, or so she says.'

There's no doubt that Bernard is, technically speaking, a superyoung person. Everything he told us about himself fits the pattern, right down to his family history: his grandparents lived to be ninety years old. Yet in his case, being superyoung was complicated by a neurotic obsession with boyhood, which may have been abetted by his genetic predisposition towards a youthful appearance but was not necessarily caused by it.

Bernard's pattern of behaviour – avoidance of adult respon-sibilities, a preference for activities associated with boyhood, and the inability to form a lasting love relationship – are sometimes called the Peter Pan syndrome, referring to the hero of James M. Barrie's novel and play about the little boy who never grew up. This phenomenon is quite distinct from that of the superyoung: Peter Pans are boys who never progress into emotional adulthood, remaining preoccupied with boyish pursuits, whereas the male superyoung continue to follow a course set in young manhood throughout their lives, enjoying activities that are appropriate to their apparent and real age groups.

The trouble begins when a man won't, or can't, leave behind his glorious boyhood. Nowadays, it's easy for a grown-up boy to flee from reality. The games of childhood can be continued, with football exchanged for less arduous ones – golf, darts and snooker progressing to electronic toys and fast cars, and a compliant wife or girlfriend indulging them, acquiescing in a necessarily maternal role.

Boys who don't know how to grow up are left behind, in a kind of limbo: whimsical, easily hurt, imprisoned in immaturity until the real world forces some sense of duty upon them. As one Peter Pan, now forty-nine years old, told me, 'The period between four and twelve was my personal golden age. To this day, I relate better to children than to adults. I'm awkward, gauche, too holding back of my feelings in adult company. With adults, you have to expect ulterior motives and suspect betrayal all the time. If that's what growing up is all about, count me out!'

Bernard shared that sense of disgust. At one point he told us, 'I cannot relate to people of my own age, male or female.' That statement was the tip-off of a neurotic personality: he phrased his situation negatively, as a disability in relating to people close in age to himself, rather than positively, as a preference for those younger than himself. The healthy superyoung, to an overwhelming extent, expressed unalloyed delight in their own youthful appearance and in the company of the young.

That delight, that zest for life, is not in itself a youthful quality, but it certainly highlights a youthful appearance. Looking young starts in the mind and radiates outwards. The facial expressions of happiness are the most easily recognized of all the emotions. It is also the most accurately identifiable, regardless of sex or widely disparate cultural backgrounds. Happiness can be ascertained visually within 12–25 milliseconds, whereas fear, by contrast, requires 300 milliseconds or more.

The ultimate secret to looking young, then, may simply be, 'Don't worry; be happy.' The superyoung have discovered a positive, upward spiral: their cheerful outlook keeps them looking young, and their youthful looks give them something to be happy about.

Questionnaire:
Do You Look As Young As You Feel?

This questionnaire, based upon our study of the subjects in the superyoung project, is designed to be widely applicable. There are no right or wrong answers, but be sure to answer all the questions, or your score won't be valid. Answer accurately and truthfully, but don't ponder over your answers too much; there are no trick questions or hidden meanings. The questions are designed to determine whether you have a superyoung appearance – the higher your score, the more likely you are to be among the superyoung.

1. Other people have told me that I look younger than I am.

    Many (2) A few (1) No one (0)

2. I enjoy wearing clothing styles similar to those worn by much younger people.

    Always (2) Sometimes (1) Never (0)

3. People have wanted to check my age, not believing me at first.

    Often (2) Sometimes (1) Never (0)

---

4.   I regard my intimate relationship(s) as very fulfilling.

   True (2) Unsure (1) False (0)

5.   I pay a lot of attention to my appearance and self-presentation.

   Always (2) Sometimes (1) Never (0)

6.   I have become pleasantly accustomed to hearing positive reactions and remarks about me from others.

   True (2) Unsure (1) False (0)

7.   I can work well with younger people.

   Always (2) Sometimes (1) Hardly ever (0)

8.   I have little time for reminiscing about the past, or pining over what might have been.

   True (2) Sometimes (1) False (0)

9.   There have been times when I've had to make myself look more mature.

   Three or   Once or
   more times (2) twice (1) Never (0)

10. I have a hard time imagining myself getting older.

   True (2) Unsure (1) False (0)

11. I socialize as easily with younger people as with older people.

   Always (2) Sometimes (1) Never (0)

12. I love to wear my hair in stylish, trendy styles.

   Always (2) Sometimes (1) Never (0)

13. I am very socially outgoing.

   True (2) Sometimes (1) False (0)

14. I dislike outsmarting other people.

> True (2) Sometimes (1) False (0)

15. I can be quite charming in a number of different settings.

> Always (2) Occasionally (1) Never (0)

Interpreting Your Responses

26 or more Your strikingly youthful appearance makes you stand out in a crowd of your contemporaries, though you have accepted this as your personal norm. You like being noticed, and have become a joyful, well-balanced extrovert. You love life, and would will yourself never to age if you could.

19–25 Your love of young people and new ideas is abundant. You stretch your sense of style to the limits, but those around you admire the *élan* with which you pull it off. You delight in meeting people, forming new friendships, and, most of all, being in love. Positivity rules your life like a benign despot.

12–18 Personable and charming, you possess a youthful appearance that can work well for you. You are a person of many accomplishments, but now you may be beginning to question the true nature of success. You might be thinking that the time is coming to settle down and devote yourself to your primary relationships.

5–11 You are a person of good taste and discretion, but those qualities sometimes inhibit your initial, spontaneous responses to life. You tend to retreat into shyness, which makes other people at times regard you as reserved or even, incorrectly, as 'stuck up'.

4 or less You don't cope well with stress, and it has taken a toll on your appearance. Self-awareness for you can be painful and difficult, more so than your family and friends realize. You may be paying a price, both professionally and in your personal affairs, for rejecting the dictates of fashion. However, you can improve in all of these areas by seeking expert advice.

Plastic Surgery

The mania to appear young is proverbially associated with the United States, where many people go to extreme lengths to maintain the appearance of youth – trying to buy their way into the ranks of the superyoung, as it were, by paying thousands of dollars to plastic surgeons to snip away wrinkles from their faces and suction out fat from their bodies. The cost of cosmetic surgery has dropped drastically since 1990, with the result that many more people than ever before are going under the scalpel in an effort to cheat time. California, the dream factory of the world, leads the nation, with more than 500,000 cosmetic operations a year.

At the moment, according to *Vogue*, the top plastic surgeon in America is Daniel Baker, whose clients include film stars such as Sophia Loren, Lauren Bacall and Christopher Walken. The waiting list for a consultation at his office on Park Avenue is a long one; for an initial appointment, expect to wait anywhere from a year to a year and a half. In an interview in his office, a palatial room furnished with antiques and leather-bound chairs, Baker said that his patients range in age from their early thirties to their eighties. 'Last week I saw five women over eighty. I have a hard time dealing with that. I always think, if this were my mother, would I operate? At a certain point, you have to ask, how much is a wrinkle worth.' He turned all five of them away – as he does 20–25 per cent of the people who come to him.

Baker, a trim, handsome man with flowing silver hair and the dashing air of a Hollywood leading man from the forties, said that many more men are seeking his services now: 'It's out in the open and accepted. Men in their fifties and sixties are working out and playing tennis with guys in their thirties, and if they have a bit of a wattle under their chin, they want to get rid of it.'

People rarely admit that they want him to make them look younger. 'They say they want to look refreshed, relaxed, rested.' Many people who come to him aren't motivated by vanity so much as by professional demands – and they're not all movie stars, either. 'Recently, I had a television producer come in, a 43-year-old woman who was starting to show her age a bit. I told her that, basically, she looked great, and that she didn't need to have anything done. She said to me, "Doctor, everyone I work with is under thirty — some of them are just out of college."'

The increasing use of sunblock and the decline in smoking, Baker believes, will soon create a society that 'looks ten years younger than its age, or at least what we're accustomed to seeing'.

The most popular cosmetic procedure is currently liposuction, which removes fatty tissue from beneath the skin. The price is down to $1,500 per operation, which puts it within the reach of ordinary people. A full-face chemical peel to remove wrinkles has dropped to about the same price range. The American Society of Plastic and Reconstructive Surgeons reports that the number of face-lifts, chemical peels, eyelid-lifts, laser treatments, and other procedures, such as collagen treatments to enlarge the lips, has more than doubled. The only decline in demand appears to be for breast enlargement surgery, which has been racked by controversy since the many lawsuits over defective silicone implants in the past ten years.

Bob Zemeckis, the Hollywood film director (whose comedy *Death Becomes Her* spoofed the desire to stay young), recently commented, 'The baby boom generation has started to age. They are the first generation to be really bombarded by images of perfection and youth, on television and in advertisements. People are desperate to stop the ageing process. It's more visible in the Los Angeles area, but the obsession with perfection and staying young forever is universal now.' In California, many men are coming to plastic surgeons for silicone implants to enlarge their pectoral and calf muscles.

Very few of the subjects in the superyoung project have had plastic surgery — for the simple reason that they don't need it. Whether anyone needs it is an open question; Daniel Baker, the man at the top of the field, himself says, 'Everyone doesn't have to look the same, thank goodness. I've always said that one's attitude, how one carries oneself, can do more to make one look younger than anything.' None the less, many of his patients get a tremendous psychological boost from surgery. 'It really does change a lot of people's lives,' he said.

J. J.

CHAPTER FIVE

IMAGES OF AGEING — THROUGH THE AGES

> *Methuselah lived nine hundred years —*
> *But who calls that livin',*
> *When no gal will give in*
> *To no man what's nine hundred years?*
> Ira Gershwin

In fact, according to the Book of Genesis, Methuselah lived to the age of 969 years, making him the longest-lived of the Hebrew patriarchs. They were a hardy lot: all of Methuselah's forebears lived for between 895 and 962 years (except for his father, Enoch, who was struck down at the tender age of 365).

The extreme longevity of the patriarchs in Genesis is one of those insoluble mysteries of the Bible. Yet there's no doubt that the attitude of the Hebrews to ageing was ambivalent. While the great prophets lived to extreme old age, and in many cases were revered for the wisdom of their years, it will be remembered that Moses, after leading the Hebrews in their wanderings in Sinai, was not permitted to enter Canaan.

Elderly women in the Bible occupied an even more uncertain position in society. In the Book of Ruth, after her husband and sons have died, Naomi tells her daughters-in-law to return to their mothers' homes. When they insist that they will stay with her, Naomi attempts to dismiss them with these words: 'Why will ye go with me? Are there yet any more sons in my womb, that they may be your husbands? Turn again, my daughters, go your way; for I am too old to have an husband.'

That conception of the aged person as a useless burden

pervades the Western tradition. People who complain about ageism in contemporary society need only to take a look into the past to see how far we have come. We tend to idealize life in the ancient world, but in fact it was a short and often brutish affair, and the prevailing attitudes towards age and the aged were often benighted. In the *Iliad*, the counsellor Nestor, usually described as 'stricken in years', is held up to ridicule as a pompous, garrulous old man who bores young heroes stiff with endless speeches full of hollow platitudes. The Greek gods were all young; the models for sculptures of Apollo and Aphrodite, the paradigms of physical perfection, were adolescents. There were a few exceptions, such as the Gnaeae, a trio of hideous old crones who shared one eye and one tooth between them.

The lyric tradition is even more astringent in its view of ageing. The seventh century BC poet Mimnermus of Colophon, one of the earliest Greek lyric poets whose works have survived, formulated the prevailing view of ageing in a poem lamenting the loss of love, which, according to the poet, inevitably accompanies old age (here, in Richard Lattimore's translation):

> Once old age with its sorrows advances
> Upon us, it makes a man feeble and ugly alike,
> Heart worn thin with the hovering expectation of evil,
> Lost all joy that comes out of the sight of the sun.
> Hateful to boys a man goes then, unfavored of women.
> Such is the thing of sorrow God has made of old age.

The obsession with youth among the upper classes in ancient Athens found its strongest expression in the practice of older men taking adolescent boys as lovers. There were strict customs governing this established paedophilia. The boy needed to be of just the right age; lads at the threshold of puberty, immediately before they grew beards, were thought to be ideal, though once the relationship was established it might continue well into manhood. It was never conceived of in purely physical or sexual terms; the older man had a responsibility to educate the young man and help to make him a good citizen. There was no limit on the age of the senior lover: the passion of the young Alcibiades for the elderly Socrates, described in Plato's *Symposium*, was one of the most celebrated love affairs of antiquity. The older man was expected to conduct the affair with wisdom and prudence, but it was by no means a field day for child molesters: the literature of classical Greece is filled with the bitter complaints of older men unsuccessfully wooing fickle young boys.

The more enlightened attitudes of antiquity towards ageing (which were, for the most part, formulated by old men) were summarized by Cicero, Rome's great moralist, in an essay called *De senectute* ('On old age'). This high-minded treatise was required reading for schoolchildren throughout most of the history of Western civilization, and much of our society's thinking on the subject arises from it. Not surprisingly for someone whose agenda was to inculcate morality and social order, Cicero takes the view that long life is a blessing, and that the wisdom of age ought to be respected by the young.

He cites many examples of writers, thinkers and soldiers who lived to a very old age yet continued to produce some of their best work right to the ends of their lives. Plato persevered in his philosophical labours until he died, at the age of eighty-one; Isocrates wrote his most famous discourse at ninety-four. Cicero's most famous example is that of Sophocles, who wrote some of his finest plays in extreme old age. When he was ninety years old, his sons sued in court to have him declared incompetent, so that they might take over the management of his estates. For his defence, Sophocles brought along the manuscript of his latest tragedy, *Oedipus at Colonus*, which he read to the judges. After he had finished, he asked them whether they thought the play the work of an incompetent man. They voted unanimously to dismiss the sons' petition.

In his essay, Cicero outlines the four main complaints about old age, and proceeds to dismiss them one by one:

It is alleged that it incapacitates a man for acting in the affairs of the world
Cicero disproves this by citing numerous examples of wise leaders who continued to exercise great influence into old age, and then asks who is more important for sailing a ship, the seasoned pilot at the wheel or the strong young men who carry out the seamen's menial chores?

Old age produces great infirmities of body
Cicero answers the second charge in a slightly disingenuous manner: he claims that those who are infirm in old age become that way because of a life spent in dissolution, while those who follow the path of virtue in youth and manhood will retain the full use of their faculties. The key to maintaining a sharp mind, according to Cicero, is to continue studying and learning throughout life – advice that is strikingly similar to our findings in the superyoung study. Solon, Athens's legendary law-giver, claimed that he learned something new every day; Socrates in his old age taught himself how to play the lyre.

Old age reduces the ability to enjoy the gratification of the senses
Cicero deals with this in a way that's not likely to find much favour nowadays – if it ever did. He concedes the point and says that it's actually a good thing, for it releases us from the tyranny of sensual passions. He goes on at some length describing the delights of a temperate agricultural life, asking if they are not preferable to overindulging at the banquet table, which only brings about drunkenness and indigestion, and chasing after women, which leads to disordered reason and aggressive behaviour.

Ageing brings us closer to death

Cicero first makes the excellent point that young people die every day, while old people can always hope to live to be older. Yet since death is the one inevitability of mortal existence, the span of a lifetime *per se* is of much less importance than the quality with which it is lived, and the old man who has always behaved virtuously will be prepared for death, which comes at the time appointed for it – yet another blessing of a long life.

Yet for all Cicero's philosophizing, the popular view of old age had probably changed very little since the time of Mimnermus. Lucian, last of the great Greek poets, writing in the second century AD, addresses this depressing advice to an old woman: 'You may dye your locks, but you can never dye your years; you will never make the wrinkles disappear from your cheeks.' The Roman poet Ovid is merciless in his description of the effects of ageing: 'The years will wear these charming features; this forehead, time-withered, will be crossed with wrinkles; this beauty will become the prey of the pitiless old age which is creeping up silently, step by step. They will say, "She was beautiful." And you will be utterly wretched; you will say your mirror lies.'

In the Middle Ages, the theme of the foolish old man who takes a young wife was a staple of popular literature. Boccaccio tells the story of a doddering old man in Pisa who marries a beautiful young girl. On his wedding night, he is barely able to perform his conjugal duties. After that experience, the old man suddenly becomes very pious, and ransacks the church calendar for saints whose honour they must respect by abstaining from sexual relations. One day when they go sailing, the young wife is carried off by a young corsair, who, heedless of the holy calendar, ravishes her daily. When her elderly husband comes to rescue her, she sends him away, preferring the lusty attentions of her pirate lover to the piety of her husband.

Chaucer takes up the theme in 'The Merchant's Tale', which tells the story of January, an old man, whose wealth allows him to marry the lovely young May. On his wedding night, he takes medical potions to enable himself to make love to his young bride: 'And after that he sang full loud and clear, and kissed his wife, and made wanton cheer. He was all coltish, full of ragery.' Soon thereafter, May deceives him with Damyan, a handsome young squire. January catches them in the act, but nimble-witted May tells January that age has dimmed his eyes, and he has made a mistake. January, too willing to believe her, accepts her version and goes blindly on his way.

One of the principal aims of medieval science was to discover the philosopher's stone, a chimerical substance which, if it had existed, would have possessed the power to transmute base metals into gold and to create the elixir of life, which would have conferred eternal youth. The conception of the elixir of life was gradually transformed into the myth of the fountain of youth. Many prints from the early Renaissance depict aged people walking into a fountain or pool and emerging at the opposite end restored to vibrant youth. This myth was so powerful that it induced the Spanish explorer Ponce de Leon, in 1512, to explore throughout the New World in search of the fountain of youth – an expedition that resulted in the discovery of Florida. In fact, it is far from clear whether Ponce de Leon actually believed in the fountain himself, or whether a popular legend to that effect sprang up around a typical Spanish expedition prospecting for gold and slaves; in any case, the myth formed a lively part of the sixteenth-century *Zeitgeist*.

In the Renaissance, alchemy gave way to real science – and thus to serious attempts to prolong life. The first best-selling self-help author was Girolamo Cardano, a sixteenth-century polymath from Pavia, in the Duchy of Milan, whose autobiography, *The Book of My Life*, was a widely read compendium of recommendations about how to lead a healthy life to a venerable age. Much of his advice is very similar to what one is likely to read in a health column in a modern newspaper: 'I eat more freely of fish than of meat, but only wholesome fresh fish . . . It seems good to me to eat my meal by the fire. At this repast I delight also in sweet new wine, about six ounces with double, or even more, the amount of water.'

What is remarkable about Cardano – who wrote more than a hundred books – is how much he got right, so long ago, in light of current research. He advocated increasing the levels of both physical and mental activity in order to promote good health. The benefits of following his regimen were well attested, not only by his followers but also by the journalists of the day, one of whom wrote that by using Cardano's method, one might attain 'a harmonious development of mind and body, good health, emotional stability, and a long, robust life'.

A contemporary of Cardano's, a Venetian nobleman named Luigi Cornaro, went even further. Like Cardano, he propounded many ideas that were advanced for their time, both in terms of medicine and psychology. Cornaro was one of the first scientific researchers to experiment on himself. He fell ill when he was thirty-five years old, and his doctors warned him that unless he reformed and made his life more sober and orderly, he would soon perish. That shocking prognosis had an immediate, salutary effect: he became obsessional about his health and adopted a course of moderation in all things, particularly alcohol, food and his emotions. He systematically studied very old people, research that led him to make his regimen ever more detailed and elaborate. His much-translated *magnum opus*, entitled *A Treatise of Health and Long Life, and the Sure Means of Attaining It*, set the goal of living to be a hundred years old.

The aspect of his research which has received the most intense scientific scrutiny in modern times was his restricted, low-calorie diet, which anticipated the findings of modern nutritionists by nearly 500 years. Cornaro also emphasized the importance of regular sleep, exercise, and the enjoyment of leisure time; he devoted himself to his garden and artistic activities. When he was in his early eighties, he wrote in a buoyantly optimistic vein, revealing himself to be an early prototype of the superyoung personality: 'The life which I live at this age is not a dead, lumpish, and sour life, but cheerful, lively, and pleasant . . . Yet I am sure that my end is far from me: for I know [setting aside accidents] I shall not die but by a pure resolution: because that by the regularity of my life I have shut out death [in] all other ways.' Cornaro's prophecy proved to be true: he missed his goal of a century by only a few years.

Shakespeare took a rather chilly view of old age in *As You Like It*:

> . . . the lean and slipper'd pantaloon,
> With spectacles on nose and pouch on side,
> His youthful hose well sav'd, a world too wide
> For his shrunk shank; and his big manly voice,
> Turning again toward childish treble, pipes
> And whistles in his sound. Last scene of all,
> That ends this strange eventful history,
> Is second childishness and mere oblivion,
> Sans teeth, sans eyes, sans taste, sans everything.

Yet he also created one of the most noble and sympathetic portrayals of old age ever written, in *King Lear*. Simone de Beauvoir, in her masterly treatise on cultural images of ageing, *The Coming of Age*, says that *Lear* is 'the only great work, apart from *Oedipus at Colonus*, in which the hero is an old man: here old age is not thought of as the limit of the human state but as its truth – it is the basis for an understanding of man and his earthly pilgrimage'.

In the eighteenth century, advances in medicine and hygiene made extreme old age much more commonplace, and attitudes towards ageing began to change. The patriarch became the symbol of a family's prosperity; as the leisure income of the emerging middle class increased, sentimentality formed an important part of social attitudes. Children were no longer regarded as chattels, easily exploited for the workforce, but rather as creatures to be cosseted and cherished; likewise, their grand-parents were increasingly revered by those in the prime of life, who began to see themselves in the aged. The leading thinkers of the age, Voltaire in France and Samuel Johnson in England, lived to great old age, and owed much of their tremendous authority and power in intellectual circles to their longevity.

In the Romantic era, sentimentality expressed itself in morbid ways. The great fascination of the age was the image of youth felled by death. John Keats, tragically struck down by tuberculosis at the age of twenty-five, was the archetypal Romantic hero – forever young. An even more spectacular example of tragic youth was that of the poet Thomas Chatterton, who, while still in his teens, perpetrated one of the greatest frauds in the history of literature. He composed hundreds of verses in an antique style, and wrote them out on old parchment, confounding some of the greatest literary experts in London. However, when Chatterton was unmasked, he became despondent and committed suicide – three months shy of his eighteenth birthday.

The modern obsession with youth may be said to begin with *The Picture of Dorian Gray*, Oscar Wilde's fable about a beautiful young man who never ages. The novel's publication in 1891 launched an epoch of youth worship which shows no sign of abating. In the story, young Dorian wishes that a gorgeous portrait of himself would reflect the ravages of time rather than his own beautiful body. Lord Henry Wotton, Wilde's thinly disguised mouthpiece, delivers this ecstatic summation of the youth-worshipper's creed: 'There is such a little time that your youth will last – such a little time . . . The pulse of joy that beats in us at twenty, becomes sluggish. Our limbs fail, our senses rot. We degenerate into hideous puppets, haunted by the memory of the passions of which we were too much afraid, and the exquisite temptations that we had not the courage to yield to. Youth! Youth! There is absolutely nothing in the world but youth!'

Dorian Gray gets his wish, of course. As the years go by, he abandons himself to a licentious life of dissipation and vice, the depredations of which afflict the portrait, hidden away in a locked room, while Dorian himself remains untouched:

Hour by hour, and week by week, the thing upon the canvas was growing old. It might escape the hideousness of sin, but the hideousnesses of age was in store for it. The cheeks would become hollow or flaccid. Yellow crow's-feet would creep round the fading eyes and make them horrible. The hair would lose its brightness, the mouth would gape or droop, would be foolish or gross, as the mouths of old men are. There would be the wrinkled throat, the cold, blue-veined hands, the twisted body . . .

In the end, Dorian's wickedness catches up with him, and when he dies his servants find a horribly withered, wrinkled old man, lying next to a portrait of their master as a comely lad, exactly as it was the day it was painted.

This macabre strain in the Victorian view of ageing received its most graphic expression in H. Rider Haggard's adventure novel, *She*, about an eternally young woman who has ruled for thousands of years over a lost tribe in East Africa. Ayesha found eternal youth 2,200 years ago by stepping into a wall of flame deep in a subterranean chamber. When she falls in love with the novel's hero, a young English adventurer, she takes him to the Flame of Life, so that he may join her in eternal youth and beauty. To show him that the flame will not burn him, she steps into it once more. That proves to be a fatal error, for her second immersion in the flame cancels out the first dose, and Ayesha ages 2,200 years. Her passage from superyoung to superold, in the space of a few minutes, remains one of the most horrific, fantastical depictions of ageing in literature:

Smaller and smaller she grew; her skin changed colour, and in place of the perfect whiteness of its lustre it turned dirty brown and yellow, like to an old piece of withered parchment. She felt at her head: the delicate hand was nothing but a claw now, a human talon resembling that of a badly preserved Egyptian mummy . . . Smaller she grew, and smaller yet, till she was no larger than a monkey. Now the skin had puckered into a million wrinkles, and on her shapeless face was the stamp of unutterable age.

In this century, the proverbial visitor from outer space, examining our films and television programmes and magazines, would justifiably assume that we earthlings live in a perpetual state of robust youth, except for a handful of decrepit old-timers, who exist mainly to baby-sit and amuse the young folk with their ridiculous ways.

Paradoxically, as people live longer, and as the proportion of elderly people in the population continues to increase, the image of humankind in our culture grows ever younger. Jack Benny, when he was well into his fifties and sixties and beyond, always claimed that he was thirty-nine years old, spoofing the absurdity of wanting to stay young forever. Today, thirty-nine is an age for grandparents – hoary old age in a youth culture which, in the nineteen-sixties, adopted as its motto, 'Don't trust anyone over thirty.' In the mid-nineties, fashion designer Calvin Klein gained notoriety for using models scarcely out of puberty.

The catch-phrase 'Don't trust anyone over thirty' was the premise of a teen exploitation film called *Wild in the Streets*, directed by Barry Shear, which was released in 1968. This dark cautionary tale about the potential dangers of America's obsession with youth follows the career of a charismatic teen idol named Max Frost, played by Christopher Jones. First he leads a national campaign to lower the voting age to fourteen, then he succeeds in getting his girlfriend elected to the US House of Representatives. In her first speech, banging on a tambourine, she says, 'America's greatest contribution has been to teach the world that getting old is such a drag.'

When she proposes an amendment to the Constitution that would lower the minimum age for the President and Members of Congress to fourteen, Max's followers spike the capital's water supply with LSD, so that the stoned congressmen will vote for it. Max Frost runs for President with a campaign song that proclaims, 'Gettin' old, lookin' old, that's a drag now/The country's into a whole new bag now.' After he is elected, he establishes concentration camps (called, with a deft Orwellian touch, Mercy Centers), where everyone over the age of thirty is interned and given doses of LSD daily. At the film's end, the absurdity of the youth culture is given a final jab: after Max sadistically kills the pet crayfish of a group of little boys, they begin to plot, whispering darkly, 'We're going to put everyone over ten out of business.'

The veneration of youth has been an enduring theme in Hollywood since the advent of the talkies. One of the earliest screen classics was the film *Lost Horizon*, an imaginative modern myth about a hidden valley in the Himalayas called Shangri-La, which shelters the secret of spectacularly prolonged youth. The film, directed by Frank Capra, was based upon one of the best-selling novels of the twentieth century, by James Hilton (which became the first paperback novel ever published and is now, at this writing, in its ninety-seventh printing).

Two hundred years before the story begins, a French missionary named Perrault stumbles into Shangri-La, where he discovers a combination of herbs and mystical meditation that slows ageing almost to a halt. In the opening scene, four Westerners in India, travelling aboard a small aircraft, are kidnapped and transported to Shangri-La. Perrault, now 250 years old, presides over a cult of ageless mystics whose mission is to preserve the best of human civilization from the coming barbarian onslaught (the novel was published in 1933, the film released in 1937). Perrault, attempting to persuade his visitors to join the cult, describes the state of agelessness at Shangri-La in terms that might almost be an evocation of the superyoung view of ageing, in flowery, ecstatic terms:

> The years will come and go, and you will pass from fleshy enjoyments into austerer but no less satisfying realms; you may lose the keenness of muscle and appetite, but there will be gain to match your loss; you will achieve calmness and profundity, ripeness and wisdom, and the clear enchantment of memory.

The film industry today has a strangely disjunctive view of ageing, which might be described as an extreme case of cultural sexual dimorphism. In Hollywood's classic era, the box office was dominated equally by women and men, who were nearly all middle-aged: Bette Davis's name in lights was just as likely to sell tickets as was Clark Gable's. Today, however, the reigning stars are virtually all men, who continue to play young protagonist roles even as they reach and pass an age that would mandate retirement in any other field. Meanwhile, their female co-stars, in picture after picture, year after year, remain the same age: young. Today, a female movie star may be washed up at forty, or even earlier, replaced by a younger beauty whose body hasn't yet had a chance to develop 'flaws' (i.e., evidences of maturity), who plays the romantic interest for a man literally old enough to be her father.

Moreover, with the advent of plastic surgery, there tends to be a certain sameness to the appearance of young female stars. When the ideal of beauty is closely focused around the lean, post-adolescent epitome of hour-glass figure and regular facial features – what might be called the *Baywatch*/Barbie babe – there is no longer any scope for the strong features and commanding presence of a Marlene Dietrich or a Joan Crawford.

The parts for elderly actors in most films today are the familiar stereotypes of the crotchety old coot with the heart of gold, or the kindly dispenser of sugary wisdom, roles patented by Lionel and Ethel Barrymore in the golden age of Hollywood. Jack Lemmon and Walter Matthau, for example, have made a string of highly successful formula films in which they play endearingly buffoonish, feuding old men, reinvigorated in their second childhood as much by grit as by the love of a good woman. There are a few exceptions to the rule: in 1981, Mark Rydell's box-office hit *On Golden Pond* featured a bravura performance by Henry Fonda, then seventy-six years old, as a lovable patriarch at the end of his life. Eight years later, Jessica Tandy's feisty old Southern lady in *Driving Miss Daisy* gave the 80-year-old actress the chance to play a dramatic role of substance. Both Tandy and Fonda won Oscars for their performances – and died shortly thereafter.

Ron Howard's enormously successful film *Cocoon* put a new spin on the myth of old age evaded. The film attempts to identify itself as presenting a compassionate view of old age, but in fact it is one of the grimmest portrayals of senior life ever made. It begins by showing a group of confused, mortally ill people slowly wasting away in a retirement community in Florida. With only a handful of exceptions, everyone is either confined to a wheelchair or Zimmer frame, or is approaching senility. A group of elderly men who are not quite as decrepit as the others sneak into a seaside estate to go swimming in the pool there, which miraculously restores them to youthful vigour. They are brimming with energy, and endowed with the sexual prowess of adolescents; one old man who had been suffering from cancer suddenly goes into complete remission.

It seems that the house has been rented by extra-terrestrial aliens (who, of course, do not age), who have been using the pool to hatch pods containing some of their race who were left behind when they came to visit this planet during the age of Atlantis. These pods, called cocoons, have infused the water in the pool with a magical, rejuvenating power. At the end of the film, the aliens generously invite all the residents of the retirement community to go back with them to their planet, where they, too, will become immortal. The final image of the frail, feeble old folks hobbling and wheeling aboard the flying saucer is a bizarre spectacle: ageing, in the view of the filmmaker, is such an awful calamity that abandoning one's loved ones and flying into space to live among alien creatures is preferable.

Television, from the beginning of the medium, has been even more exclusively the province of the young and the beautiful than has film. In the classic era of American television, the elderly were segregated into the by-now-familiar ghetto of the peppery old grandpa, epitomized by characters such as those played by William Frawley in *My Three Sons* (replaced by William Demarest after Frawley's death) and Walter Brennan in *The Real McCoys*, and the well-meaning but befuddled grandma, as portrayed by Irene Ryan in *The Beverly Hillbillies* and Aunt Bea on *The Andy Griffith Show*, played by Frances Bavier.

In the seventies, the male characters in television dramas were allowed to age into authority figures and tycoons, but, as in film, they were usually paired with much younger women. The classic case is that of Blake Carrington, in the hugely popular soap opera *Dynasty*, an oil millionaire who leaves his middle-aged wife, Alexis, played by Joan Collins, for the younger Kristal, portrayed by Linda Gray. Yet, whereas John Forsythe, who played Blake Carrington, was allowed to show his age, with silvery hair and a tranquil, detached mien, the two women were lighted and made-up to look younger than their years.

One notable exception to this rule was the role of Mrs Pynchon on *Lou Grant*, a stately matriarch of a newspaper dynasty, played by Nancy Marchand, in a part transparently modelled on Katharine Graham, the publisher of the *Washington Post*. Without doubt the most enduring portrayal of an active, independent elderly woman on television was Angela Lansbury's dauntless mystery novelist–amateur sleuth Jessica Fletcher, in *Murder, She Wrote*, which was one of the most popular drama series ever broadcast in America (see profile, page 43). Another notable exception was the eighties sitcom *Golden Girls*, about four retired women in Florida, who manage to get as many dates as high-school cheerleaders.

In Britain, there has in recent years been a rather peculiar spate of programmes about elderly people: *Keeping Up Appearances* portrays the powerful personality of a terrible snob named Hyacinth Bucket (she wages a constant, losing battle to persuade the world to pronounce it 'bouquet'), whose bourgeois pretensions make life miserable for her husband and neighbours; *One Foot in the Grave* centres around a curmudgeon named Victor Meldrew, who takes a jaundiced view of everything going on around him – a character that traces its lineage back to Sheridan Whiteside, the irascible Man Who Came to Dinner in Kaufman and Hart's play. Another popular British sitcom, *Waiting for God*, concerns the lives of a group of people at a private home for the elderly.

The hit comedy series *Absolutely Fabulous* revolved around the exploits of two ageing baby boomers, Edina and Patsy, played by Jennifer Saunders and Joanna Lumley, who desperately – and ludicrously – cling to a young, trendy lifestyle. Edina's mother, portrayed by June Whitfield, is a classic revival of the theme of the confused granny. In the series' final episode, she comes under the influence of two friends from Florida, Mac and Millie, savage caricatures of swinging American seniors, clad in pastel-hued, pyjama-like sportswear, designer sunglasses, and T-shirts proclaiming 'I don't do cookies' and 'I'm spending my kids' inheritance.'

The generation that came of age in the sixties identified itself with youth more explicitly than any that had preceded it – particularly in its music. In 1966, the Rolling Stones had a hit single called 'Mother's Little Helper', which began with Mick Jagger singing 'What a drag it is getting old.' Pete Townsend and the Who took it a step further in 'My Generation', declaring 'I hope I die before I get old.' As the baby boomers aged, they were forced to confront the fact by seeing the fresh young faces of their pop idols becoming lined, their defiant mops of hair growing thin in advancing middle age. Yet many of the rockers of Jagger and Townsend's generation, including Paul McCartney, Eric Clapton, Elton John and others, are still very much at the top of the business, though they have turned to mellower musical styles commensurate with their dignified position in the pop firmament.

The glossy printed media are, if anything, even more dominated by images of youth, virtually to the exclusion of middle age: our visitor from outer space, after reading the fashion magazines, might deduce that the life expectancy in America and Western Europe is twenty-five, at best. One very amusing exception to the rule is *The Oldie*, a gently satirical magazine for older people which began publication in Britain in 1992. Edited by Richard Ingrams, formerly editor of the satirical magazine *Private Eye*, the humour is sophisticated and wry, but the overall tone is nostalgic: things were better back then. The first issue included an article entitled 'What Is Heavy Metal?'; since then, the magazine has published articles about such trendy entertainers as the Everly Brothers and Barbara Stanwyck, an interview with Richard Wilson (who plays Victor Meldrew in *One Foot in the Grave*), and pin-ups of Tim Rice, the portly, silver-haired lyricist.

Ambivalent and negative views of old age are by no means confined to popular culture; they are just as likely to crop up in experimental literature as in best-selling pot-boilers. In *The Counterfeiters*, André Gide wrote: 'Why do books have so little to say about old people? I believe it is because the old can no longer write them, and because when one is young one does not bother with the old. An elderly man – he no longer interests anyone at all.' Samuel Beckett also dealt with ageing in devastating fashion. Some of his most famous works explored the theme of crumbling memory: its loss, in his view, is tantamount to the loss of self. In *End Game*, one of his most famous stage works, two old people sit in dustbins and ramble on bitterly about all that they have lost. The eponymous hero of Beckett's novel, *Molloy*, is a feeble old man at the beginning of the book and, as it progresses, his body becomes more and more broken down: his limbs stiffen, he loses half his toes, and by the end, unable even to hobble on his crutches, he can only crawl about, helpless as an infant.

These grim depictions are counterbalanced by some celebrated works of American literature that portray elderly men as heroes. William Faulkner's *Old Man*, published in 1939 as part of *The Wild Palms*, and Ernest Hemingway's *The Old Man and the Sea*, published twelve years later, both take as their subject men at the ends of their lives, valiantly battling against forces of nature: in the former a black convict survives a terrible flood of the Mississippi River in a rowing-boat; in the latter a Cuban fisherman hooks a great marlin, only to lose it to the sharks.

On the stage, Tennessee Williams created one of the most poignant and painful depictions of the transition to old age in the character of Blanche DuBois, the faded Southern belle in *A Streetcar Named Desire*, who clings neurotically to her vanished youth. Blanche only comes out of her room after dark and always avoids direct light, in order to conceal her age; in one of the play's climactic scenes, her brutish brother-in-law Stanley drags her into the lamplight, unmasking her bags and wrinkles.

As far as the sciences go, Simone de Beauvoir once made the excellent point that while the popular conception of elderly people had improved continuously throughout the nineteenth and early twentieth centuries, when the industrial revolution brought greater wealth and more leisure time to the newly emerging middle class, by the middle of the twentieth century 'the standing of old age has been markedly lowered since the notion of experience has been discredited. Modern technocratic society thinks that knowledge does not accumulate with the years, but grows out of date.' The images of the great American inventors of the late nineteenth and early twentieth centuries,

Samuel F. B. Morse and Thomas Edison, are wise old men with bushy white beards; today's great technologist is the fresh-faced computer buff epitomized by Bill Gates (who himself, in many respects, fits the superyoung profile).

In the electronic age, politicians and diplomats are tantamount to media stars. Many of the towering figures of this century kept power into very old age: Clemenceau was seventy-seven when he became premier of the French Third Republic, in 1917; Churchill was eighty-one and Konrad Adenauer eighty-seven when they retired from office. The Chinese have always revered old age, but in this century they have outdone themselves, retaining first Mao Tse-tung and then Deng Xiaoping as supreme leaders until the ages of eighty-three and ninety-one, respectively. Some of the most powerful images of ageing in recent years were the television advertisements for Ronald Reagan's re-election in 1984, which showed the 73-year-old president chopping wood and riding a horse – the very picture of the rugged Western cowboy.

Today, elderly Americans have an independent political image of their own, that of the Gray Panthers. Founded in Philadelphia in 1970 by Margaret Kuhn, the Gray Panther Project Fund, as it is officially called, is an outspoken advocacy group that exposes ageism and promotes a positive attitude towards ageing. The group began by using some radical tactics, borrowed from other political pressure groups such as the Black Panthers, which earned them their sardonic nickname in the press; in 1971 they officially adopted the name. It is largely because of their advocacy, allied with the more moderate American Association of Retired Persons, that the elderly wield considerable political clout. Even as the Federal budget was being slashed throughout the eighties and nineties, social security and Medicare remained untouched: every politician knows that old people vote in much greater numbers than the young – and, like everyone else, they vote with at least some attention to their wallets.

Al Hirschfeld

Artist Al Hirschfeld has been an important figure in American show business since 1921, when, at the venerable age of seventeen, he was made head of the art department of Selznick Pictures. 'L. J., the old man – that was David's father – took a liking to me,' he explains. 'He suggested that I take over the art department. I couldn't believe it.' After four years with the Selznicks, and later a stint with Warner Brothers, Hirschfeld took off for Europe, to travel around freely and live the bohemian life for a few years. He returned to America in 1927, and imme- diately signed an exclusive agreement with the *New York Times*, to cover the Broadway scene with his witty, whimsical cartoons. Seventy years later, his illustrations are still a familiar feature of the paper's Sunday arts section.

Today, Hirschfeld lives with his wife, theatre historian Louise Kerz, in a spacious old townhouse on Manhattan's Upper East Side, comfortably furnished in antiques and crammed with – what else? – Hirschfeld drawings of actors and musicians, spanning the eight decades of his career. His studio, on the top floor, is lit by skylights with a northern exposure. Sitting at his drawing board in an old barber's chair upholstered in red leather he says, 'I'm never aware of my age until someone points it out to me. Throughout much of my life, I was always the youngest one.' In order to compensate for his youthfulness, he says, he began wearing a beard, which has proved to be a life- long companion.

When asked what he attributes his longevity to, he shrugs and gives the right answer: 'Genes. My parents both lived into their nineties. I remember once reading an interview with Shaw, when he was in his nineties, and he said it was because he was a vegetarian and didn't drink. Soon after that I saw a story about Winston Churchill [who lived to ninety], in which he said he drank a quart of brandy and smoked ten cigars a day, and never ate anything but rare beef. Ever since then, I've believed it doesn't matter much what you do.' Easy for him to say!

His one concession to the healthy life was to quit smoking. Thirty years ago, he says, he met his friend, legendary Broadway showman Billy Rose, at Sardi's restaurant. 'Billy told me that he had just come from the doctor, who told him they might have to amputate his leg, because of nicotine poisoning. My cigar went out while we were talking. I was going to relight it, but then I thought better of it.' That was the end of Hirschfeld's smoking days. (As it turned out, Rose's leg was saved by his heart surgeon – who just happened to be Michael DeBakey, see page 22).

At ninety-four, Hirschfeld remains in excellent health. Except for a slight limp, he would easily pass for seventy: his pale eyes have a piercing gaze, and his hand is steady as a rock – essential in his line of work. His beard is now white but it remains thick and bushy, making him look like one of Michelangelo's Hebrew prophets on the ceiling of the Sistine Chapel. As he has always done, he works seven days a week, turning out some 200 finished drawings a year (an output far below what he produced in his prime, he says).

Hirschfeld exemplifies many of the cardinal traits of the superyoung. Throughout his life, he has always had close associations with people younger than himself – though now, as he points out, it's hardly a matter of choice. Most of his friends from his youth and middle years are dead now, but he reminisces about them cheerfully. In 1947 he went on a trip around the world with the humorist S. J. Perelman. 'We were doing a book together, called *Westward Ha!*. In Nice, we went into a barber-shop, and there was an old man there, as wrinkled as an elephant's behind. It was Somerset Maugham. He came up to us and shook Sid's hand and said, "Mr Perelman, I presume?"' Later, after they had got better acquainted, Hirschfeld worked up his courage and asked the author about his working habits. 'He told me that he only wrote an hour and a half a day. I said I was amazed, considering the great body of work he had produced, and he told me, "If you live long enough, it piles up." I've certainly found that to be true.'

Hirschfeld's romantic life has also followed the superyoung pattern. 'I can't remember being single,' he says matter-of-factly.

His first wife was a chorus girl from the *Vanities*, a popular musical show on Broadway. After they divorced, he married a well-known European actress named Dolly Haas, in 1943. Two years later, he celebrated the birth of their first child, a daughter named Nina, by concealing her name in his drawings, which has been a Hirschfeld trademark ever since. When Dolly died, in 1995, he immediately married again, to his present wife, who is more than thirty years younger than him. They attend the theatre three or four times a week, and frequently entertain friends at home.

Al Hirschfeld has received countless awards, including Tonys, citations from the Players and Friars clubs, and honorary degrees from universities. 'I think they're mostly for staying alive,' he says, 'not for what I do. Now I'm constantly getting parchments and little crystals for growing old.' When asked which award means the most to him, he replies with a wry little smile that it is the one given him by his native city of St Louis. 'They gave me a plaque with that McDonald's arch they have down there, and they misspelled my name. I'll always treasure that.'

J. J.

CHAPTER SIX

A NEW SCIENCE OF AGE CONTROL

To get back my youth I would do anything in the world, except take exercise, get up early, or be respectable.

Oscar Wilde

All living things have secrets to reveal, new science to be unravelled by the ancient process of discovery, investigation and analysis – which sometimes leads to answers, and sometimes to even deeper mysteries.

A plant physiologist at the University of California at Los Angeles named Jane Shen–Miller has proved that embryonic life can be preserved for centuries, which also suggests how ageing may be slowed and life prolonged. Shen–Miller has managed to grow a shoot from a 1,288-year-old lotus seed from China. It is believed to be the oldest seed ever germinated. 'This sleeping beauty, which was there when Marco Polo came to China in the thirteenth century, must have a powerful genetic system to delay its ageing,' said Shen–Miller. She obtained seven of the brown, oval seeds, each about the size of a marble, from the Beijing Institute of Botany. She planted the first of the seeds to be germinated, which was a mere 332 years old, in a decorative pool in the courtyard of her home. It sprouted dozens of leaves, and resembled a modern lotus in every respect, except that its leaves were a bit smaller.

Shen–Miller's research team cited several reasons for the seed's longevity, including the presence of L–isoaspartyl methyltrans-ferase, an enzyme whose main function is to repair protein. It does its job by preventing the build-up of abnormal residues in the protein of ageing seeds. Such residues can limit the viability of the embryo, and hence its ability to germinate.

This enzyme also repairs itself, or rather it repairs amino-acid damage in its own DNA sequence, thereby protecting the efficiency of its crucial protein-repair role. This important enzyme can be found throughout nature – including within the human body, where it is present in large quantities in brain cells. This substance and others similar to it may be partly responsible for slowed ageing and prolonged vitality in living creatures – the chemical equivalent of the elixir of youth, which helps the superyoung to maintain youthful vitality and appearance into their middle years, and beyond.

The body is constantly repairing itself, from the level of molecules to that of tissue and organs. The largest known molecules, those of DNA, are repaired exclusively by enzymes. As we age, this process becomes less efficient, making more and more errors, and ultimately it breaks down. Bruce Ames, a biochemist at the University of California, Berkeley, has worked out that the DNA in every cell of the human body sustains about 10,000 destructive 'hits' from oxygen free radicals alone (highly reactive unstable forms of oxygen liberated when oxygen is used by the body). The DNA repair system is highly reliable, and can put nearly all these cellular wounds right again, but over time damage accumulates. In 2-year-old rats there are about 2 million DNA lesions per cell – twice as many as in young rats.

This fatalistic view is bolstered by what is known as the Error Catastrophe theory of cell ageing. According to this school of thought, the cells of complex creatures (including human beings) themselves become increasingly complex. The strands of DNA contain the codes for every protein the cell builds. When a cell makes a protein, the applicable part of the genetic codes must be accurately replicated. As this process is repeated over and over, imperceptibly small errors creep in – like blue-prints based upon photocopies of photocopies of photocopies. These little mistakes are amplified and compounded until the genetic codes transmit destructive, meaningless messages; the cells themselves get run down by all this fruitless but effortful work, and eventually fail. It is one of the basic principles of science that everything made of matter will finally run down, sooner or later.

Mutations also accumulate with age. Cells generate waste products and defective proteins – cellular garbage – and when the cell divides, some of these substances are passed along. This residue builds up over the course of many cell divisions, polluting the inner environment.

Some biologists now believe that slowed ageing results from more effective cellular repair work, and that the process can therefore be controlled to some extent by diet, environment and behaviour. While these discoveries and ideas explain how such effects may take place, they do not adequately explain *why* they do. But the fact that the 'how' is underpinned by knowable biochemical reactions hints strongly that the 'why' lies in the direction of evolution. Long life and good health do indeed run in families, as we discovered time and time again from the subjects of the superyoung project. It's not simply a matter of good genes: healthy, life-prolonging habits are also passed along from parent to child, and they can't be disentangled from the genetic factors.

The health of the individual is always in a fine balance with the rest of nature. Human survival is more precarious than we realize in our day-to-day lives; essentially it's no different from that of any other species. From an evolutionary point of view, *Homo sapiens'* greatest accomplishment has been the prolongation of its lifespan through the advances made in medicine and public health in the modern era. Our species won out at the dawn of the human era because our brainpower was greater than that of our nearest competitors, the other anthropoids, and that distinguishing mark has continued to serve us well.

Longevity – survival and recurrent hereditary traits – must have a function and, in science, function must have meaning.

Apparent improvements in a species, such as effective protein repair at the cellular level, and slowed ageing, confer an advantage to the whole species by improving its chances for survival, regardless of what perils the environment might throw its way, even those of its own making. When biologists speak of species survival, they aren't talking about our physical selves but rather our genes. The individual has relevance only in so far as he is a carrier of his species' genetic destiny. That line of reasoning is the basis of Richard Dawkins's concept of the 'selfish gene': if an individual leaves behind no progeny to help shape the ongoing genetic profile of the species, then he is irrelevant, even meaningless.

Throughout my clinical work and the research conducted by the superyoung research team, I have been led to ponder, and attempt to answer, one powerful, overriding question: what selective advantages and endowments accrue to the human species by retaining youthfulness into sexual maturity and beyond?

When people talk about the 'good genes' they have inherited, they are usually referring to the previous two or three generations – more remote ancestors are generally known to them, if at all, only by family legend and old portraits. The knowable proportion of information about all of our forebears' heritable characteristics is a fraction of the infinitesimal.

Natural selection works incrementally, very slowly, requiring hundreds if not thousands of generations before the tiny, reactive bits of trial-and-error tinkering result in physical changes in the species itself. Evolution normally works slowly, but humankind is now near to being able to speed it up considerably. The breathtaking changes in human ageing brought about by science in this century have stimulated a simultaneous desire to stay younger longer. Each generation over the past fifty years has looked younger than its predecessor, and remained so for a longer period, well into middle maturity.

Most people nowadays, it seems, want youth, not only the

superficial, outward appearance of youth but also its vibrant optimism, that intangible zest which arises from the instinctual awareness that one is in one's prime. Youthfulness has now become the mirror-twin of beauty and glamour: looking younger has a halo effect, which associates it on an intuitive level with what is good and desirable. Such preconscious evaluations are global, made across diverse macro- and micro-cultural divisions.

Now, to pose the question in evolutionary terms: is it possible that the positive identification of youthful attractiveness is some sort of biological cue, operating beneath the obvious patterns and strategies of human mating? Is beauty more than skin deep?

If youth and attractiveness were related in a statistically provable way to fecundity, then passion would nullify the supremacy of cold logic. Here, the emotional side of the mind helps to determine some behavioural life-choices which have implications for who we are and what our offspring will be like. Here, the irrational intersects with our species' innate need to love and be loved, to form cooperative social systems and alliances, to protect and defend our own flesh and blood.

Several theories can be advanced as to why some lucky ones retain youthful characteristics longer than others do. The progenitors of such people may have been perceived as more personable, more positive, and therefore more sexually attractive. Their own choices of partners might even have had something to do with the evolution of this winning cluster of traits.

Such optimistic people, especially in the era before efficient birth control, might have been more willing to risk sexual intercourse and the commitments of parenthood than were somewhat more pessimistic people. Our data, both in terms of general optimistic outlook and more specific, health-related optimism, suggest that this factor could well have played a part. There might seem to be a contradiction between this line of reasoning and the finding in my research that the superyoung subjects tended to have fewer children and smaller families. If such 'optimism' genes do exist, they would have come into existence many, many generations before the current crop of superyoung people was born. The opposable thumb evolved because it enabled early man to climb trees and pick food, but today most of us find it useful more often for holding a pencil, a fork or a tennis racket.

Conversely, one might look at what has happened to those less well-endowed with beauty and other positive physical traits. The widespread cultural bias against women has operated cruelly throughout history. Although the great majority were quite capable, physically and emotionally, of childbearing, some were rejected. They were committed to nunneries by their fathers, abandoned, even sold into slavery. These abuses persist to the present day, particularly in certain backward parts of Asia, where the practice of murdering female infants has given way to aborting foetuses that have been identified by ultrasound examination as female – one of the most insidious instances of science abused, an interference with natural selection.

In our own culture, female offspring with disabilities have sometimes been barbarously subjugated by specious mental-health 'therapies': Rosemary Kennedy's lobotomy and the shock therapy given to Tennessee Williams's sister Rose are only two of the best-known examples. For centuries, the belief in the inferiority of women was so deeply ingrained, the attitude so universally accepted, that however repugnant it might appear to us now, it was once considered a fundamental natural law.

The foregoing analysis is based solely on historical data. In the far greater extent of prehistory, it's likely that unprepossessing daughters were treated even more harshly. Patriarchy was hardly likely to have been *less* powerful then than it is now. The patterns of sexual dimorphism in height and strength that had evolved by the historical era suggest quite the reverse, that in prehistory the tyranny of the male sex was even greater. Beauty is power, and the powerful are attracted to beauty as if by a magnetic force.

113

If my theory is correct, and human beings have always tended for one reason or another to choose their sexual partners based upon youthful appearance and optimistic attitudes, then the genes related to these traits would be passed along more effectively. A preference for youthful, comely partners that might have initially been slight, perhaps even fortuitous, would still be adequate to explain some of the individual differences that ultimately came into being.

Beauty, proverbially, is in the eye of the beholder. However, people whose physical appearance is widely admired are usually endowed with a heightened sense of self-confidence, and hence greater self-assertiveness and sociability. Only at the extreme end of the spectrum does this lead to pathological narcissism or, incongruously, to crippling levels of neurotic self-doubt and insecurity, as in the case of someone such as Marilyn Monroe or James Dean, who felt isolated and were taken advantage of on account of their beauty. Youthful comeliness may signal, at a glance, both robust good health and fertility. This is an instance of what is known as gene-environment co-variation, in which possessing a particular attribute helps to create a social environment that is conducive to enhancing it: nothing succeeds like success.

And what more potent factor could there be in this context than that of erotic attraction? As the feminist psychologist Janet Sayers put it, 'Good-looking men are as flames to a moth for many women. They can make a woman feel beautiful. With a good-looking man attached to a woman's arm, her looks are given credence.'

It's important to see this from the woman's perspective. In the superyoung project, we sought to interview as many of the younger female partners of these exceptionally attractive super-young men as we could. Most of these women felt that they had benefited from their age-gap relationships, that their personalities and character strengths complemented those of their partners. The women themselves often couldn't believe that they had fallen so hard, so easily, without any resistance, like teenage girls. Before meeting the men in question, they had been self-confident, and after they started dating them, they became even more buoyant. They found themselves thrust into the social limelight.

Yet the women firmly denied that they had been looking for a father-figure, either consciously or unconsciously. They also denied that they were seeking to shock or upset their families by getting involved with an older man. Often, they were amazed by the men's physical responsiveness and expertise at lovemaking, compared with the younger men they had dated. Elaine, twenty-nine, is one such 'moth woman'; her flame, Joe, is nineteen years older than she is. She told me, 'He was every woman's dream. He has so much going for him – a good job, a great car, he's well liked, and of course he's so gorgeous and young. I would have felt terribly let down if he hadn't looked at me twice – but then he did! That was obviously a tremendous boost to my own self-esteem.'

In the beginning, Joe was reticent, playing hard to get. 'He looks so passionate and sensitive, and although my rational side kept telling me "Look out – danger!", I also knew that his looks couldn't tell me anything about what he was really like. But down deep, I expected him to be terrific in every way – most especially in bed. I was afraid he would be vain, but he wasn't as vain as most other men I've met – he didn't have to be.' Elaine said that, after they began dating, her best friend had warned her that Joe was a heart-breaker – and then she tried, unsuccessfully, to date him behind her back! Elaine and Joe married soon after they were interviewed for the superyoung project.

The seductive energies emanating from a person who looks young, and who attracts others who find that exciting, exude an intensely appealing power. In our research we found that there were wide differences among individuals in the strength and duration of their 'youthful' sexual impulses. Many men and women, especially among the superyoung, had maintained virtually the same quality and amount of sexual activity and libido well into their middle years. If one member of a couple looks much younger but is in fact older, he will at first recreate the sexual excitement of his younger days, and then, self-validated, prove himself able to attract a mate whom others regard as being as attractive as himself. Similarity of physique and personality have been established as major attractants for both genders. If, for whatever reason, assortative mating – similar people choosing each other – takes place, inherently healthy people will tend to mate with other very healthy people, and their offspring will share that trait as a natural advantage. This phenomenon could be described as the survival of the sexiest.

As we have seen, the superyoung are much more likely than ordinary people to be in a permanent relationship; and if it should come to an end, usually due to the death of their partner, the superyoung, regardless of their age, almost always go out and find a new lover. The fact that they have smaller families is irrelevant; superyoung men often have *more* families, and frequently father children until later in life; Ben Bradlee (see page 65), who in his late fifties settled down with a younger woman and had a baby, is only a public example of a superyoung man exhibiting the virility of a young man at an age when most men are finally taking life easy, enjoying the peace and quiet of an empty nest with their wives.

Sexiness – in so far as it is possible to generalize about so subjective a quality – might be perceived as a consequence of fitness, in the Darwinian meaning of the word. To apply a cellular analogy, if the individual cell reproduces successfully, then it has satisfied its *raison d'être*, and is therefore among the fit. As Freud put it, 'The individual himself regards sexuality as one of his own ends, whereas from another point of view he is an appendage to his germ-plasm [Freud's term for the as-yet undiscovered gene], at whose disposal he puts his energies, in return for a bonus of pleasure. He is the mortal vehicle of a (possibly) immortal substance – like the inheritor of an entailed property, who is only the temporary holder of an estate that survives him.'

This bleakly unromantic interpretation of the reproductive process runs counter to the emotional immediacy experienced by a person in love or possessed by sexual lust; yet achieving a great orgasm and climbing ever upward on the evolutionary ladder are both purely human notions. Nature isn't something out there: nature is us. Humankind may have produced the most exotic, widely varying repertoires of behaviours, sexual and otherwise, on the planet, yet we are none the less a part of the whole family of terrestrial life. If we begin to think of ourselves as superior to nature because of our ingenuity, then we risk cutting ourselves off both from biological reality *and* from our innermost selves. Natural selection derives in part from sexual selection; I would propose that this has advanced to involve a degree of emotional and psychological selectivity, as well.

From the individual's point of view, strong emotions have evolved and been transmitted in such a way that they give one 'intuitions' about what to do when one is in doubt or in danger. The mysterious power of love and sexual attraction is that our hearts – or, more accurately, our glands – often overrule our heads. As the psychologist Henry Plotkin has put it, 'Emotions are postcards from our genes telling us in a direct and non-symbolic manner about life and death.'

Instinct-led behaviour works very well, most of the time, for probably 95 per cent of the animal species on the earth. Despite extremely recent developments such as conscience and reason, human beings, when it comes to matters of the heart, revert to older, 'hard-wired' programmes. Indeed, some sexual signals are under hormonal control. Those who become the emotional victims of their sexual passions often wonder why they act so irrationally. There has always been a conflict between society's demands for order and the individual's lusty, sensual impulses. Traditionally, a balance was struck by the imposition of taboos.

The preponderance of sexual taboos throughout all cultures in the world is an indication of how sensitive and problematic this pressure point is in our nature; yet despite the great weight of guilt and shame attached to violating taboos, society has never been able to prevent or suppress what used to be known as 'sins of the flesh'.

A deep connection exists between sex and love, above and beyond the obvious one. For example, during orgasm a woman's body produces the hormone oxytocin, which acts upon the emotional centres of the brain. Oxytocin has been shown to be responsible for stimulating nurturing maternal behaviour; in the laboratory, mammals treated with oxytocin nuzzle their pups more frequently than those who don't receive the extra dose. In human adults, a lover who regularly stimulates his mate's oxytocin will be rewarded with warmer feelings of affection. Intense mutual pleasure increases bonding. Ongoing sexual frustration probably has an equal and opposite effect: most marriages that crack up are preceded by a decline in the rate of female orgasm (though the question of cause and effect there remains an open one).

There is no doubt that nature invented sex so that we could have fun in bed but, as a scientist, I must believe that this instinctual behaviour has an underlying evolutionary purpose, that it promotes the future of the species. The challenge of dealing with the uncertainties of life was the fuel that stoked the engines of evolution. One theory that has earned much credence in recent years is known as the Red Queen theory. In Lewis Carroll's *Through the Looking-Glass*, the Red Queen tells Alice that where she lives, 'it takes all the running you can do to keep in the same place'. Originally propounded in 1980 by biogeneticist Bill Hamilton of Oxford, and independently by others, the theory argues that sex is a mechanism for continuously reshuffling the genetic deck. The theory's metaphor places us and all other sexually reproducing species on an evolutionary treadmill, perpetually changing our encoded genetic defences in an endless war against microbes and other competitors.

However, it is a simplistic notion that genes are the only factors that need to be considered in evolution. Reproduction is not necessarily at the centre of evolution, but is one key facet among many. That brings us to the question, what else runs in families besides genes? The short answer is, many things do, but in particular, styles of childrearing, approaches to sociable interpersonal behaviour, and a wide variety of coping strategies. Taken together, a child's genes and childhood experiences will coalesce in his adult personality, for good or for ill.

Human beings have become adapted to living in much larger social groups than other primates (now, indeed, the entire population of the earth may be regarded in many ways as one huge social group). In order to live amicably and constructively with as large a group as we do, we have made networking the forte of our species. When the family circle is widened, various other kinds of reciprocal needs have a better chance of being met. That is why extended families and even broader tribal groupings have been the norm throughout most of human history, and probably in prehistory as well.

The fracturing of the nuclear family and the withering away of the extended family are unprecedented anomalies, social aberrations with unforeseen consequences that could cause major rifts in the social fabric. To ensure the survival of the young, emotional security and good values should be transmitted to them over a long period of time.

Human development might be defined as the increasing ability to build mutually empowering and self-affirming relationships. The learning phase of social upbringing, throughout childhood, is more prolonged and intense in our species than anywhere else in nature. As slow as the process of growing up is, it is followed by a seemingly interminable intermediate transitional phase, adolescence, a time of rebellion which some people can never quite outgrow emotionally. Angry boys grow up to become angry young men, and finally embittered old men. Young parents who are still literally growing up with their children may lack the maturity to prepare their offspring to cope with the demands of adult life, something which they are only in the process of discovering for themselves. As the psychotherapist Anthony Storr has written, 'The hand that rocks the cradle erects the playpen . . . Development is often impeded by the immaturity of parents, and it is true to say that the less a parent is mature the less can he tolerate rebellion in his children, and the more does he require their subservience and their agreement with him. Neurotic, insecure parents tend to have neurotic, insecure children: and it is largely because immature parents cannot tolerate differentiation from themselves that this is so.'

In such families, it is often the grandparents themselves (frequently not much older than the normal age for parenthood nowadays) who must undertake the responsibility for child-rearing. Their genes have already been passed on, but they have an even greater gift, ready and waiting to be tapped: knowledge and wisdom. They should be able to exert this benign influence without being the victims of bias, yet such prejudices persist, and it is to this we turn our attention in the next chapter.

Jack LaLanne

Jack LaLanne is the undisputed father, godfather and eternal patriarch of the physical fitness movement in the United States. In 1936, he opened the first modern health club, in Oakland, California, launching one of the most profitable industries of the modern era. In 1951 he started a live daytime television programme, in which he showed the folks at home how to get fit and stay that way. *The Jack LaLanne Show* ran for thirty-four years, making it one of the most successful programmes in American television history.

Today, he lives in a ranch house in Morro Bay, California, north of Los Angeles, with his wife and partner of forty-seven years, Elaine. He long ago sold his nationwide chain of health clubs, and now devotes most of his time to personal appearances, delivering the health gospel to corporate and public audiences. At eighty-three, he is still in great shape. His 150 pounds are perfectly distributed across his five-foot, six-inch frame, with a forty-six-inch chest and a trim thirty-inch-waist. At one recent personal appearance for a men's underwear manufacturer, he handily beat the company's 39-year-old chief executive officer at sit-ups and pull-ups.

Like most superyoung people, LaLanne has strong beliefs, and he loves to share them. When he begins to give his spiel – the word isn't meant pejoratively, but no other would be accurate – his face is transformed by a visionary gleam, and the pace and delivery of his speech become increasingly dynamic and emphatic. (Norman Vincent Peale once told him that he should have been a preacher.) 'If you have pride and discipline,' he says, his voice ringing with conviction, 'you cannot fail. And if you commit yourself to a programme of exercise, that takes pride and a hell of a lot of discipline. I get up every morning at four-thirty, hit the gym by five, and work out for two hours. To leave a warm bed and a hot woman, to go to a cold gym, that takes dedication.'

Like any good preacher, LaLanne has a full repertoire of anecdotes and analogies. 'I just bought my wife a new Cadillac and myself a new Corvette. Now, what's the one way you can hurt a car? The more you drive 'em, the quicker they wear out. But how about the human machine? How do you hurt it? Inactivity – that's the killer. Mentally, morally, spiritually, sexually – inactivity, that's the killer. Sex and exercise are synonymous – just try and overdo 'em. You can't.'

Born to a family of French immigrants in San Francisco, LaLanne was sickly as a child. 'My whole life was sugar, sugar, sugar. I was addicted to it,' he says disgustedly. When he was fourteen, his mother took him to a lecture by a noted dietitian of the day, and his life was transformed. He became a vegetarian and started exercising, beginning a health regimen that has lasted for seventy years. He built his first gym at home, while he was still in high school. 'The local policemen and firemen would

Superyoung

come and work out there,' he says. 'I used those guys as guinea-pigs, to develop my exercise machines.' LaLanne invented the first weight selector machine, which allowed the level of resistance to be increased by the use of pins rather than lugging heavy plates. He also invented the leg extension machine, a staple of every gym in the world, and the first calf machine.

Then, in 1936, he opened his first health club. 'It was in downtown Oakland. Oh, it was beautiful. I had chrome equipment, carpets on the floor, nice showers. I was paying forty-five dollars a month in rent.' But those early years were hard. 'It was just not accepted then. They said I was a kook and a charlatan. Even my family thought I was nuts.' What turned it all around, he says, was the television programme, which introduced the concept of physical fitness to American families – and unleashed the formidable power of Jack LaLanne's personality and passionate belief in his message.

'If you came to my health spa, I knew your first name, your girlfriend or boyfriend's name, your mother and your sister. I knew everything about you, because I was your counsellor. If you missed two days at the gym, I'd call you at home and say, "I don't want your money. How am I going to get you in shape if you're not here?" We cared. Today, if you join a health club, you get zero instruction. They just take your money and turn you loose. You have to get a personal trainer, but who can afford that kind of money? Today, that's all it is – money, money, money.'

He emphasizes that it isn't necessary to join a health club to get into shape. 'People can do everything at home. They can run in place, they can do sit-ups, stretches in the doorway.' He endorses the use of exercise video tapes, but with the caveat that you need to vary the programme every three weeks. 'And remember: you're never too old to start. Even if you're ninety-five years old, you can double your strength and double your endurance. At least half an hour, three or four times a week – and never miss it, regardless of what happens.'

He is at least as persuasive on the subject of nutrition, though he is no longer a strict vegetarian. His guiding maxim is, 'If man made it, don't eat it.' He eats ten raw vegetables and three to four pieces of fresh fruit every day, with lots of pulses and rice. His main sources of protein are fish and egg whites. One of his favourite dishes is an omelet made from five or six egg whites, with bean sprouts, celery and mushrooms, cooked in Pam (a commercial preparation of lecithin, in spray form). 'If I eat bread, it's a hundred per cent whole wheat. If I eat dessert, it's fresh fruit. Once in a while I might have a non-fat yogurt, but that's real seldom. The whole key is moderation and variety: the more variety of natural foods, the better.'

At times LaLanne can be almost overpowering, but whenever he senses that he's getting carried away, he will pause and say 'Shut up, Jack,' and tell a joke. Yet there's no doubt that he is deeply sincere in his message of healthful positivism. 'If you want to live long,' he declares, 'you have to believe in something. That's the key: believing. Get a hobby. Learn a language. If you're single, go out and start dating. And dress well: too many old people dress like old coots. Women should get their hair coifed, have manicures and pedicures. Don't think about retirement – think about giving something.'

J. J.

CHAPTER SEVEN

FIGHTING AGE OR AGEISM?

Da Dios nueces a los que no tienen muelas.
'God gives nuts to those who have no teeth.'
Spanish proverb

Life may not always be getting better, but it's undoubtedly getting longer. Increased lifespan and improved health are among the principal human achievements of the twentieth century. In every recent decade the average lifespan has risen by about two years, a trend which shows no sign of abating: now middle-aged Americans outnumber pre-adolescents by more than two to one. If medical advances could continue at their present pace, by the year 2050 about 90 per cent of the population would live to see the age of ninety. America has more than 20,000 centenarians – ten times the number forty years ago. Survivors are becoming better at surviving, maintaining their hardiness for longer, with briefer periods of infirmity throughout life, including extreme old age.

The average age in Western technological societies is certain to continue its upward climb, which means that the new elderly generation at the turn of our century will confront unprecedented challenges. The major concern is the decline of a powerful, visible role for retired adults in a society which does not appear to value the contributions of its elders – an attitude defiantly rejected by virtually all of the participants in the superyoung project.

As they make the transition from middle age, older people

124

have many more years to live, and yet many more empty hours to fill. Many of them, if not all, will need to redefine the terms of engagement in this new, unstructured territory, and to seek out new sources of strength. Despite the wisdom and experience they have acquired, the lessons of the past may not always prove to be relevant.

Most of the elderly patients I see tell me bitterly that they are patronized and treated unfairly, or at least differently from when they were younger. In 1968, at the height of the great wave of youth worship and youthful rebellion, Robert N. Butler, a psychiatrist in Washington DC, coined the term 'ageism' to describe the spread of pejorative images of the elderly and the discriminatory practices arising from them. Despite concerted efforts and the passage of a few palliative laws, ageism still persists in many quarters to this day. In surveys conducted by myself and others, as many as three-quarters of people over the age of fifty said that they had directly experienced such prejudice themselves. Many Americans were shocked – though not all were surprised – to hear the former Governor of Colorado, Richard Lamm, say in 1992 that 'older people have a duty to die and get out of the way'.

The negative behaviours encompassed by ageism include anything from off-hand insults ('grumpy old geezer', 'she's no spring chicken', 'mutton dressed as lamb'), straight through to ignoring, rejecting, ostracizing, ridiculing, belittling and vilifying people solely on account of their age. Much of this occurs behind the victim's back – but that, too, carries deleterious effects: it alters how other people perceive the person and, more pertinently, how they behave towards him.

The negative stereotyping of the elderly in the mass media amounts to a crude code – they're portrayed as doddering codgers and absent-minded old busybodies, hobbling along with bent backs and quavering limbs, who sponge off their adult children rather than living independently, and who never go anywhere or do anything constructive. Such stereotypes are obstacles to knowing, understanding and loving, and can cause well-meaning young people to overestimate the frequency and severity of age-related problems, the degree of adversity older people suffer, and, by implication, what they themselves can expect to suffer in the future.

For some people, reaching the middle years can induce a state of insecurity approaching panic – the so-called 'mid-life crisis' – but if it is viewed objectively and embraced positively, the way the superyoung do, the ageing process can give more than it takes away. These life transitions don't have to result in tumult: most people don't fall away from what they had previously thought was a firmly supportive nucleus of ambitions and core beliefs when they reach mid-life, but enough do to warrant a more sympathetic look at what is going on during these crucial periods.

First, there is denial: the psychological defence which tells the self that what is happening isn't happening at all. Yet as the toll of the years becomes more obvious, we need to open up these blind spots. How can we progress beyond these often unreasonable fears and prejudices? How can we break through the stalemate that denial produces to reach some sort of acceptance of the inevitable?

Defensive denial serves a psychological purpose: it allows us to cope with life by dismissing or pushing out of active consciousness thoughts that are inconsistent with how we view ourselves – the way we present ourselves to others, and the way we would like to be. When allowed to take on a life of their own, such thoughts threaten our inner balance. In other words, denial is a form of self-censorship. Whether it is deliberate or not, whether absurd or manageable, denial has the power to falsify our sense of personal integrity.

Making the tally of birthdays the final arbiter of our behaviour, of what society expects or allows us to do, permits bleak, unhappy feelings about ageing to arise spontaneously, so that they need not be triggered by any particular event. My interviews with thousands of ordinary older people have revealed some striking patterns: for many of them, emotional high points and declines are seen more as the consequence of social expectations than of actual life experiences. They look at themselves almost as objects, thinking about themselves in the third person, always trying to work out how others will see them – and then, often, only on the basis of looks and behaviour. Small wonder that those affected come to see themselves in old age as used up, cast adrift, without purpose.

Because cultural ageism is based upon attitudes about what is *not* acceptable, it also restricts what the mind can imagine. Ultimately, these negative emotional constructs reduce the ability of elderly people to think and act like independent adults: after a lifetime of being told to prepare for childishness, it comes to be seen as an inevitability. The melancholy mood that results leads to defeatism, and finally the fulfilment of the prophecy. Some people go even further in the negative direction: they conclude that there are no more opportunities in the future, no more romantic or sexual experiences, no more triumphs of the intellect or the spirit – indeed, that there's no future in the future. The problem of this 'diminished horizon', as gerontologists call it, is compounded by the sufferer's reluctance to contemplate change and growth – and, above all, by ageist prejudice.

For example, in America many older people have been tempted to relocate to so-called retirement communities in the Sun Belt, stretching across the South West, or in Florida. Meanwhile, in Britain some of the coastal resorts fringing the south coast have gradually become such communities in a more ad hoc way. And the sunnier climes of the Mediterranean beckon continually, and are now home to many British expatriates. Although there are sometimes very good reasons for making such decisions to move, these grey enclaves can become age-based ghettos, cut off from the mainstream of society, inevitably resulting in generational prejudices.

Ageism, like certain other prejudices, may have its basis in compassion, but paradoxically it results in reducing the autonomy of the target individual – even bringing about unnecessary dependency. When her children decided to put their mother in a nursing home because she was becoming a little forgetful, they may have done her far more harm than good. Many older people resist such well-meaning treatment, because they see it as a diminution of choice, variety, social life and intellectual stimulation. They fear it as a bland way of becoming a non-person. As the desire for independence grows, such institutions will more and more become a last resort for those with disabling medical conditions, who are too frail to remain within the community.

Ageism ought to be viewed as primarily a psychological reaction, because its existence is not based upon the biological facts of ageing. Indeed, those who are most prejudiced about older people frequently know the least about them. There are few, if any, real connections between biological ageing and the social behaviour produced as a response to it. Therefore, discrimination on the basis of age should be confronted and combated whenever it occurs. The remedy lies in the direction of social influence, by education, working to alter public opinion by persuasion, and, where necessary, by making the laws against such discrimination tougher.

In recent surveys, about half of those over fifty said that they believed they wouldn't be able to get a new job if they became unemployed. People in this group who are highly capable and well motivated can start up their own businesses from scratch, but those who are able to face such a challenge with equanimity in late mid-life are rare. This approach is sometimes combined with another, frequently mooted alternative, that of multiple part-time jobs. Both options require a high degree of resilience – one of the signature traits of the superyoung.

Jessica Morrell, a participant in the project, was a successful physiotherapist, but when (she was then 61) her husband's career called for him to move hundreds of miles away, to the Pacific Northwest, she resigned from her job and followed him. One year later to the day, he left her for another woman. For a while she was crushed by the sense of betrayal, but when she learned that she couldn't count on receiving alimony from her ex-husband, she had a breakthrough. She decided to try to do something she had always dreamed of, to turn her hobby, ceramics, into a business. She began turning out highly stylized, sometimes humorous coffee mugs, teapots, fruit bowls and other collectibles. She also began giving lessons. As she progressed in her career, Jessica discovered abilities within herself that she didn't know were there.

Often, people feel fairly positive about their future goals when they reach retirement, but immediately afterwards there may be a feeling of let-down that can become catastrophic. My research has shown that for most men, satisfaction with retirement decreases over time – so much so that, for many, a crisis is sometimes produced long after they have become used to the idea of being retired, when they realize that their lost dignity and prestige will not be recovered. While some retired people increasingly value their new, easy-going lifestyle, and the feel-ings of pleasure and contentment that come with it, they also become more timid, less sure of their abilities, more inarticulate about their emotional needs. When a man is retired but his wife remains employed, disagreements over who does what at home can cause serious marital strife where none may have existed before. Men who feel they were forced into retirement fare worse than those who chose it freely. Yet in some cases, this sense of failure or rejection can motivate the reluctant retiree to move forward and bounce back to a highly developed stage of personal renewal.

The changes induced in this way tend to be deeply personal, and are often religious or spiritual in nature, sometimes embra-cing the tenets of New Age mysticism. A good example of how this may come about was described to us by one of the super-young participants, Kirk Collins, who is now happily retired, living on his boat in Key West:

> It might be melodramatic to say that I nearly lost my faith. I was one of the earliest victims of down-sizing. What really got me was the cold, clinical way the cuts were imposed. I came out of it OK in the end, but that was thanks to our minister and my good friends in the church. Once I got over the idea of being a workaholic, I began a more stress-free time in my life. A new sense of inner quiet gave me back the joy which should have been there all the time.'

For women, ageism can be even more devastating. Different prejudices have a way of combining and reinforcing one another, an insidious process which results in senior women being doubly marginalized. For instance, female workers in the public eye are often transferred or eased out from their jobs at an earlier age than are their male counterparts. And while there now exists a substantial body of case law giving ageing women legal recourse against discriminatory practices, the burden of proof rests upon the victim. Many of those most profoundly affected are often too vulnerable and demoralized to embark on such a bold course of action.

In a youth-oriented culture, the superficial aspects of youth — especially appearance, speed and energy — are given excessive weight, sometimes supplanting the qualities of age, such as wisdom and kindness. Derogatory comments about a person's appearance are much more apt to be directed at older women than at older men or younger women. We say that we believe, and perhaps we do, that true beauty comes from within; but well-documented research has consistently shown that attractive-looking people, whether young or old, are perceived by strangers to have more favourable personalities, and to have achieved more success, whether they have done so or not.

Why do we find it so hard to see the beauty in an ageing face? Perhaps it's our fear of death which makes the effects of time in others so difficult to overlook, and even harder to accept in oneself. Wrinkles aren't simply symbolic; they are bitter truths which cannot be denied. It's a part of being human to harbour such massive contradictions within our psyches – we sense that the finest values in a person aren't visible to the eye, yet we worship the vapid young fantasy creatures of the electronic dream factories, whose ephemeral beauty is only retina-deep. We want to live forever, although we know that that is impossible. Left unresolved, such inconsistencies lead to mental conflict.

Ageist prejudices are so widespread that the victims themselves often come to adopt, albeit unknowingly, some of their tenets. The phenomenon of the victims' gradual self-denigration isn't confined to age-based bias. There are those who prefer self-delusion to self-development, who end up as victims because they collude in defining themselves primarily in terms of age and appearance.

English anthropologist Dorothy Jerrome, after a great deal of observational field research, explained how this comes about: 'Old age is a moral category. Responses to it are a matter of virtue and moral strength or weakness. To be happy and make the best of things in spite of pain and hardship is a moral and social obligation attached to the status of an old or handicapped person. Those who fail are blameworthy, and tend to blame themselves.' Self-blame is hostility turned upon oneself, one of the first, crucial steps towards depression. Under the control of guilt or low mood, judgment can become impaired, distorting thoughts about oneself, the world and the future.

Of course, to 'be happy and make the best of things' is a quintessential superyoung trait, but those who lack that inner buoyancy, and who have been repeatedly exposed to ageist prejudice, begin to apply the stigma inwardly, and then to segregate themselves from others and become isolated. Bereft of a social context, their choices, actions and environments are likely to become ever more restricted in scope. In such a state of negative self-image, reassurance from others counts for almost nothing. The sufferer's real or imagined invisibility becomes integral to his self-concept. He will begin to feel incapable of bringing about any positive changes in his life.

The absence of vital social contact underlies a pervading sense of meaninglessness, an existential malaise that can be found in any period of adulthood, but especially in later life. Moreover, as people age, the experience of loss increases. One's circle of friends shrinks because of death, which not only deepens the sense of isolation but also makes the spectre of death ever-present. Such losses impede the person's ability to engage in desirable new relationships and maintain existing ones. The result is loneliness: old people caught up in this process of progressive isolation attribute their condition to their advancing age, and therein lies the connection between ageism and loneliness. Most at risk of loneliness are those who retired from poorly paid positions, divorced people and widowers.

The diversity of human behaviour and values in a pluralistic world should mean that greater, rather than fewer, allowances are made – greater tolerance rather than diminished horizons. But such is not the case. Collective fears are exploited for various reasons, from the banal (product advertising) to the ridiculous (conflicting exhortations from the voices of conformity to behave differently from one's own nature).

As the literary critic Kathleen Woodward has pointed out, these are symptoms of angst, and as such are actually cultural signposts, warnings to all of us: 'Old age is a time in our lives about which many of us feel anxiety and fear. The symptoms of these feelings of apprehension are denial and repression of the very subject of ageing and old age. But a fear of ageing is not necessarily only a "personal" problem. Our culture's representations of ageing are predominantly negative and thus are inextricably linked to our personal anxieties – for ourselves and for others.' At the same time, images of youth in our society are now so pervasive that they are impossible to ignore, intruding into all spheres of life. That doesn't mean that we should pin blame on all these portrayals, only that we should acknowledge that they don't contribute anything positive to the lives of older people.

Rather than retreating from the world, the victims themselves, *for themselves*, need to mount their own counter-arguments in the face of prejudice. When the 'facts' as presented are not facts but rather dubious impressions distorted by bias, they must be evaluated carefully, analytically. Simply accepting yourself as you are helps to break down many of the polarized preconceptions held by others. Learned prejudice can be opposed and unlearned. The helplessness it produces can also be unlearned, tough as the process may be. The resulting self-empowerment brings with it the feeling of raised confidence and the expectation of effectiveness in producing change.

Improving sociability takes one out of a repetitive and unchanging environment, and opens access to a range of new people, some of whom may have divergent or even challenging viewpoints. Good social participation and integration is strongly linked to health, a sense of well-being and longevity. There can be no doubt that committed friendships prevent depression more effectively than Prozac. Most of us still need to learn how to better imagine an optimistic, creative life course. In the next chapter, we will examine the coping strategies and insights of the superyoung, to see how their novel, alternative ways of coping with life can work for everyone.

Cecilia Hurwich

Cecilia Hurwich has made a science of feeling young. Now seventy-eight, she travels the world to spread the gospel she calls Vitality in Ageing. She served on President Clinton's White House Conference on Ageing, in 1996, which charted a national ageing policy for the twenty-first century, and leads Great Old Broads for Wilderness, an informal group of elderly women who climb the mountains and trek the forests of the American West. Hurwich's career as a professional Great Old Broad began at the age of fifty-nine, when her mother died. 'I realized that I didn't know any women over seventy. I asked myself, Where are my role models? Who was I going to learn from?'

At an age when many people are thinking about early retirement, she went to graduate school in psychology, motivated in part by a desire to meet vigorous women who might fill that need in her life. She undertook a 10-year longitudinal research project called 'Vital Women in their Seventies, Eighties, and Nineties'. She studied the lives of a group of a hundred older women in the San Francisco Bay Area, where she lives, to determine what factors contributed towards maintaining youthful vitality in later age. 'My favourite subject was a woman named Ann, who enrolled in a Spanish class when she was ninety-five. I told her, "Oh Ann, that's great! Are you planning a trip to Mexico or Spain?" And she replied matter-of-factly, "No, I just want to keep the cobwebs out of my head."'

There are certainly no cobwebs in Hurwich's head. She and her life partner, a man six years younger than herself, share a redwood house in Berkeley decorated in retina-searing shades of orange and pink, with leopard-skin patterned carpet and paintings and folk sculptures she has collected on her eight visits to India. A petite lady with glossy brown hair and dark, sparkling eyes, Hurwich moves with the grace and sure dexterity of a woman thirty years younger. She radiates enthusiasm about the possibilities of later life, without sugar-coating the physical downsides. 'You don't have to have perfect health to be active.

I have arthritis and glaucoma – so what? I concentrate on what I *can* do, not what I *can't* do.'

Like many superyoung people, she reinvented herself in late middle age. 'My forties were a bummer,' she says cheerfully. 'I had a bad divorce and a bad back. In my fifties and sixties I began to find my way, and in my seventies I blossomed. I got my PhD from Berkeley just as I turned seventy. It was a great party.' Her back was in such bad shape that the doctors all told her to wear a brace and take it easy. 'Then I found a wonderful doctor who told me to take off the brace and exercise.' Hurwich's career as an avid outdoorswoman began with a trek in Nepal when she was fifty, the beginning of her interest in the art and thought of the Indian subcontinent. 'My x-rays look terrible, but I just keep going,' she says proudly. On a visit to Bombay in 1997, she amazed her audiences with the agility of her yoga demonstrations.

Hurwich's longitudinal study revealed five general characteristics of people who preserve the vitality of youth in later life, all of which emerged to a significant degree in the superyoung project. She reported that the Great Old Broads in her research:

- find life meaningful,
- are optimistic,
- have friends of all ages,
- continue to grow (Hurwich says of herself, 'I've shrunk two inches, but I've grown inside'), and
- consider spirituality important.

In 1992, she organized a group in Bombay for a trek to Hunza, a tiny Asian kingdom on India's western border, which was taken over by Pakistan in 1947. She had read an article in *National Geographic* that said the people of Hunza continued to be remarkably vigorous until extreme old age. 'I interviewed women who were still working out in the fields in their seventies and eighties,' she says. The Hunzaites endure a severe winter, which leaves them very thin by its end; Hurwich believes that their longevity and good health may be partly explained by this periodic near-starvation diet (a view supported by some recent, well-publicized experiments with mice). But her most important finding in Hunza, she says, was the worshipful respect shown towards the elderly. 'When an old woman comes into the room there, the children kneel and kiss her feet.'

J. J.

CHAPTER EIGHT

AGEING WITH GRACE: THE SUPERYOUNG IDEAL

> *You think it horrible that lust and rage*
> *Should dance attention upon my old age . . .*
> *They were not such a plague when I was young*
> *What else have I (now) to spur me into song?*
>
> William Butler Yeats

> *Though much is taken, much abides; and though*
> *We are not now that strength which in old days*
> *Moved earth and heaven, that which we are, we are;*
> *One equal temper of heroic hearts,*
> *Made weak by time and fate, but strong in will*
> *To strive, to seek, to find, and not to yield.*
>
> Alfred, Lord Tennyson

'Population ageing will be one of the most important phenomena of the next half century.' That solemn judgment was the considered opinion of a panel organized by the US National Research Council, in 1994, which had as its mission to formulate a national policy on ageing for the twenty-first century. Now, while the policy makers are busy making policy, and the social planners are planning, what can older people do for themselves, to make their lives rich and rewarding?

In the preceding chapter, we examined some of the problems encountered by older people – boredom, enforced idleness, age discrimination and loneliness. Sooner or later, despite their natural advantages, the superyoung like everyone else are forced to confront these problems in some form. Indomitable optimists that they are, they don't succumb to such difficulties but rather find solutions to them. The ingenious strategies for successful ageing devised by the remarkable people in my study provide instructive models for us all. What are their approaches to the key areas of work, leisure, lifestyle and intimate relationships? Can the superyoung show us how to construct winning, flexible alternatives for what is, after all, an inevitable part of life? Or are they simply the exceptions that prove all the old rules?

In the first place, the superyoung don't feel that they deserve any special rights or entitlements, solely because of their age. The majority had not even actively considered the question. When pressed on this issue, they said that they favoured absolute freedom to choose how they lived their lives – by extension, they felt that this should apply to everyone, regardless of age and without limit. Margot Bryce, a vinegary 84-year-old woman from New Orleans, who has worked both as a photographer's model and later as a photographer herself, told me:

> Control your own destiny, or someone else will try to. I've found *my* niche, a precious space for myself. I'm comfortable now being me. I'm not letting anyone else direct me or dominate me ever again. I don't want to be exempted from anything – including my obligations to others. If people see you asking for help, they will come to see you as being in need of it. Not bad, you might say, but bingo, the next thing you know, they take away your first and most important role, that of an adult with choices. So keep on being sparky right to the end.

The superyoung see ageing as a natural process to be accepted, albeit a very slow one, so they tend not to take note of particular milestones or events normally connected with age. For them, a fiftieth or sixtieth or seventieth birthday isn't likely to be observed as a portentous turning point but rather celebrated with the same gusto with which they approach every other activity in life. Physical difficulties are perceived merely as inconveniences, obstacles to be surmounted by whatever means are available. Here is how Victoria Mason, who had taken up windsurfing at the age of seventy-six, described her attitude towards health issues:

> I'm in the prime of my life. I believe there's nothing I can't do if I put my mind to it. I have been diagnosed as having high blood pressure and osteoarthritis, but you have to *make* yourself fit and healthy. With a feeling for sublime humour, life loses some of its excessive serious-ness. By tolerating personal suffering, we can treat it with a light touch. You have to keep going, and make yourself get up in the morning. Sometimes it's hard, and I've felt that I couldn't be bothered, but I always try to think positive and find something good about the day ahead.

Because the superyoung have been optimistic in outlook throughout most of their lives, they continue to be positive in their responses to advancing age. In the instance above, the ingrained practice of optimistic, healthy thinking had direct implications for what Victoria would actually *do*. Her affirmative handling of her situation in her mind was translated into positive behaviour. And she followed through — it wasn't just a one-off resolution which was broken soon afterwards. If the new behaviour succeeds, then it leads to increasing self-confidence in other situations, and reinforces the view that it is possible to find ways to cope in a constructive way.

Nina Rulenskya, a former professional dancer, is one of those people who delights in trying new activities, diversifying her daily routine on a regular basis. At the age of seventy-seven, she helped to set up a social club to encourage her contemporaries to be more active. 'Age is irrelevant to me, and my heartfelt attitude is that it would be nice if others could see it that way too. All you have to do is ignore how old you are, keep busy, and never, ever say or think, "I can't do that, not at *my* age." That kind of talk is simply not allowed.'

Jack O'Mahoney, age seventy-eight, a former jet-propulsion engineer living in southern California, also believes in the benefits of positive, active ageing. Throughout our talks, he seemed to radiate a kind of energetic contentment. He was adamant about how his beliefs had affected his lifestyle: 'I really do believe – and it isn't just wishful thinking – that getting old is an adventure. Especially if you've managed to keep your marbles, there are all sorts of things going for it. The way ahead is only difficult to see for those who dither and refuse to make choices for themselves.'

O'Mahoney said that he looks for parallels and correspondences between fields of thought that are usually seen as being in opposition, such as science and mystical spirituality. 'My approach has become more open and eclectic. I also approve of the gung-ho way that the Gray Panthers moved our goal posts of ambition so decisively, especially when they first started their pressure tactics. I didn't realize how important freedom of speech was until they got going. There is no reason to become the passive pawn of external circumstances; we shouldn't be put off by the weight of problems facing us, but make a start toward addressing them.'

Retirement is a delicate psychological moment for most people; and while some firms do have pre-retirement preparation programmes in place, nearly all of them are woefully inadequate. The retiree is suddenly thrust out there on his own, cut adrift from the world of work and its many varieties of social interaction. As one forthright pre-retirement instructor told me, 'It takes most of us nine months to be born, but when we are launched into the retired life, we might receive, at least, six helpful lectures to prepare us for the rest of our lives. It's usually quickly popped in near the end, and when it comes, it's all a bit of a shock.'

The superyoung view retirement as practically meaningless, for it in no way signifies a retreat from or a diminished commitment to the concerns that absorbed them previously. It's not a time for disengagement in any form, neither from work nor from social contacts. Sophie Hart, a lady of eighty-six now residing in Bury St Edmunds, England, who earlier in life had founded an educational charity, said matter-of-factly, 'The subject of retirement itself needs a bright spotlight cast upon it. I am sure that those of us who have lived through the world experience of the last seventy or eighty years have insights that *need* to be shared. Society is waking up to an ageing population that won't be ignored or put away. I hope that we can turn that to good effect, for the sake of those who will follow.'

People at this time of life are still energetic and eager to remain involved in the world. There is a need for them, for themselves, to find outlets for their energies as well as their social needs. According to the official estimates, a quarter of all retired Americans return to some sort of paid employment, mostly part-time, after they retire from their career jobs. The participation rate in the labour force of people sixty-five and older has increased, though only slightly, since 1985. But these data are underestimates; probably as many as 50 per cent of retired people return to some form of work, even more if you include voluntary and charitable activities.

For the superyoung, retirement is a time for self-discovery and reviewing one's life, especially for those who had little time to contemplate such personal issues in the past. Sophie Hart told me, 'Inevitably, too, I have been thinking about the basic philosophies for living we all work out for ourselves. I feel we are only paddling in the shallow end of the learners' pool as yet. You have to be able to tie up where you have arrived with your beginnings and your falterings, now that you're nearer to the end.'

Margaret Jaye, a retired schoolteacher, sixty-two at the time of our interview, had just taken up ski-orienteering in the Rockies and mountain biking in the Alps – both for the first time. She explained how she got started: 'My problem was an inability to get past the "But I haven't done that before" attitude. Then I joined a new discovery programme, in which there was an option for a research project. Most of those joining the scheme seemed to be pretty active folks already. However, this experience gave me more commitment and forced me, thank God, to complete things.'

The healthy ageing process includes accepting the mistakes, omissions, foibles and grievances of one's youth – all those dreadful moments one might have wished would be forgotten. It's a matter of owning up to oneself. The acceptance of responsibility for one's own fate seems to be almost essential to the discovery of individual meaning. Perhaps by only aspiring to this, or perhaps by actually attaining it, one can transcend the limitations of the self, through trust in real intimacy. This should be the major goal of any life review – whether undertaken later in life or earlier.

In order to change one's way of thinking, one should take every opportunity to examine all the relevant evidence. In the case of an honest life review, this would include all the key choices made, why they were made, the constraints placed in the way, and, despite all these factors, what lessons may have been learned about things done or left undone. In the recent past, women began to face up to this at an earlier stage in their lives than men did, usually when all their children had grown up and left home; men tend to postpone such reappraisals almost indefinitely, or at least until retirement hits them hard.

Some people do engage in such reviews throughout life, especially in times of stress – after divorce, serious illness, or a major career setback (or, indeed, after a professional triumph). Patterns emerge; guiding principles and common themes can be seen sharply. Such reviews permit one to explain and clarify the events that have shaped one's life. Subjective ideas and objective realities can be integrated into a more coherent biography, which can be revised and amended as necessary after further reflection and self-examination. Why permit yourself to be troubled and dismayed by unfinished business? Why go into retirement with surplus baggage?

Arranging the best conditions for a successful life review is often easier to attain in the less distracting period that follows the 'honeymoon', immediately after retirement begins. A life review at this time facilitates further psychological and social integration near the start of this next major stage in life. It lends itself well to a self-help approach, though it can also be undertaken within the framework of psychotherapy. For the self-aware, it is simply another step in an ongoing, systematic introspection.

For the superyoung, there is no gradual slowing down prior to retirement – that would be unthinkable for them. Darla Shaw, a superyoung subject who lives in rural Connecticut, described her last year before retirement: 'I had a number of firsts: my first graduation speech at a prison (how's that for a captive audience!), my first time to teach an Elderhostel course, my first appearance in a low-budget film [*Pink Pumpkins*], my first time to do a voice-over for a TV commercial.' During this *annus mirabilis*, she also served as a consultant to a military museum, performed stand-up comedy, toured China, and wrote a children's book, *Queen of the Jellybeans*, as well as a serious study of Tourette's syndrome (a neurological disorder characterised by an excessive amount of nervous energy, together with many unusual sounds and movements).

In the decades preceding retirement, in the prime of life, the superyoung typically construct lives with numerous meaningful strands, comprising several different roles. Therefore in old age they feel less need or inclination for a retrospective life review focusing on prior problem areas. To them, that would be akin to a negative form of looking backward – a very un-superyoung thing to do. That is not to say that the superyoung reject their pasts, or fail to draw lessons from their experiences; they simply refuse to live in the past. The present offers a new perspective on the past, and exciting new prospects for the future.

Simply piling up the years is no guarantee of mature emotional development. Lee McMahon, for most of his life a successful insurance salesman and sportsman, and now retired and living on the shores of Lake Hopatcong in rural New Jersey, proposed another kind of project for himself: he has undertaken a quest for a new inner equilibrium: 'I've discovered that in some ways we know less – and in other ways more – than we think we do. This is a time for balancing the books, not waiting to square your final accounts but doing something about it. When you get to this age inevitably you think about it being the last chance you'll ever have to put things right, and what that might involve.'

The superyoung believe that they only deserve the regard and approval of others if they pitch in and do their share. In an enlightened way, they aspire to take on new roles that are primarily selfless in nature. This is mainly determined by their emotional empathy, for on a profound level they feel what other people are feeling – not only what can be perceived from words and outward behaviour, but also, often, what others are experiencing on the inside. Empathy is a learned skill, and it improves with practice, particularly in retirement. Other people naturally tend to seek out such empathic, socially knowledgeable people to unburden themselves to. It was clear from my research that the superyoung subjects who were able to provide this sort of support to their neighbours, for whatever reason, improved their own self-esteem as well as that of the person they helped. Perhaps as a consequence of all this, they became even more socially active, and, over time, suffered fewer illnesses themselves compared with those who were more isolated.

Agatha, seventy-one years old, is a remarkably gentle, quiet person. Her inner peace is almost palpable. Yet it wasn't always so: as a child, she was taken away from her mother and forced against her will to live abroad with her father. She was physically abused for years by the woman who later became her step-mother. For most of her adult life, Agatha was the literal embodiment of the poor, struggling artist. She now meditates daily, drawing on Asian philosophy, primarily Zen Buddhism, which she studied for a while at a nunnery in Kyoto. Expressing herself with a neat Zen paradox, she told me:

> If I am older, I am now also younger. I think that civilized society has grown away from childhood innocence. To overcome ageing, you have to relinquish your bonds to all those things that are not really needed: this is for the good of your soul. It's extraordinary how selfless you can become when the circumstances call for it. Believe in yourself, but nurture and encourage others' dreams too. In this way, you combine a sense of doing and being in communion with others. Nothing can replenish your feel-good factor better than hearing other people's needs, or being of some small service to the community.

Barbara, a long-retired medical missionary, was just beginning to lose her eyesight when we interviewed her, at the age of ninety-three, but her outlook remained undimmed:

> I was just an old-fashioned girl longing to do some good; it took me most of my life to cotton on to the fact that others did not necessarily share goals similar to mine. The sense of life is within us, but that's not the same thing as saying that it *is* us. I had to get my own ego out of the way, and get back into being involved in other people's needs. When there is a chance that life is offering this kind of opportunity – to get involved with living life to the full – we should take it. One life, if it's one's own, is more than plenty. I learned that to concentrate more on others is, ultimately, better for your own soul.

The altruism of many of the elderly superyoung subjects in the study harks back to a notion first enunciated by both the early Christians and the neo-Platonic philosophers of imperial Rome, and independently embraced by the native American peoples: the concept of stewardship over nature and responsibility for other people, for the sake of succeeding generations. Those who take on the steward's role work to improve conditions for the benefit of all. They not only strive to preserve, protect, and transmit the lessons and heritage of the past – they are actively committed to changing the world for the better, and feel this duty with the force of a moral imperative.

The classical, romanticized image of this kind of steward is that of someone planting a sapling to grow into a tree for the benefit of posterity. What is being transmitted is not only the tree itself but also the symbolic good example. Stewardship simultaneously conserves and cherishes that which is the best of the past and looks forward to the future, to develop and to build for the common good. Stewards are a part of the social glue, holding together the links between the generations.

The superyoung really like people as they are, not as they should be. They give other people emotional support, and receive at least as much as they give. Such behaviour, when it is practised consistently, contributes directly to increased emotional well-being, and indirectly to a lower probability of illness. Sound personal relationships are effective buffers against stress; conversely, if emotional support is sought after but not received – or worse still, withdrawn – additional stress may arise, leading to further frustration and depression. People with a well-developed primary group of family members and confidants are substantially better protected against some certain psychological symptoms, including high anxiety, alienation and disturbed feelings of failure or futility.

The superyoung are social creatures *par excellence*, and because of this, like many others, they are animated by the desire to be as popular as possible. That comes easily to them. Their company is enlivening and exhilarating, and other people want to have them as friends. However, amidst this lifelong pattern of making and keeping friends, there are many instances in which the super-young feel it right to depart from the majority view. They do this even if it makes them stand out more – even if it means that they disappoint the expectations of their friends. That's a sure sign of emotional maturity: the superyoung don't commit the error of fearing to err. Any of them would be happy to say, 'The way you see me now, that's the way I really am, and it's the only way I can be.'

Because they mix with a broad spectrum of people, the superyoung are exposed to many alternative views, which creates a rich counterpoint to the received wisdom of the majority. Just as they tolerate differences within themselves, so they tolerate differences between themselves and others. By giving themselves permission to be exceptional, that's precisely what they become. Yet the superyoung aren't outspoken just for the sake of being so; their non-conformity is several shades more subtle than that. They're gently, patiently persistent, but never offensive.

Robert Frost said that he hadn't dared to be radical when he was young lest it make him more conservative when he was old. Jenny Lansdowne, an English war bride who settled with her American husband in Indiana, sixty-nine at the time of our interview, agreed with this view but took it a step further:

If you have any subversive potential, wait until you're over sixty: you're better able to carry it off then, and to get away with it, too. For instance, I don't stand for older women being dismissed out of hand. I won't be airbrushed into being something I'm not. Society expects us to conform to what is seen as the natural way of growing older – that is, slowing down, reaching out for the knitting, and watching daytime TV till you've got rectangular eyes. But it needn't be that way if we don't want it to be. Time is too precious, and our stay here can be pretty precarious. Always has been.

At the age of fifty-five, Celeste Hayden took early retirement from her position at a large fashion house in Europe. In our interview, she said that she was annoyed with the status quo she had tolerated for many years, and embarked on a new phase of non-conformity. She said,

> By trying to please men, men, men all the time, by doing whatever they wanted, by playing the part they had cast me in, I perpetuated their pathetic behaviour, always under-mining who I was. That was truly dispiriting, and was eventually unsustainable as a way of life. I learned later that things could be done much differently. The greatest thing in the world to know is how to belong, and to whom, if you will. The freedom I have earned is precious to me.

Celeste, like the other superyoung participants, found the ability within herself to accept her changing position in the world – and the courage to adapt to it. The superyoung, empowered by a talent for empathy, a sense of stewardship, and a healthy open-mindedness, make ageing a process of liberation. Such healthy habits of the mind can contribute towards a superyoung out-look, leading to mental and physical vitality at any age.

In Part Two, we will present a concrete, comprehensive plan, based upon the experiences of the superyoung, which allows anyone to make these life-enhancing changes.

Making the Most of Retirement

Longer lives require better planning: the experiences of the superyoung in their transition to retirement can translate into specific advice for those approaching retirement, and for members of their families.

Some people may find that over the years their social circle has narrowed down to a few close friends and work contacts. Thus, when they leave the workplace, they lose touch with a large number of people all at once; work mates' promises to stay in touch tend to go the way of most good intentions. Yet those who actually do manage to keep in contact with both their contemporaries and other age groups are more likely to maintain a strong, positive self-image. Therefore, one of the most important parts of preparing for retirement is to widen your social circle beforehand. Renew contacts with old friends with whom you may have lost touch while you were busy working.

Married couples sometimes need to make adjustments and learn to cope with a new set of routines. Try not to become an exclusive, rigidly self-contained unit: husband and wife are less likely to fray each other's nerves if they have a mixture of shared and independent interests. The transitional period of retirement can be particularly difficult when one partner has already been at home for some time, because he or she will usually have established a pattern of living, and may well resent having it disturbed. Homemakers sometimes complain of less freedom and independence after their partner's retirement. However, when both husband and wife were employed, retirement offers the opportunity to develop a more equal and cooperative relationship.

To make the most of retirement, planning and preparation are of paramount importance. As the time approaches, a couple should sit down together and draw up an action plan. Sometimes designating private spaces, separate rooms if possible, may be a good idea. But remember, having so much more time together can also give you the opportunity to make your relationship even better. Marital partners follow different paths to personal development. In their later years, women are happier, feel more empowered and less vulnerable than they did earlier in the marriage. These trends are related to a change in the balance of power within the relationship. As the parental role reduces, some women become less dependent on their husbands and find other avenues of satisfaction and support.

Sexual problems can sometimes arise in retirement, because of the husband's or wife's loss of self-esteem when he or she is no longer working and putting bread on the table. Yet retirement also provides the opportunity for man and wife to become lovingly re-acquainted, and a sensitive wife with the ability to empathize with her husband's feelings of loss can overcome this challenge.

The leisure time that retirement brings with it allows the individual to concentrate on creative pursuits, which, for the first time, can become full-time intellectual vocations rather than mere hobbies. According to the Oxford social psychologist Michael Argyle, leisure time can give people of all ages the chance to attain 'a deeply satisfying quality of subjective experience, an intense and highly agreeable state of "absorption" and loss of self-awareness'.

Such freely chosen activities are typically accompanied by a higher level of 'positive hedonic tone', psychologists' jargon for good mood, as well as a heightened sense of power, less physical tension, and improved mental concentration. Leisure pastimes usually bring both extrinsic and intrinsic rewards, and demand more effort and commitment than purely passive leisure activities such as sunbathing, viewing television to excess, and catnapping – though, interestingly, not daydreaming. And don't be afraid to draw upon your past experiences to be a teacher and mentor. However modestly this role is assumed, young people will learn much from your wisdom, and you will learn an equal amount from their fresh perspectives.

Retirement brings with it more unstructured time than any other period in one's life, including childhood (children sleep longer and deeper than older people do). Many retired couples look forward with relish to establishing a less complex and demanding lifestyle. The superyoung are particularly good at coping with this new abundance of time, by imposing upon it loose structures of what they want to do. The superyoung subjects of sixty and older told the researchers that they had added new leisure activities to their repertoire from time to time throughout their earlier lives, and continued to do so in retirement.

Superyoung participants living in rural areas are more active in their leisure pursuits, and more positive about them, than are the urban superyoung. The family structures and beliefs of the rural superyoung are more conventional – it might be said 'old-fashioned' – and despite the greater distances involved, they maintain closer contact with extended family members and old friends than their counterparts in the big cities (though one needn't equate frequency of visits with the degree of emotional closeness).

The most contented retirees among the superyoung sample maintain some form of physical exercise into advanced age, which helps them to maintain the *mens sana* as well as good physical health.

Michael Tilson Thomas

Throughout history, many of the greatest composers and performers were reported by their contemporaries to have possessed childlike innocence and zest throughout their lives – Mozart, Schubert and Satie come to mind immediately. (Of course, they were balanced by the saturnine patriarchs such as Brahms and Wagner.) Today, classical music is big business, yet it still attracts the young at heart. Foremost among them is Michael Tilson Thomas, music director of the San Francisco Symphony. The man is quick: tall and lanky, he lopes rather than walks, and talks at a rapid-fire tempo, emphasizing his points with gestures eloquent enough for the conductor's podium. At fifty-two, he looks a fit forty, and maintains the hectic pace of a pop star in his twenties.

Last night he was up until one a.m., working on a recording; at eight this morning he was back at his office in Davies Symphony Hall, preparing for a concert – one of seven he is conducting over the course of a ten-day festival – yet he is effervescing with energy. 'I get it from the music,' he says, relaxing in a chintz-covered armchair in his office. 'It's the same for me now as when I started making music. You experience such delight and wonder when you turn the dots and dashes on the page into the living voice of a composer, supposedly dead for centuries.'

Longish black hair, only slightly softened with grey, falls around his intense, angular face, which is dominated by a strong, aquiline nose and bronzed by the California sun. Tilson Thomas fits the superyoung profile to a T – or rather to an MTT, as he has come to be known in the San Francisco area: even his nickname is quick and to the point. One important superyoung trait is his lifelong association with people of all ages. In addition to leading the San Francisco orchestra, Tilson Thomas is also the director of the New World Symphony, in Miami, a training orchestra for the most gifted graduates of American music conservatories, most of whom are in their twenties. 'When I'm working with them, I sometimes forget that I'm not the age they are. Then I look in the mirror and realize, "Oh my god, I'm not a kid any more." My mother always used to say that when I was eighteen, all my best friends were fifty or over. Now I'm in my fifties, and I'm constantly in the company of young people.'

He could hardly be more creative and professionally active, unless he gave up sleep altogether, yet he still finds time for hiking in the redwood forests north of the city. Tilson Thomas, a native Californian, attributes his active lifestyle in part to the local culture: 'In Europe, it would really be bizarre for typical music lovers to imagine themselves riding on a motorbike or wind-surfing. But here in the Bay Area, it's quite natural to wake up and read your Sophocles, practise Chopin, and then run out to plant some cactus, or go rock collecting in the hills. Air has a lot to do with it.'

More than any other American conductor, Tilson Thomas has vigorously attacked the problem of how to bring young people into the concert hall. While the symphony orchestras on the East Coast, led by convention-bound, foreign-born conductors, continue to programme primarily European music of the nine-teenth century, MTT conducts a great deal of contemporary American music, particularly that being written by composers living on the West Coast. While the audiences in the cultural centres back East grow ever greyer, the crowds turning out for the San Francisco Symphony include a large proportion of young faces, some of them coming to a symphony concert for the first time. 'Last week,' says Tilson Thomas, 'when I was hiking up at Point Reyes, I ran into some other young hikers who had been at the concert the week before. We had done Mahler's Third, and they told me how much they had enjoyed it. It was the first time they had ever heard his music. They told me, "Do more Mahler!"'

Paradoxically, Tilson Thomas stays young by carefully observing the passage of time. 'I'm intensely involved in Jewish consciousness, and I find it very comforting to light a *shabas* candle to mark the sabbath on Friday evening, even if I'm conducting that night. It's a demarcation of time.' He also delights in the changing seasons of the year: 'I love to take note when the apricots come into season. Or, "Aha! Now the lavender is appearing. Let's crush it in our fingers and smell it." I believe in savouring every moment to the absolute maximum. Sitting up on Point Reyes, eating oysters in the fresh air, a crisp wind blowing – a moment like that makes me grateful to be alive.'

Like many superyoung people, Tilson Thomas believes that he inherited his intense, energetic approach to life from his parents. 'In those days, it was unusual for people to remain active in later life, but they never thought they had to be like everybody else. They always had friends much younger than themselves. We used to say that my father never lost the twinkle in his eye, that lively sparkle, until the day he died, at the age of eighty-eight. Up till the end, he was always busy gardening, playing the piano, reading, cooking.' Tilson Thomas's mother also lived to an old age, to eighty-two.

He jumps up from his chair and shows me a photograph of his grandmother, Bessie Thomashefsky, a great star of the Yiddish Theater in New York. The sepia-tinted picture discloses a strikingly beautiful woman with long, flowing hair, in an extravagant theatrical pose. 'Even in her late eighties, she was still electrifying audiences. She had flaming red hair, and wore lots of bangles, puffing on a cigarette in a long holder. I remember she once told me that it was said of her that every performance she gave was impassioned. She looked me in the eye and said, "Darling, remember, it is impossible to give an impassioned performance without some raw material."' Dramatically, he rubs his fingers together, recalling the actress's gesture, then flashes a great smile. 'I've never forgotten that.'

J. J.

PART TWO

The Superyoung Plan

INTRODUCTION

One of the most fundamental characteristics of the human condition is our ability to look into the future, to compare what we are now to what we might become. The gift of foresight, the capacity to create a design for living, is perhaps the greatest endowment of our species. The purpose of the Superyoung Plan is to permit each of us to apply this ability for constructive vision to our own lives, to take positive steps that will promote physical and mental health and well-being.

The Superyoung Plan is based directly upon my observations of the lives and thinking of the participants in the research project – the concrete strategies the superyoung have devised to improve the quality of their lives. They have provided many specific, practical pointers to the Plan, in the areas of mental agility, exercise and nutrition. I have reinterpreted these concepts, based upon the best current health research, in order to offer a programme that will work for as many people as possible, which may be followed over the course of a lifetime.

On the physical side, the Plan is designed so that the average person, after four weeks, can expect a weight reduction of five pounds, a 20 per cent decrease in cholesterol, and a 35 per cent improvement in physical strength and stamina. The ability to perform gradually more strenuous exercises – particularly when it's recreational and unpressured – has been shown to be a strong predictor of longevity. Although the maximum aerobic capacity tends to decline with age and prolonged inactivity, that can be turned around by following the incremental method of the Superyoung Plan. Because it begins at an easy, self-paced level, this programme is designed to be easily tolerated by previously sedentary middle-aged – and older – people.

The brain is the body's most miraculous possession, the seat not only of intellect and sensation, but also, even more importantly, the monitor of every physical process. It directs everything we do: the thoughts that arise in our consciousness, the movements we make, the manifold bodily functions that keep us alive and feeling well. The brain determines who we are and what we are. Only recently have biologists begun to discover the full potential of a healthily integrated mind and body; these findings are reflected in the Plan, which allocates as much attention to the feeding and maintenance of the brain as it does to the good care of the body.

Genes and behaviour are constantly interacting: the super-young aren't passive creatures, allowing themselves to be manipulated by their environment. Rather, they make their own judgments about every aspect of their lives, combining reasoned thought and intuition to satisfy the needs of their bodies and souls. They are their own best inspiration – and their ideas can offer the same benefits to you, too.

CHAPTER NINE

THE BRAIN PLAN:
IMPROVING MEMORY AND THINKING POWER

Problems are solved, not by giving new information, but by arranging what we have known since long.

Ludwig Wittgenstein

We have all experienced the frustration of forgetting a name or a face, having to read the same paragraph several times before taking in what it says, or not being able to remember what it was that we went into a shop to buy. What do such lapses tell us about our brains? Are they of any significance, or is it just information overload, a normal side-effect of our fast-paced lives?

In fact, such incidents may be real early warning signs that the brain's performance is declining, and that we need to exercise it more than we do. Most of the time the brain is under-used and under-stretched. Any passing anxiety can distract it, or focus it too narrowly. Depression disrupts concentration – to the point that reading a book like this one can be rendered impossible. Yet if even a small part of its potential is realized, the human brain is the most powerful force on earth.

The Memory Systems

Memory is how the brain creates our continuous sense of selfhood. Every single experience and thought and idea you have ever had, every hope and projection into the future, every feeling about the present – all are stored in your brain at this moment in your memory. It goes back in time to your first recollections and projects forward from a stable sense of the here and now into a future of plans, progress and growth. Yet such concepts are very much culture-bound, and therefore somewhat artificial stop-gaps to cover our collective ignorance of an exceedingly complex area of thought, every bit as mysterious and fantastic as subatomic physics. For instance, in some parts of China, you cannot assume that the people will see the future as being located in a linear way, extending before them, as many people in the West do. For them, past, present and future are all one, not three separate states.

A working memory is a smoothly functioning process, comprising a universe of sensations, ideas and emotions. In order to analyse it better, psychologists break it down into its constituent parts.

The first of these is *very short term memory*, also called iconic memory or perceptual memory. This component can only be studied by using a tachistoscope, an instrument which flashes a visual display of letters or symbols for brief durations, usually measured in fractions of seconds.

Next comes the acquisition of knowledge, the new learning phase. When we receive a stimulus, it is dealt with first by being assigned into a discrete category – usually along the lines of old or new; signal or noise; something that requires immediate action (tiger leaping at you) or something that can be ignored without consequence (a cloud drifting across the moon). If this initial evaluation shows that the stimulus is new to the brain, it is routed into the *short-term memory* system. This is rather like a self-erasing chalkboard, easily over-written but limited both in how many items can be recorded on it and the length of time they can be held. If the new perception is to become a part of the *long-term memory*, some heavy brainwork is required. The more conscious effort there is devoted to the new information, the more deeply embedded it will be in the memory.

One common, effective technique is simple repetition, as in rote memorizing, a useful, reliable skill foolishly denigrated by liberal educators since the sixties. Alternatively, the new perception can be moved more firmly into the brain by making single or multiple associations, forging links with previously stored knowledge – connecting the taste of a new wine with the taste of familiar vintages, or fitting a new political pronouncement about an issue with what the politician has said before on another, similar issue. The memory can also use more complex strategies, such as concept learning, which is involved in absorbing complex ideas that require disparate data to be organized coherently, as in certain aspects of higher mathematics. Concept learning also embraces methods and techniques of discovery, such as the experimental method, which can lead to new ideas.

Information Storage and Retrieval

The learning phase is crucial, because if new information is not properly incorporated into your body of knowledge at this point, it is simply not going to be available later in the form of a memory. Three major factors interfere with the new learning phase and prevent us from absorbing information properly: concentration deficits, anxiety and ageing.

Most of us are aware that if we don't concentrate on what we are doing, we'll soon forget it. New research has shown that high anxiety also plays a part in this. Older people have higher levels of free fatty acids in their bloodstream during the learning process (especially if they're in ongoing, high-pressure situations), indicating that they are suffering from increased anxiety. If given a beta-blocker to reduce the jittery physical feelings that go with high anxiety, they will temporarily increase the amount of information they can memorize. You can reduce anxiety and thereby improve concentration without drugs if you learn how to relax properly – an art that can have enduring positive consequences (see Chapter 12).

The more we learn about memory, the more we realize how profoundly it depends upon language. Language guides most of our thoughts: it controls how we frame questions, how we organize our arguments, how we solve problems with logic and reasoning. The best proof of that has been the boom in computer software, which has created new languages to solve new logical problems.

Most people have a decided preference for coding even visual images as words. Psychologists have gone to great lengths to create new shapes so abstract that they cannot possibly have a name, using computers to generate weird geometrical figures and chaotic fractal contours, and even resurrecting the long-forgotten Rorschach ink blot – to no avail. The human mind is not so easily deflected. Faced with such artificial shapes, time and again the test subjects immediately give it a name: 'It's a tree', or 'It's a wigwam.' Even when the association is far-fetched, it's tagged and remembered by its name.

The most vivid memories of all are those that are encoded dually, simultaneously in image and word. For instance, actually seeing a neighbour's house burning to the ground will be a far more potent memory after fifty years than merely having read an account of it. A special class of dual encoding is the so-called 'flash-bulb' memory. For instance, what were you doing when you heard that President Kennedy had been shot, or that the Berlin Wall was coming down? Most people have strong visual memories of what they were doing when these events occurred, accompanied by robust recollections of their immediate emotional responses.

Some tests suggest that the brain is able to sort memories into personal and impersonal categories. It used to be assumed that all bits of information in the long-term memory store were equal, but there may be some crucial differences. Certainly we feel more confident about retrieving remote personal memories than impersonal ones. For instance, when asked which of two events fairly close to each other in time came first – say, the freeing of the hostages at the American Embassy in Tehran, or the election of Margaret Thatcher as Prime Minister – most people, young and old alike, expect to perform badly. If the question is: which came first, the day your eldest child spoke his first words or that summer you went camping in Yellowstone National Park, there is more confidence about answering. Yet in fact, when people are asked in standard tests to put old news stories in chronological order, they do very well, between 80 and 90 per cent correct.

This relates in turn to a factor known as subjective memory – how good we *think* our memories are. Many extraneous factors besides sheer brainpower influence these judgments. Extroverted, outgoing, impulsive people tend to confuse right and left, to forget appointments or be late for them, and attempt to do too many tasks at once more frequently than do introverts. Unhappy or pessimistic people tend to underestimate all their mental abilities, even when objective tests verify that they perform better than their peers. People whose moods fluctuate markedly during the day, and from one day to the next, have real difficulties in putting their personal memories in a sequenced, chronological order; their ability to recall brief prose passages, especially those of an emotional nature, will be weak as well.

Our understanding of other areas of memory remains shadowy. For example, psychologists still do not understand very well how we remember our future intentions. When you wake up in the morning and mentally run through all the things you intend to do that day, and plan how you will do them, why do you carry out some of these plans but overlook others?

What we remember and what we forget is partly determined by a mental function called predictive planning, or foresight. It is exhibited in its purest form by chess players and musical improvisers. Within this capability to look ahead are numerous feedback loops in the memory system: foresight is best served by the ability to access the correct information held in the memory with precision and speed. The chess player contemplating seven moves ahead needs to keep them all available in the front of his mind.

Another area that is still obscure is how we manage to pick up some perceptions easily, unintentionally, almost as an incidental by-product of being conscious: a flower on the side of the road that you might have seen on the way to work, only half noticed at the time, may be remembered later in connection with whatever you were actually thinking about at that moment. If we could understand better how this type of memory works, it might be possible to help people learn more effectively, and perhaps to learn things that they once thought were too difficult.

Then there is the fascinating topic of meta-memory, which helped me to understand and explain to a young woman suffering from amnesia why there were some things that re-peatedly slipped her mind, while other thoughts and words recurred too repetitively, intruding and interfering at inap-propriate times in her running commentaries and day-to-day recollections. The emotional side of this resulted in her being overwhelmed by nostalgia – but not understanding why. When visual and temporal connections could not be made, she ex-perienced feelings of *déjà vu* over and over again. Her thoughts became very surreal. The initial treatment involved a simple explanation of her condition, repeated hundreds of times, to help her get around and through the barrier of her amnesia.

Thousands of people suffering from problems with their memory could benefit from such specific help, but they never receive it. That is one reason why I have compiled these exercises. Many of the subjects in the superyoung project have devised techniques and systems similar to those presented here, and I have incorporated them into my own regimen.

For most people, the ability to retrieve data from the long-term memory store is guided by the rule of the magical number seven, plus or minus two. Seven objects, or seven chunks of information, or even seven nonsense syllables, is the number the average person can cope with. As specific memories are distributed, at least in part, throughout the brain, it is language, that unique organizing principle we humans have evolved, which enables us to search our memory banks by back-tracking with key words from the particular to the general, from the concrete to the abstract, and vice versa. The memory problems encountered by people suffering from senile dementia are compounded by the simultaneous destruction of the brain systems that language serves – the speaking, receiving and interpreting of verbal information.

The more we understand about how we learn and memorize new information, the more we see it to be a process full of paradox and contradiction. How do forgetful people even realize that they are forgetful? Yet they do, and this is perplexing. Memories are both robust and fragile, enduring and fleeting; much can be discovered about how memory works by seeing what happens when it fails.

Causes of Memory Loss

Memories can be lost in many different ways, some unsurprising, some sinister. It can happen imperceptibly, over many years, or in a split second. Those staples of melodrama and farce, the blow on the head or the sudden traumatic shock, are common causes of memory loss. Since the divorce laws have been liberalized, far fewer spouses now step out for a pack of cigarettes and vanish off the face of the earth, but people do still turn up in airports and shopping malls, not knowing their identity or how they got there. A proportion of mysterious disappearances are probably the result of hysterical amnesia or so-called 'fugue states', in which the victims, under great internal stress, just drift away.

Much more common are the long-term effects of excessive alcohol consumption and, less well known, of chronic cigarette smoking. The memory tends to worsen noticeably after fifteen years of alcoholic drinking, or much sooner in people who go on massive binges. The effects of cigarette smoke are subtler because the poisonous effects of carbon monoxide in each puff are temporarily offset by the alerting effects of the nicotine. The first clear evidence of tobacco's deleterious effects was revealed by tests in which smokers showed significantly poorer ability at connecting names to people's faces – even though they were allowed to smoke during the tests!

Brain activity is also hampered by the use of some so-called minor tranquillizers, because the overall psychomotor speed – the speed at which any message to or from the brain is translated into action – is slowed by up to 35 per cent. Head injuries from car and motorcycle accidents produce brain damage and amnesia in hundreds of thousands of cases, and electric convulsive shock treatment also causes enduring memory loss for some patients.

However, Alzheimer's disease and other forms of dementia are the most significant causes of severe memory disturbance. Because of our increasingly ageing population, unless new treatments are found, it is projected that the numbers of such cases will continue to rise for at least the next fifteen years. There is also a milder but commoner disorder known as 'benign senescent forgetfulness'. This diagnosis is controversial – it isn't known whether it is a mild form of true dementia or the severe end of normal, though somehow accelerated, ageing of the brain.

Simple ageing is, of course, the most common cause of mild memory loss. From about the age of thirty, many people begin to notice that their memories are not as sharp as they once were. For many years, experimental psychologists had heated scholarly debates over whether the basic problem was defective storage of memory traces (or engrams, as they were also called) or defective retrieval from the memory storehouse, but recent research has thoroughly discredited the former explanation. Normal memory stores have been proved to have practically infinite capacity: you can't run out of space to store your new memories, and most memory traces – the mass of everyday information we all take in with little apparent effort – can be startlingly accurate. In one such piece of research, undergraduates in a series of key experiments were shown thousands of unremarkable landscape paintings. When asked weeks and even months later to pick out the paintings they had seen before from an even larger array of thousands of similar paintings, the students' visual memories were remarkably accurate, with 'hit rates' in excess of 96 per cent.

The fact that the memory store is such a large and complicated system makes it like a large library in which some parts are well organized and catalogued, such as formally rehearsed learning, and other parts, perhaps the greatest amount, are relatively chaotic, lacking any kind of filing arrangement at all. Most of our personal and interpersonal relationships, and our emotional responses to them, would come into this significant category. Very few real people ever approach the extremely logical and rational cognitive organization of Sherlock Holmes or Mister Spock.

To make matters worse (and to mix metaphors), the brain, when in many of its recall or recognition modes of operation, is also like a rather noisy radio transceiver, for even as it tunes into the appropriate signal, it also captures some additional noise. If a person were to learn a dozen new words and their meanings, and learn them to perfection, after the passage of several hours he would probably be able to recall only seven of them. He might also confuse some of them with other, very similar words, particularly ones with similar meanings that he had not learned before.

Both of the above effects – the mixed-up library and the noisy radio – become worse with age, the former simply because there are more bits of information to be misfiled, and the latter because the electrical impulses between brain cells fire randomly, for no apparent purpose, more frequently as we age. Yet overall the effects of ageing on memory are negligible and can be compensated for in a number of ways – not least by doing mental exercises such as those I have created.

Maintaining Brainpower

The brain thrives on intellectual challenges, and it really does excel when faced with the unexpected. Yet most people considerably underestimate their ability. For example, if presented with an anomalous test sentence such as 'Colourless blue ideas float perilously by baseball', most people initially think they will not be able to repeat it back without error, but more than 90 per cent do so successfully.

Marta Kutas and Steven Hillyard, psychologists at the University of California, carried out an experiment some years ago in which they asked young volunteers to read somewhat less abnormal sentences out loud. The subjects were wired with sensors attached to their scalps which measured the electrical activity taking place at various points in their brains. Kutas and Hillyard found that when their volunteers read a sentence ending in an unexpected fashion, the electrical activity peaked much more sharply than when they were reading sensible sentences. The 321 sentences used in the study were carefully structured to provide semantic booby traps – for example, 'The cat sat on the television aerial.' The research team paid particular attention to one wave-form of electrical brain activity, which they called the N400 wave, because it peaks around 400 milliseconds after the brain receives a stimulus. They found much higher N400 activity when the subjects read sentences with unexpected endings.

What does that mean? It appears that N400 activity can be used as a good tracking index of the brain's activity, especially in the context of deciphering meaning. The N400 wave can be used as an objective qualitative indicator of when and how well the brain is working at targeting novelty, as opposed to passively operating on automatic pilot – as we increasingly must do in these highly automated times. This research supports the notion that the mind is meant to be curious and exploratory, to seek out novelty and diverse stimuli. It also proves what I already knew from my clinical experience: exercises for the brain keep it operating more healthily.

All mental stimuli are not created equal; apparently, some are much better than others. One of the best types of mental stimulation is active social exchange and interaction. When brain-imaging first became widely available, an influential group of medical researchers in Tokyo used the new technology to study a group of business executives over the age of fifty-five who worked for a large electronics firm. These men were divided into two very similar groups, each comprising men of equivalent intelligence, educational background, age, social class and level of seniority and responsibility in the firm. But there were two key differences – the men in Group I had been required, by the nature of their jobs, to interact with other people significantly more often than those in the second group. The experiment showed that the brains of the men in Group I were in better shape, with slightly lower levels of age-related atrophy than their counterparts in Group II.

When the memory does begin to fail, anxiety is often the crucial villain. People are reluctant to acknowledge it as a cause of their problems, and even if they are able to, they are sometimes at a loss to connect the cause in their personal environment with the effects on their mind and body. Yet anxiety can attack, directly or indirectly, practically every part of the body; it's little wonder, then, that it can also induce forgetfulness. Yet it's possible to intervene constructively at any point in what often turns out to be a continuous downward spiral; self-managed prevention can short-circuit the entire sequence.

Mnemonics can be learned. They work best when they are acquired early in life and when they are practised regularly. The ancient, much-favoured method known as Loci, relies on vivid, even bizarre, visual imagery, but the optimum approach is to mix this technique with verbal or numerical methods. All these mnemonic procedures can be learned easily in childhood or adult life. Research has shown that this is one thing that should not be left until too late in life – older people are less likely to use mnemonic aids if they are learned late, even if they are specially trained to use them.

Learning to Relax

Deep muscular relaxation can induce the appropriate degree of intellectual peace in which to learn. In fact, this is now the treatment of choice for most people suffering from high anxiety. The relaxing person empowers himself, becomes increasingly self-confident, and thereby makes it possible to become more creative. A profoundly relaxed state enhances a person's ability to daydream, to augment the normal patterns of thought with vivid visual imagery, and to meditate.

Relaxation exercises consist of tightening then relaxing each muscle of the body in turn, then tightening and relaxing combinations of muscle groups, all the while visualizing pleasant scenes in the mind's eye, and repeating relaxing or strengthening phrases to oneself, such as 'Calm and relaxed and peaceful'.

The beneficial effects go beyond the expected psychological ones. People with mild to moderate high blood pressure can lower it to the same point with relaxation training as they can with medication. The two forms of treatment are not mutually exclusive; they can work together even more beneficially than either therapy on its own.

Self-hypnosis is a variant on the theme of relaxation; some people find it more conducive to their needs. It should be borne in mind that learning to relax is usually only the first stage of a more systematic stress-management programme. For many people, it's all that's needed to improve the quality of their intellectual life.

Stress Management

A graduated stress-management programme begins by examining all the sources of stress in one's life. They are listed from the mildest irritant to the most terrifying fears. The problem with many hidden sources of chronic stress is that they become enmeshed with a person's life, to the point of seeming – erroneously – to have become a part of the personality.

However, there are some recurring personality patterns for people more prone to anxiety. The Type A personality describes someone who is driven, unable to delegate responsibility, an intensely linear and overly directive thinker who feels pressured by a chronic lack of time. Small details are always attended to meticulously, and the normal hassles caused by minor setbacks make him feel disconcerted and irritable. The Type A personality is more prone to suffer a premature heart attack, duodenal ulcers, and other so-called psychosomatic disorders. But research has shown that he can be helped to change for the better. The Type B personality is almost the reverse of the Type A: unruffled and unflappable, a Type B person is one who habitually behaves in a stable manner, using his reasoning to solve problems, even in stressful situations. Guided by calm judgment, he plans ahead and may delay gratification in the interests of reaching a long-term goal.

The Type A/Type B dichotomy is a familiar staple of psychology, but some recent research has challenged this static dialectic. Now psychologists are finding evidence of a third personality type. The Type C person thrives on stress, enjoys taking intellectual risks, and seeks out new and different sources of excitement. He rises to the occasion by trusting his initial intuitions and by having a playful attitude towards innovation, and he refuses to tolerate circumstances which make him feel unhappy. Such people often feel energetic when others would begin to flag, and they may look significantly younger than their years. Aspects of Types B and C personality sound very similar to the superyoung.

Stress management can help a Type A person gradually become more like a Type B or Type C personality, through exercises that emphasize the 'loosening up' process, regaining perspective and a sense of humour, and solving problems while in a relaxed mental state. There are many other ways to overcome or compensate for difficulties that the mind encounters. Visual imagery is a formidable aid to memory, which can be built up with practice; rehearsal can reinforce learning, and a fine command of language improves the way your memory works.

Most people, most of the time, vastly under-utilize the brain's true potential. The exercises which follow will restore the functions of this supremely important organ to the levels that the superyoung have demonstrated in my research over the past decade.

Switch on Your Brain

Start here with the first programme of exercises to build up your brainpower. In this section we concentrate on aids to reinforce your memory, so you don't forget the things you learn. Next, we will play some games with words, and teach you other simple techniques to help unblock your memory and focus your concentration.

Seeing is Remembering

One way of remembering a list of things you have to do is to take a familiar environment, such as the streets in your town, and imagine walking through them in your mind, distributing the items on your list as vividly as you can along the route. The more bizarre the image, the better this system works. Then, when you want to recall your list, you retrace your walk in your mind, and the images you see on your mental journey will jog your memory.

This memory system, called the Loci method, has been used successfully for thousands of years, from Roman senators, who used it to remember the main points of a speech, to the Renaissance mnemonists, people who became famous for their ability to memorize hundreds, even thousands, of items almost at a glance.

With practice, you can use the Loci method quickly, matching images to items instantaneously as you glance through a list, and then be able to recall them weeks or even months later. Our example comes from an artist who is experienced with this method; in this case, he used it to remember a list of things to do before going on a skiing holiday. All of the following steps were done entirely in his mind's eye:

> Going down his main street on the left side, he records the need to cancel his newspaper delivery by visualizing an elephant's trunk carrying a giant newspaper; he checks his toiletry case for essentials like aspirin and Band-Aids by seeing a row of aspirins stuck on the next roof; he remembers to buy film for his camera by imagining a large camera upright against the next building; he makes a note to order travellers' cheques and foreign currency by seeing a bright gold coin lodged in the bank's wall; he reminds himself to take out travel insurance by placing a leg

in a plaster cast outside the insurance office; and he remembers to buy something to read by imagining two massive paperbacks like bookends around the bookshop. Returning down the right side of the same street, he then provides equivalent paired images to remember to buy ski-goggles (a ski-goggle hanging from a road sign), to do preparatory ski exercises (ski outfit sliding down the roof of the next house), to locate his passport (a large one leaning on the next corner). He remembers to check his sewing kit (buttons and needles dangling from a street lamp) and to pack his thermal underwear by imagining them with hot water bottles in the next shop's front window. In the central plaza, he visualizes both suntan oil and his schedule for making it to the airport on time by mounting a Swiss cuckoo clock telling the time he must leave on top of a huge jar of suntan oil.

Many other sorts of conscious reinforcements will work as memory aids. Some are verbal, and most of us still remember at least one mnemonic device we learned in childhood: Every Good Boy Deserves Favour for the notes on the lines of the treble clef; My Very Educated Mother Just Served Us Nine Pumpkins for the correct order of the planets revolving around the sun. Whenever you have to make up a list, or want to remember someone's name permanently, you can make up your own mnemonic aid, using words, numbers, images, signals, even gestures – whatever you find most vivid.

All memory aids work best if you start using them early in life, and use them regularly. Research shows that older people are less likely to make use of mnemonics if they learn them late in life, because they tend to be more anxious about learning new things, which mars their performance. The good news is that relaxation training exercises can alleviate this problem.

Change Tack

The better your range, grasp and use of language, the better your brain performs. One of the best ways to build up your ability to handle words with fluency and imagination is to read new books, and to challenge your mind by trying new categories, such as the Latin American novel, or young African writers. For instance, if you've always thought that science fiction was juvenile, ask your librarian what are considered to be three good books in the genre and read them. Afterwards, ask yourself if they measured up to a high literary standard. What did the books have in common? What questions did they pose?

Try tracing themes in fiction, or investigate the novelists who are grounded in a particular region of the country. Why was *Peyton Place* the bestseller of the fifties? What are the qualities of a John le Carré thriller? Or have a fresh look at a familiar classic. What books are children or teenagers reading today? What do they have in common? What marks them out as special? If it looks interesting, then go on to explore the top twelve contemporary writers of children's books. Always try to pursue the next higher level, especially if you enjoyed the one preceding it.

Grow Your Grammar

As well as building up your vocabulary, you need to learn how to vary your use of language. The standard sentence form is subject, predicate, object; very few people use subordinate clauses, or rhetorical flourishes such as the paradox, in everyday speech. If you can gradually increase the complexity of your verbal language, you will increase the complexity of your thought, so try to extend your use of words, sentences, clauses and phrases: be creative with grammar – it is not the inflexible vehicle that many of us were taught.

Try to write as long a sentence as you can on any subject. Aim for at least a hundred words or more. This is how Marcel Proust did it in *Remembrance of Things Past*:

On one occasion he had looked in for a moment at a party in the painter's studio, and was preparing to go home, leaving behind him Odette transformed into a brilliant stranger, surrounded by men to whom her glances and her gaiety, which were not for him, seemed to hint at some voluptuous pleasures to be enjoyed there or elsewhere (possibly at the Bal des Incoherents, which he trembled to think that she might be going on to afterwards) which caused Swann more jealousy than the carnal act itself, since he found it more difficult to imagine; he was already at the door when he heard himself called back in these words (which, by cutting off from the party that possible ending which had so appalled him, made it seem innocent in retrospect, made Odette's return home a thing no longer inconceivable and terrible, but tender and familiar, a thing that would stay beside him, like a part of his daily life, in his carriage, and stripped Odette herself of the excess of brilliance and gaiety in her appearance, showed that it was only a disguise which she had assumed for a moment, for its own sake and not with a view to any mysterious pleasures, and of which she had already wearied) – in these words which Odette tossed at him as he was crossing the threshold: 'Can't you wait a minute for me? I'm just going; we'll drive back together and you can take me home.'

Questions
What purpose does the length of this sentence serve?
What does the sentence tell you about Swann's character?
What mood is Proust trying to convey?

Does he succeed?
What does the sentence tell you about Odette's character, even though she is seen through Swann's eyes?
Does the sentence tell us anything about Proust himself?
Could you write this sentence in a more succinct fashion?
How would another great novelist, e.g. Melville or Hemingway, handle the same scenario?

Travel Beyond the Book

Play the film director game: imagine you are making the novel you've just read into a film. Which scenes would you cut? Which ones would you highlight? What kind of visual imagery or special effects would you employ? Why? Would you change the sequence of the plot? Who would you cast in the main roles?

Writer and columnist Frances Edmonds tried this exercise with Tom Wolfe's book *Bonfire of the Vanities* shortly before it was made into one of the biggest fiascos in cinema history. These were her initial thoughts and recommendations:

A brilliant book revealing social mores and showing how the fragile patina of yuppie existence can be brought crashing down. I wouldn't want to cut anything out – there are masses of great scenes and it would make a brilliant three-hour film. You could start with the end scene of McCoy being carted off to jail, but I think I'd rather stick to the chronological sequence of the book. I wouldn't want to cast actors in the roles, basically because they're over-priced these days, so I'd look for people wanting to start second careers. I'd cast a certain now-disgraced politician as Sherman McCoy, the main character – master of the universe, wheeler-dealer, high flier – who has an affair on the side and is brought down by one mistake, a car accident in New York which kills a black man. His long-suffering wife Judy might be played by a much-admired and dignified socialite, and Maria, his lover, could be played by a reformed high-class call girl. Likewise for the roles of the charismatic demagogue, the Reverend Reggie Bacon, the not-so-hot gossip columnist, and the assistant district attorney looking for publicity.

Pushing Back Boundaries

The brain thrives on new experience – and you can provide it with the extra healthy stimulus that it loves by regularly offering it a new chunk of information. Read a good specialized magazine from time to time, such as *New Scientist*, or an architectural or medical journal. Challenge the idea that your mind isn't up to reading such things. Often your ideas are self-censoring, that little voice that tells you, for example, 'I can't read chemistry, it's too hard'; yet if you just try it, you may find that you can get the gist of it.

Stretch your mind by purchasing a newspaper or periodical of diametrically opposing political views to your own, and take on the ideas one by one in a mental argument. Compose a letter to the editor or the author of an article you particularly disagree with, putting your point of view as clearly as possible. (You don't have to post it!)

Improve Your Language

Most of us, most of the time, think and remember with words rather than with images. Images are there too, but language is the brain's workhorse. So the more words and names you have at your disposal, the better your mind can work. You can boost your vocabulary by playing with language lists while you're stuck in traffic or commuting on the train. With practice you'll notice you can add more and more words to the games you play, and become more inventive at thinking up new variations.

1. Try playing the category game, where you name as many birds as you can (or trees, or means of transport, or dishes using eggs).

2. List the twenty or more words you think are the most beautiful, then the ugliest, words that express joy and other positive emotions and those that signify violent, negative feelings. Come up with a new category each week.

3. Try the A–Z game, where you choose a category and try to find one example for every letter of the alphabet, starting perhaps with foreign capitals, boys' first names, or film titles. Michael Gough Matthews, director of London's prestigious Royal College of Music, made this valiant attempt at listing classical composers, in the space of ten minutes:

A	Albéniz	**N**	??
B	Beethoven	**O**	Offenbach
C	Chopin	**P**	Poulenc
D	Dvořák	**Q**	Quilter
E	Elgar	**R**	Rameau
F	Fauré	**S**	Stravinsky
G	Grieg	**T**	Thomas
H	Hindemith	**U**	??
I	Inglebrecht	**V**	Vierne
J	Jongen	**W**	Wagner
K	Kalliwoda	**X**	Xenakis
L	Lully	**Y**	Ysaye
M	Massenet	**Z**	??

Say It Again

Memories are not inanimate objects; they are artificial constructs which can be made more enduring by using various mnemonic aids. When there is something you want to commit to memory, you should reinforce the impression it makes on the brain with a further stimulus – an image, a gesture or a feeling – which will double the signal and make it easier to recall later. One often-neglected memory aid is repetition. Repetition puts the information more securely into the memory – which is why we can still remember the rhymes and songs we chanted as children.

Study pages of material you wish to remember, then revise and condense them into three or four pages, then revise these into a single page, and finally reduce it to two or three sentences. Any work or operation performed on words or images effectively places that material into the memory better, by increasing the depth of processing you actively exert upon it.

Dreamwork

One good way to improve your memory is to work at remembering your dreams. Dreams are not just neurological noise or debris: they give us significant clues about our unfulfilled desires, uncompleted goals, and what makes each of us uniquely ourselves. Remote memories freely flood forth during sleep because of their strange form and content, and truths hidden in them can sometimes be revealed.

Dreams often continue on similar lines to the waking thoughts and preoccupations that precede them. Knotty problems can sometimes be solved by dreams, provided the person trusts them. If a dream contains associations with waking ideas, they can continue into sleep. Dreams hunt out lost or escaped meanings. The form of these fragmentary, vague and elusive clues often changes from words to pictures.

In waking life, you miss a lot of clues and cues when they occur, because you're distracted by other events. If they're dredged up and rearranged in our dreams, we get a second chance to notice them. And because these traces of dream memory are so faint, learning to capture them is good memory-retrieval practice. If it's done on a daily basis, you'll soon see an improvement in the power of your memory.

CHAPTER TEN

CREATIVITY AND THE SUPERYOUNG

No truth is so sublime but it may be trivial tomorrow in the light of new thoughts.

Ralph Waldo Emerson

Much more goes on in the mind than linear, conventional thinking. The superyoung have taught me that it's never too late – or, for that matter, too early – to become more creative. Creativity isn't a gift that a lucky few are born with, which enables them to produce works of art or scientific ideas; it plays a part in everyone's life, and enhancing it can give us all more effective ideas and expand our choices throughout life. What's more, it can be great fun, allowing us to be innovative, flexible, and ready to adapt to change – whatever our age.

On an objective scale measuring creativity, the superyoung occupied the high end, from 'bright normal' to obviously 'above average'. Some of their creativity may have been based, at least initially, on a wish to escape from whatever limitations or frustrations they encountered on a daily basis. This escape route into fantasy play is perfectly healthy and beneficial; it sets the stage for the mind to make conscious unusual, unexpected perceptions of the world around us – and within us. Particularly for the superyoung who said that they felt younger or thought younger, it was almost a ruling factor in their lives, the way they approached their work, their continued passion for learning, and their leisure pastimes.

The successful creators among the superyoung trust their intuitions, even vague hunches. Such instinctual mental processes permeate even their everyday behaviour, yet they are balanced with a greater than average degree of objectivity and cool detachment. Nikko Silvano, a computer software whiz, exemplifies these qualities very well. He's in his late thirties, but still retains a boyish appearance, lanky and thin, with a sheepish grin and tousled hair, like the young Robert Redford. Other people regard him as charismatic: men are either jealous or admiring; women become possessive in his presence, or want to mother him. Silvano certainly gives the lie to the sterotype of the 'computer nerd'. When I first met him at an inventors' forum, held in conjunction with an international science festival, he told me about his early life and experiences as a publicly-identified gifted child. He was told at the age of seven that his IQ was 'off the scale, at least 150'. At that point in his life, some subtle disadvantages began to emerge. He felt compelled to adopt social camouflage, to second-guess his schoolmates so that he wouldn't be bullied, exploited, or otherwise coerced into cheating for them. Over the years, his ruses became more deceptive, until, by his early teens, he thought of himself as a social chameleon, developing pseudo-selves to fit whatever situation he found himself in. Each of these personas was very well-adjusted: I doubt if I have met a more stable or well-balanced person. To compensate for his adolescent loneliness, his inner imaginary life became greatly enriched.

When I first interviewed him for the superyoung project, I was surprised at his admission that he had given these issues only the slightest, passing consideration. Nothing he did seemed unusual to him. He believed 'superstitiously' (his own word) that to over-analyse his thought processes would somehow spoil their intuitive fluency. However, his gifts have equipped him to be creative across many spheres of activity – artificial intelligence, robotics, interactive game design, movie FX (special effects). He is also exceptionally creative in his leisure: he paints nudes from life, writes poetry, and composes piano music.

When I asked him, 'How do you do it all?', he said, 'I get a buzz, an overwhelming delight, simply from thinking ahead, using my God-given intuitions, extrapolating several steps ahead. While I'm still learning something new, my mind is already going, whirring, trying to fathom new possibilities. When I was twelve, I captained a football team, a dream team, totally in my mind. I visualized the plays, the moves, the feints. Now that's really not very far removed from designing the concepts behind a new computer game, visualizing the graphics, exploring how it will look on the screen. When this is happening, time seems to stand still – like one continuous "now".' Silvano's style of intuitive creativity can be thought of as a transitory return to primitive, even childlike modes of thought, so-called primary-process thinking, but when it's combined with mature, reflective thinking, it can lead to a deepened understanding.

Where did the creative drive of the superyoung come from in the first place? The secret, as with gifted children, seems to lie in a stimulating intellectual environment. One of our superyoung subjects, Donna Wright, who writes biographies and historical novels, described how she created these conditions for herself: 'I plan interesting and stimulating experiences, experiments in living. I have almost a compulsion to keep driving myself ever onward; there has to be some project in the works. I couldn't imagine life any other way – none of that putting-your-feet-up-and-relaxing stuff for me. And I don't tolerate boring or unhappy circumstances for long, believing fundamentally, as I do, in positive action to change such situations.'

Several of the creative superyoung described their formula for success with this equation: 90 per cent perspiration, 10 per cent inspiration. Donna Wright continued to describe this vein of thought to me: 'I am an infinitely inquistive soul, and I want to know everything that's going on. This is positive and it leads to much pleasure. Maybe, after all, keeping alive the spirit of curiosity keeps one young. I have an insatiable appetite for knowledge, experience and philosophy, and in refusing to grow old I remain very probing. I see reading as independent research. Recently, spurred on by Stephen Hawking's accomplishments, I have started brushing up on my theoretical physics and cosmology again.'

As the creative superyoung described the way their minds work, a pattern emerged. The creative process takes place in four distinct stages: **preparation, incubation, illumination** and **verification**. The **preparation** stage is essentially a cycle of searching. Margaret Donne, a superyoung bioengineer and inventor working in Boston, described the process to one of our researchers: 'I don't think about such matters consciously. The way a new idea comes to my mind is mysterious to me. What I do know is that if nothing constructive emerges in the key, early stages, I have to go back a step and put in more research – and more thinking too, of course – to find another way to interpret what could be going on.'

In this preparatory stage, the thinker recognizes that a problem exists, or that an idea can be exploited somehow. The idea may eventually be the nucleus of a book or an interactive computer game, a scientific theory or a marketing campaign. This leads to more analysis and research, which the creator sees as enjoyable in its own right, even when it seems laborious.

Then there is sometimes a hiatus, when the solution remains elusive, despite all the work on the project. During this exasperating period, there is a good deal of ambivalent emotion, restlessness and doubt, and the creator often considers abandoning the quest. This is the beginning of the **incubation** period, when the preparatory thought and information gathered by the creator sink into the subconscious, which mysteriously probes and reshapes the data. Some creators are more aware of this aspect of the process than others, and go about it somewhat more consciously. For instance, here is how Henry James described how he developed the plot for his novel *The American*: 'I . . . dropped it for a time into the deep well of unconscious cerebration: not without the hope, doubtless, that it might eventually emerge from that reservoir, as one had already known the buried treasure to come to light, with a firm iridescent surface, and a notable increase in weight.'

Next comes **illumination**: Eureka! A possible solution swims into full consciousness. Finally, the solution must be **verified**. The invention or theory or course of action is put to the test, confirming the original idea (or invalidating it – not every act of creation is successful). If an idea has potential, it usually resonates with other constructive ideas, which can lead to new and unexpected applications.

Given that we all need a potent, vigorous creative talent, how can we go about improving our own abilities? A number of qualities have consistently been detected in highly creative people – including, of course, the superyoung. There is no reason to believe that these traits cannot be learned and emulated. They include the ability to take an unconventional approach, a penchant for intellectual risks, openness to novel experiences, persistence, versatility, and what might be called emotional intelligence, an imaginative, empathic transaction between the individual and the problem or project he is working on.

Ray Milner, a superyoung scientist working at an Ivy League university, described his experience with this last characteristic: 'When I get stuck in a quandary that I can't resolve, when one avenue of thought has been temporarily exhausted, I look *inside* the problem more searchingly, to examine what could be vexing my efforts. I project into every angle, every intellectual nook and cranny. If I can reach a state of oneness with it, a little like meditating, the answer flows then and there, or comes to me in quiet fantasy or dreaming. Then there is a realization that I'm inside that imaginary world, a world and a mental space without end, which is always full of immediate wonder.' Milner applies the same philosophy to his leisure pursuits: 'Even in my every-day life, my hobbies and vacations, concretely feeling my way

186

still works for me. For example, James Joyce has become my favourite author. And why? Because many happy hours have been spent following his footsteps in Dublin and elsewhere in Europe, wherever he went.'

His deep immersion grew into a total commitment to understand more – much as one biographer described Henry David Thoreau's approach to life: 'The process of his poetic creation is one of discovery and unfolding carried on by a sensitive and acute artistic mind immersing itself in the flux of life, attempting to fix as well as possible through art the ceaselessly changing nature of reality.'

You can follow Thoreau's lead, and make his method an intentional strategy. First, you need **originality**. Learn to break away from habitual ways of thinking so you can restructure problems in unusual or unique ways. Highly original people are unimpressed by any sort of stereotype or over-generalization. They are receptive to new ideas from others, often seeing them from a different angle very quickly. Original people tend to come from small families; females are often only children, and the males first-born. They are independent by nature, and are frequently described as gifted in their childhood.

To have original ideas, you need to be able to draw on all your resources, including your emotions. Both sides of your brain can experience different feelings at the same time; even more astonishing, the two halves of the brain may at times be in conflict with each other. We are most likely to be alert to new ideas when we are aware that there are many extraordinarily dynamic feelings within us, which sometimes pull us in different directions. These multiple tendencies force us to think more effectively, to make decisions in more complicated ways.

You will also need **fluency**, the ability to come up with lots of ideas. Some of them will turn out to be false leads: 83 per cent of Nobel prize-winning scientists claim frequent or occasional assistance from unconscious intuitions, but only 7 per cent say that such hunches were always correct. The remainder estimated that they were temporarily led astray by false trails anywhere from 10 to 90 per cent of the time. Albert Einstein, the 1921 physics laureate, once said that he lost two years on an erroneous intuition.

Dr Felix Mantee is an eminent psychiatrist and participant in the superyoung project. His life goal has always been nothing less than to win the Nobel prize. He described how true discovery can elude one's grasp: 'Being perceived as ahead of your time means that you take conceptual risks all the time. Sometimes you take an inference too far, and then you pay the price – totally inadvertently, you lead yourself, and sometimes others, into the proverbial cul-de-sac. It can cause friction and, academic rivalry and vendettas being what they are, career setbacks. But if you're an innovative thinker, you accept this, shrug it off, and move on. In the beginning you may be a little more cautious about taking the plunge – or so you tell yourself, until the next time you wake up at four in the morning in a cold sweat, with a revolutionary insight.'

Creative thinking also demands **flexibility**, a willingness to attempt various solutions without being tied to any particular one until it reveals itself to be the most promising. Don't play favourites: 'facts' can be wrong. Experiments fail and still contribute to the development of science or culture. Creative thinkers instinctively feel a continual need to adapt to change. Barbara Crufts, a school principal in her sixties who is now earning a PhD for a second career, told me: 'What is stressful to many of my contemporaries is stimulating and exciting to me. I love the unexpected, the serendipitous, and can always improvise and adapt myself to it and find in it a stimulus for further creation.'

Just as a weight-trainer warms up with gentle flexing and aerobics before moving on to the heavy lifting, it's important to loosen up the mind, and the best way to do that is with humour. Humour has the power to liberate, to unzip reality and free us to think outrageous thoughts. A professional comedian in our superyoung group told me: 'Comedy is a challenging way to think. All my life, wonder and curiosity have been my twin mistresses. They have let me say a giant, glorious 'YES!' to exploring funny, touchy issues.' Wit provokes insight; incongruity is common to humour and creativity, and both manage to integrate apparently opposing elements.

The creative superyoung are strongly energized by the desire to realize their potential. Barbara Crufts told me, 'Appraise yourself positively – you're not old, you're experienced in life. You can also gain a lot by learning from those who make good despite everything bad that's been thrown at them. I think one stays young by living life to the full and not expecting the world to come to you. And I do most profoundly believe that an absence of dependency upon others is a major factor in maintaining a young approach to ideas.'

The superyoung show us that it's possible to develop these skills and attitudes throughout life. Many people prevent themselves from drawing upon their nourishing insights, the great welter of ideas that lies within. They see it as an activity for other people – for intellectuals, for scholars, the chattering classes. They allow their natural curiosity and intuition to wither away. When I recognize this phenomenon, I see good minds and worthwhile people stagnating. But curiosity can develop and increase throughout the entire span of life if you nurture it. Just a little more emotional sensitivity can make a difference.

Be prepared to take a chance.

The Brain Plan:
Exercises to Increase Creativity

Over the past ten years, I have developed a series of mental exercises to expand and exploit the brain. In order to acquire the creative skills needed to accomplish the lifelong benefits described throughout this book, it is important to practise the various components of creative behaviour at the appropriate level. In Budapest, Erno Rubik, he of the Cube, has arrived at similar conclusions by planning a model series of puzzles. I have come to view the creativity exercises that follow as training for freedom.

The Metaphor Exercise

Learn to bring even dull words to life. Playing language games can be an amusing way to increase your verbal ingenuity and fluency, and of encouraging your imagination to let rip. Try taking ten nouns at random from a dictionary and concocting a satisfying metaphor for each – the more far-fetched, the better. Here are some examples:

mother	tower of strength
alibi	exonerating evidence
marriage	licence to divorce
ballot	politician's showdown
reputation	personal public relations
grape	embryonic tipple
student	education elongator
connoisseur	appreciation specialist
kettle	whistling pot
vest	insulation for chests

Finding Alternative Uses

A brick isn't just for building walls. It can also be used as a doorstop, to block a car from rolling downhill, or for an artwork. Thinking of alternative uses for familiar objects requires lateral thinking, and practising it improves both your originality and flexibility.

Pick one of the objects from the beginners' list below. Quickly write down as many uses for it as you can, trying to come up with some unusual, ingenious functions. Do one or more objects a day until you note an improvement, then move on to the advanced list. There is no time limit, although most people complete all the beginners' list within twenty minutes or so.

Beginners	**Advanced**
barrel	picture frame
brick	panties
blanket	compact disc
pair of tights	toothbrush
paper-clip	wine flagon
tin of shoe polish	hair from a wig
elastic band	old radio

Here's what a class of twelve-year-olds at University College School in London came up with, working with the beginners' list:

barrel – stool, table, raft, house for a homeless person, place for keeping a pet, place for children to play

brick – weapon, foot rest, paperweight

blanket – dust cover, insulated tent, fire escape, hammock, stuffing for a teddy bear

pair of tights – mask for bank robbers, emergency fan belt for a car, support for a strained ankle, blindfold, safety net for a flea circus

paper-clip – lock pick, key ring, earring, toothpick, brace for teeth, tool for etching, fishing hook, instrument of torture

tin of shoe polish – camouflage paint, hair dye, apply to the nails to prevent biting, wheel for model car, for writing

elastic band – catapult, to hold up socks, hair band, tourniquet, to power a model car

One of the superyoung participants, a children's art teacher named Anthony Harrison, added these imaginative suggestions:

barrel – sending a message down river, winding up a long rope, hiding place, platform, latrine, use two ends for wheels, marker buoy at sea, diving bell, casing for a bomb

brick – tombstone for pet, hammer, fishing weight, testing the depth of a well, knocking fruit out of a high tree, fulcrum for a lever, use to rub down wood, to get hard skin off the bottom of feet, to mark position

blanket – flag, cloak, curtain, bandage

pair of tights – bag, belt, fish net, water filter, rope

paper-clip – wire, ear picker, needle, broach, staple, electrical conductor

tin of shoe polish – waterproofing for cloth or paper, burning lamp, use the inside of the lid for signalling with light

elastic band – tie-dyeing, for making a mousetrap, to stop a leak in a tube, to hold a bandage in place

The Main Character Exercise

Imagine that you are the hero or heroine in the first act of a play you haven't seen staged, or in the opening chapters of a novel you've just started to read. If you were the character, what would you do next? Try to work out the rest of 'your' story as fancifully as you can. How far can you go in spinning this out on the basis of what you have seen or heard, and what you can infer from that? Here are the opening paragraphs of an unwritten novel, *Latitude of Ghosts*, which I have used in my work with professional writers who suffer from so-called 'writer's block'.

'No more murder for me. I've had enough.' The lugubrious detective turned to Christian Savage and shrugged. The studio was small, too small for the furniture up-ended inside the archway door. Christian twitched nervously. He too had decided then and there never to get involved in a murder again, if he could help it. In a flash, another idea hit him like a thunderbolt. This time, he would be a serious suspect. Very serious.

He knew his friend's investigation would follow a case-hardened formula. He also knew his prints were all over the place, in places they shouldn't have been. The deceased artist's model, lying at his feet, had photos of him in her locket and her wallet, and probably there were several more in her apartment. It had been a very improper relationship. They had once been lovers, but last year they drifted apart, after only one argument. But last night they had met again. Now, Vanessa had met a sticky end. How was he going to explain that? As sheer coincidence?

The detective struck a casual pose as the scene-of-crime officer started his comprehensive video recording programme. Christian knew how the detective's dirty mind worked. But this time he was innocent. Well, relatively so. There were more fake paintings in this room than he had ever seen before in one place. Would the police notice? Surely, someone in the department might, but not his friend in Homicide. But Christian knew he wouldn't be able to move them now without engineering an elaborate hoax. No, they would have to stay.

He glanced down at Vanessa's unseeing eyes. It came to him, a presentiment from foreboding, what he could do to absolve his guilty conscience – make a clean breast of things, surely an irretrievable step if ever there was one. He knew he had sinned, but he also felt he had committed no real crime. To confess, to throw himself on the mercy of human justice. He sanctioned his other self to act; it would be a total and complete unburdening.

What do you think Christian Savage will do next? Why? How many different versions of his 'total and complete unburdening' can you imagine?

The 'Who Are You?' Exercise

You can direct your creative powers to come up with fresh thoughts about your own personality, as well as to shape the world about you, and this can be very worthwhile.

Write down a list of all the significant people in your life, grouping them into threes, each composed of yourself and two others. Select several entirely different roles for yourself, by way of contrast, for instance, 'Myself as other people see me', 'Myself as men (or women) see me', 'Myself as a particular other person sees me'. Then take each trio in turn and consider which two of the three people are most alike and write down why that is so; usually it will be in the form of an adjective such as 'intelligent', 'long-haired', 'deceitful', and so forth. Then go down the list of adjectives and rate yourself on each one, asking yourself which of these traits you would most like to improve.

If there is a trait you would particularly like to change, ask yourself by how much. Write down or imagine how you would behave with the changed trait in a range of diverse situations, then conduct a brief experiment, with yourself as the guinea-pig, by exhibiting more of your chosen trait for a week. During this experimental period, note if anyone is even aware of a change in you and, if they are, how they respond to you in your new role. Is it worth making the change permanent? Are you happier with the new, modified personality? Experiment with different characteristics until you find a balance that seems to fit you best.

Weave a Web of Strangers

There is a clear relationship between levels of curiosity and adventurousness and overall creative output. Curiosity is another of the intrinsic motivations of the creative superyoung. Yet in many of us the expression of curiosity has somehow become inhibited. The reasons for this are our fear of embarrassment, of inadvertently giving offence, or of appearing to be ignorant.

Surreptitiously observe a small group of people in a public place, and weave a story around them, based upon their expressions, demeanour and behaviour. As one of the creative superyoung participants told me, 'By using this method, I can witness the blandest everyday incident, such as two people meeting, and, because of their actions, I can imagine what they are saying, or put them into a different, dramatic situation. If I see a stranger looking particularly unhappy or upset, I can weave a plot around the person to account for it, and guess what will happen to him next. By doing this exercise, I have trained my imagination to place me in situations where I am articulate, or romantic, or really quite sexy.'

The Goethe Exercise

'One ought, every day at least, to hear a little song, read a good poem, see a fine picture, and, if it were possible, to speak a few reasonable words.'

Dream Enrichment Exercises

Sleep is a transition in the flow of consciousness. In this light, dreams are a product of life style and personality. For some, dreams can help foster a close relationship between vivid imagery and an all-absorbing, totally concentrated style of imagination.

For about an hour and a half each night, the mind intermittently lets down its guard and drifts into a magical universe, mysteriously and spontaneously created, which offers a rich source of inspiration, if only we can learn how to tap into it. During vivid visual dreaming, the right and left sides of the brain work more independently, in a far less integrated way, than at any other time. The more rational left brain's dominant control is weakened, partly switched off, unable to affect the stray images that arise from the latent, emotional, and more creatively oriented right brain.

Two psychologists at Cardiff University have undertaken research which shows that a dream's symbolism can produce clues in circuitous ways. David Fontana and Myra Thomas believe that dreams are a necessary part of problem-solving. They gave their subjects anagrams, such as SCNACEDELIHSKR, the solution to which is Charles Dickens. One subject hit on the answer, in sleep, through an elaborate chain of reasoning involving a dream about a team of detectives on British television named Dempsey (an American) and Makepeace (a Briton). The female star of this police programme, set amidst the mean streets of London, had a hairstyle like the research volunteer's friend, a woman called Carol; that reminded her of Dickens's *A Christmas Carol*, and from this she free-associated the answer.

'The interesting thing here,' said Fontana, 'is the kind of reasoning used to get from the dream symbolism to the anagram solution. It isn't logical, linear thinking, it's not lateral thinking, and it's not trial-and-error. It exposes a whole different pattern of thought which seems much more linked to intuition and creativity.'

To do this exercise, keep a notebook by your bedside. When you wake up, scribble down whatever fragments of dreams you can recall, but do not, at this stage, try to organize them into coherent narratives. Later, when you are physically relaxed or feeling meditative, try to invent as many possible meanings for your dreams as you can. Later, when you are your 'normal' self, rate each of the alternative interpretations in terms of plausibility, and give reasons for your choices. Finally, try to work out how you would have liked each dream to have continued, had you been able to let it do so. Be confident in the certain knowledge that, even for sceptical and cynical people, dreams can identify and solve problems. They can also reveal your true feelings and desires, especially those which have been inhibited.

Here is one week's dream diary, kept by a young student, with her own attempts to make sense of the clues they are giving her:

February 4 I come down a huge, dark staircase into a church. I'm pretending to be another woman and cast myself down dramatically on a rug in front of the altar rail. I am aware of having to play a part in order to infiltrate the mysterious body of the church that lies behind the altar rail. A priest comes and blesses me. I'm worried that I'm not crossing myself properly and will be found out. I'm looking at a woman who looks like Vivien Leigh as Scarlett O'Hara in *Gone With the Wind*. She has purple eye shadow at the edges of her eyes, and she's smiling. It is sunny and breezy. She sits daintily on a stone, and the hem of her skirt ripples in the wind. She seems to be the woman I was pretending to be in the church.

Coming down stairs = sexual act?

Woman in church = feminine part I have to play to get at the mysteries (of sex?) behind the altar, i.e. where the male priest is allowed to go. Feel inadequate in the part and that I will be found out.

Woman on stone = successful femininity

Happy, smiling, easy, rippling skirt is womanly and subtly sexual.

Eye shadow = artificiality?

February 6 I'm in a café in Italy with my family and friends. I slip out and cross a piazza. A man on a Lambretta motorscooter drives towards me. I'm frightened and run back into the café. In the lobby, a group of Italian men stand silent and watchful.

Café = family, security, my country

Piazza = space, freedom. Italy is where I'm going to study next year.

Man on scooter = my worries about how I'll cope with living abroad on my own during my exchange programme year

February 7 I'm lying on the beach where I grew up. It's very cold. Three children are there, the older boy goes swimming and I think how nice it would be to swim if only the water was warmer.

I'm lying naked, face down, and my father is further down the beach. Suddenly, the water comes higher, wetting the beach. Everybody's belongings float away and I start to search for my lunch in the water. As I'm swimming, a boy with a mole on his back swims by under the water. I find the three oranges and take them to my father.

The water forms a huge hill and I'm looking up at it. At the peak there is a line of swans with chains around their necks, held by people standing on a platform. It's like a zoo. A swan swims near me and the strong current forces me downstream with it. The swan is threatening – I spit water at it and then realize this is provocative. The swan grabs my hand in its beak and crushes it. I escape, swimming away, thinking how lucky I am to get away with my hand.

Three children = my flatmates and I

Sea = disorder in our apartment

Three oranges = posted Dad his birthday present yesterday

Boy with mole = my eldest brother has a birthmark on his back

Swan = narrow escape I had last week when an old-fashioned window fell on my hand and broke my finger

February 8 I'm straddling a deep pit or grave. A man is telling me to dig, but I cannot reach the bottom with my shovel and I fall in. A woman appears with a strange, yellow, wet face. She's just been on holiday with her boyfriend to Trinidad or somewhere else exotic. Then she tells me that she 'fell in'. I ask her if she swallowed any earth. She says that she got some in her mouth but the doctor said they were all dead.

I meet the same woman in the supermarket looking very pregnant.

Pit = extended essay I've been trying to write for weeks now

Man = my conscience nagging me to get it done

Woman = friend who's worried that she might be pregnant

The Brainstorming Exercise

One of the best-known uses of creative thinking is brainstorming, whether you're trying to predict the major innovations to come in the next millennium, or simply trying to find an ingenious solution to an immediate problem. The technique is used by groups of people, especially those whose professional lives depend upon new ideas, such as think-tanks or advertising agencies. However, an individual can apply the same principles independently.

It's important to start by identifying the problem properly before rushing around looking for the solution. Too many business executives, with their all-out 'can do' approach, look for answers before they've thought hard enough about the question. It could be that the problem starts further back in the organization or the technical process than it at first appears, and unless you get close to the real problem the right solution will not emerge.

The *raison d'être* of a brainstorming session is to elicit as many ideas as possible in a short time. The most valuable ideas are the ones that act as catalysts, provoking everyone to come up with new lines of thinking. Some people like to suspend their analytical judgment during a brainstorming session, in order to liberate the free flow of ideas. It's sometimes fruitful to adopt a free-wheeling attitude in which, initially, all ideas are accepted without the intellect censoring any of them, however unlikely they may seem at first glance.

An important step in boosting the flow of ideas is to break down the artificial partitions that have grown up in the trained, compartmentalized brains of most adults, which block the creative process. Breaking through the barriers between different disciplines and separate chunks of knowledge allows you to link up ideas from various sources, and permits bits of useful knowledge that are normally considered to be incompatible to come together. These fresh juxtapositions of ideas may then produce valuable new insights.

One good way to help this process along is for someone outside the immediate team to sit in on the session, to cross-fertilize the run of ideas by bringing in knowledge about related – or unrelated – topics. If you're brainstorming on your own, you can do this by turning your attention to many different subjects, which you can then bring to bear on the topic at hand. You should feel free to develop these 'outside' interests without being self-critical and feeling you might not understand the more abstruse elements. Just try to find the most clearly written explanation of something you're unfamiliar with, in a popular science magazine or specialist journal.

It helps to use a tape recorder to keep track of the ideas as they pour out, and to make drawings or diagrams if necessary. Then you have a complete record of even the wildest proposal – for when all else has been considered and discarded, that may turn out to be the one that works best.

The Knight's Move

The Knight's Move refers to a devious association of ideas which is so unorthodox that it is hard to follow – like the crooked path of a knight on a chessboard. However, when such a thought process is looked at consciously and deliberately, there is a link between successive ideas; the deviousness may arise because of an intermediate step or concept that isn't expressed. Try to work it out whenever possible. This will not slow down the flow of ideas, but will make finding them more efficient, and the entire process more powerful. The perceived deviousness may also simply be the ability of a particular individual to perceive a link or remote association that others cannot.

A good example of the Knight's Move is the television advertising campaign for the Peugeot 405, in 1989, which used vivid images of flaming fields of sugar cane. The logical connection between burning cane and a smooth-driving French car is far from obvious. Peter Ward, the creative director of the agency that created the campaign, explained his imaginative leap in this way: 'A friend of mine went on a walkabout in Australia and described how miles of sugar cane were burned. The enormity and power of the image struck me, and I tucked it away in my head for future use. Ten years later, when we needed to create a dramatic event around the Peugeot 405 which people just couldn't ignore, that breath-taking image occurred to me.'

The advertisement was remarkably successful, Ward believes, because it left viewers room to make their own imaginative links between the flaming fields and the car. Research showed that viewers associated fire with cleansing, purifying and cathartic properties, and connected the 405 with 'something new' or 'a phoenix rising from the ashes'.

Sometimes in the course of the day, your mind jumps straight from A to D instead of going through the usual A, B, C, D. It can be hard to follow the association from one idea to the next, to see what led from A to D, because the mind has left out the connecting steps. That jump from A to D is the Knight's Move. When you notice it happening (in a brainstorming session, for instance), try to work out the sequence of thought, as a way of observing how the creative mind works. You'll usually be able to find the missing links.

The Remote Associations Exercise

Choose a word at random from a dictionary and write it down. Then, looking at this word, write down the first word that comes into your mind which is somehow associated with or connected to it. Continue to build up a sequence, following the chain of associations wherever it goes. See how long you can keep the chain going. If you like, do away with the paper and pencil and start word associating in your head – or out loud in the bath.

After a few tries, vary the game to make it more challenging. Try to arrive at a remote, rare, word from the first word you choose, following the shortest route possible. Alternatively, try going off on tangents, creating incongruous, ambiguous, or fantastically out-of-context associations. Remember, making unusual verbal juxtapositions is every bit as good for developing your creativity as visual ones.

Here is an example, a chain of associations from one of our superyoung research subjects, starting from the word 'lobster':

Lobster, crab meat, claws, pots, nor'wester, raincoat, New England, navy, coastguard, life jacket, Mae West, staircase, siren, mermaid, *Odyssey*, illusion, magic, tropics, fever, dice, luck, lottery, exploitation, gold, pan, fried rice, ricotta, saffron, silk, shimmer, glow, warmth, contentment.

The Tolerance for Ambiguity Exercise

Just as a problem can have several answers, so a story can have more than one ending. In his novel *The French Lieutenant's Woman*, John Fowles teases the reader with alternative denouements. Creativity means opening up the possibilities of different but equally valid solutions to problems and narratives.

Start reading a short story, but stop reading before you have completed half of it. Now put the book away, and try to hold the plot and characters in your memory for at least twenty-four hours. Then see if you can portray the mood or atmosphere of the story visually.

Here's how Amelia Burke, a third-year fine arts student, went about painting 'The Dead', by James Joyce. Her trained imagination was sparked by the following phrases in the story: 'a cold fragrant air from out-of-doors escaped from crevices and folds'; 'the gas in the pantry made her look still paler'; 'fleshy and pallid'; 'from the back room came the clatter of plates and knives'; 'ten trembling fingers on the tablecloth'; 'Gabriel was surprised at her stillness'; 'he would make himself ridiculous by quoting poetry to them which they could not understand'.

Next, try to complete the story, at least as far as its climax:

- as you think it will end;
- as you would like it to end, if you were the writer;
- as someone you know personally would finish it;
- as a famous personality would finish it, e.g. Madonna, Bill Clinton, or anyone else you care to think of.

See how many different endings you can devise. Which is best? Why? Try to finish the story in as few words as possible.

Once you have become reasonably proficient at this, try to repeat the exercise after reading less and less of the stories you choose. Yet another variation is to try and find an author that you find it practically impossible to be diverted from. Then find one whose stories are practically impossible for you to get through. Who are these different authors? How do they or their writings differ from each other, and from your own improvisations for their stories?

Poetry Reconstruction Exercise

Take a couple of lines of poetry from any great or mediocre poet, for example:

> *Like a long-legged fly upon the stream*
> *Her mind moves upon silence.*
> W. B. Yeats

or

> *And succumbed by the bold bare momentum*
> *The kinetic windsong glows with the keening*
> *Of rockets.*
> *A continuum of stars, flashing in lightning.*
> Nick Bolden
> former coal miner and amateur poet

Read each poem fragment three times. Then try not to think of anything. Read them again, and try to visualize what they're about. Now write an outline of your theme for the poetry.

For those who like poetry, compose a poem making use of either one of the above, or both in combination. Those who prefer to write in prose, write an essay; if your creativity is visual, paint a picture.

Picture Expansion Exercise

Look through books of art that aren't familiar to you; the works of surrealist painters such as Salvador Dali or Giorgio de Chirico are particularly good for this exercise. Look at one picture which captures your curiosity or imagination in some way and work through the following steps:

Jot down the free associations that pop into your mind when you look at the picture.

Write down what you feel the picture is about.

Does it remind you of anything?

Try weaving a story around the image, just letting your imagination drift.

Most pictures will trigger different feelings, memories and associations in everyone who explores them in this way.

Musical Modality Exercise

Shut your eyes and listen to a piece of music you have never heard before. Then, with the music still playing:

Try to imagine what it's about.

Write down what you think the music is expressing.

Can you think of any other music that evokes the same mood or images?

Attempt some of the variations described in the Poetry

Reconstruction Exercise and the Picture Expansion Exercise, above.

The Induced 'Risky Shift' Exercise

The 'risky shift' is a psychological process, whereby if someone becomes more relaxed, they are less suspicious and more apt to take slightly greater risks in their thinking and behaviour. This means that if they are in a context requiring creativity, they can relax and are able to give more ideas 'off the top of their head', ideas which tend to be somewhat more original than otherwise because there is less self-censorship.

To help you take more intellectual risks, first do the Picture Expansion Exercise, or any of the other exercises described above. Record your results. Now do thirty minutes of progressive deep muscular relaxation (as described in the next chapter) or any form of quiet meditation, and immediately afterwards try the same exercise a second time. Research has shown that this can lead to a significant increase in originality and flexibility, but does not enhance fluency or elaboration. Physical relaxation increases the likelihood of taking intellectual risks. It also suggests that stress, even routine stress, is detrimental to creativity. In these experiments, highly creative people showed greater gains in originality than less creative people when both were given an extra bit of time, but there were improvements for all.

CHAPTER ELEVEN

KEEPING YOUNG, KEEPING FIT

> *An awful debility,*
> *A lessened utility,*
> *A loss of mobility,*
> *Is a strong possibility.*
> *In all probability*
> *I'll lose my virility*
> *And you your fertility*
> *And desirability,*
> *And this liability*
> *Of total sterility*
> *Will lead to hostility*
> *And a sense of futility,*
> *So let's act with agility*
> *While we still have the facility*
> *For we'll soon reach senility*
> *And lose the ability.*
>
> Tom Lehrer

> *Exercise and temperance can preserve something of our early strength even in old age.*
>
> Cicero

A love of regular, vigorous physical activity, in one form or another, is one of the major defining characteristics of many participants in the superyoung study. Keeping yourself in motion not only promotes a heightened sense of physical well-being but also improves intellectual functioning at any age, particularly later in life. People who exercise regularly develop a healthier, more positive attitude towards life, and maintain a better self-image – at least in part – for the simple reason that exercise does, in fact, make you look better.

Why Exercise?

My superyoung research strongly suggests that an active life style improves the chances of longevity by burning excess calories and reducing fat deposits. There are many ways to do this, but the best programmes also maximize **aerobic endurance**, maintain a **supple and flexible** range of motion, and build muscular **strength**.

Endurance enhances your ability to keep going under stress, whether jogging or walking briskly, without getting uncomfortably out of breath or tiring too quickly; it also helps protect you from heart disease. Body fat steadily decreases over the course of an intensive aerobic exercise programme – not only because you're burning calories but also because, for reasons that are not entirely understood, the desire to eat foods high in saturated fats and cholesterol declines. The best activities for increasing stamina require a bit more energy than you may be accustomed to. Such exercise will make you slightly out of breath: that's just the point, to increase the heart rate and the flow of oxygen (hence 'aerobic', which combines the Greek words for air and life). In order to obtain the maximum benefit from aerobic exercise, you need to keep up the momentum for at least twenty minutes, though thirty to forty minutes will enhance its effectiveness even more.

Suppleness is all about being able to stretch, bend, twist and turn through a full range of motion. You need this ability all the time – for tying your shoes, reaching a high shelf, even getting into and out of cars. If you're supple, you're less likely to get injured from falls or a new strenuous exercise, or to lose your balance. Flexibility is sometimes the forgotten factor in fitness. Exercises that increase suppleness ensure that a variety of joints and muscles are put into action, thereby keeping them in healthy condition and contributing to faster reflex reactions. Afterwards, the muscles are better able to be tensed and stretched, which is a helpful first step towards inducing a state of physical relaxation.

Strength is the ability to exert a directed force for pushing, pulling or lifting. You need some strength nearly every waking moment – to move around, to carry objects, to climb stairs, even to sit up straight. Gradually building muscular strength protects you from strains and sprains. Strengthening the large groups of muscles in the back and stomach will give you a more erect posture, as well. Weight resistance training leads to the best improvements in muscular strength and function. It's possible for the average woman to increase her strength by up to 40 per cent in this way, even though the female body is not as efficient biochemically at producing muscle mass as the male body is.

Like nutrition, exercise should be balanced to meet the needs of the individual, taking into account the wide physical variation among people, for exercise can be as much a source of stress as its release. However, a bit of stress can be a good thing for people who have led a sedentary life: it induces alertness, a feeling of excitement, faster reaction speeds, heightened acuity and, perhaps most important of all, a feeling of accomplishment when a goal has been attained. A safe amount of physical stress 'inoculates' the body and mind against stress in the future. A similar process minimizes, over time, the objective and subjective levels of difficulty experienced during exercise; the person becomes better able to cope with progressively more difficult programmes. Regular stress release can be as healthy and invigorating as laughter or a good night's sleep.

The life of a couch potato is an easy one, and it can be addictive, but in the long term it leads to serious health problems. Sedentary people are far more susceptible to the adverse accumulation of weight due to their greater sensitivity to the effects of dietary fats. Physical inactivity carries with it a number of proven risks; in general, it means that you will be three times more likely to be in poor health. On the other hand, if a mature person makes a resolution in mid-life and undertakes an intensive exercise programme, it's important that he doesn't overdo it, particularly in the beginning. Vigorous, high-intensity exercising, especially for the uninitiated, is likely to produce some unwanted physical side-effects, and may drive them back to couch-potatohood – just as a crash diet can sometimes be worse than the bad diet it replaced.

Getting Started

If you're not very active now, the first step towards getting fit might be simply to walk more. Why stand in a queue waiting for a bus or sit in a traffic jam when, with a bit of planning and effort, you can walk or cycle instead, either for the whole or part of your journey? When you do go for a walk, move at a faster pace than you're accustomed to. Walking briskly has been shown clinically to result in a more profound state of neuropsychological relaxation, and is believed to have a moderating effect on anxiety. Walking quickly for twenty to thirty minutes, at least three times a week, will soon improve your stamina noticeably.

Even if you are fairly active at home or at work, you probably still need other activities to make any real gains in stamina, suppleness and strength. You will find that it's best to get such exercises in a programme that is as well balanced as a good nutritional plan. To do so, the following cardinal rules of exercise, and our core exercises, are provided for your guidance, and as an introduction.

Get Moving

First of all, get moving! Don't postpone it. Use some imagination in finding more active ways to do the things you do every day, and by taking up new activities. There are literally hundreds of pastimes to choose from. Opt for those you will enjoy, which you can do regularly and accommodate easily into your everyday routine. It's better to find activities near home or the workplace: if it takes you half an hour to get to the gym or the tennis court, you'll soon be using that as an excuse not to go there. It's also a good idea not to choose exercises that are dependent upon the weather or other unforeseen circumstances.

Build up Gradually

Once you've started, build up the work rate gradually. It takes time to get to within striking distance of peak fitness. Exercise just hard enough to get a bit sweaty and out of breath, but never to the point of extreme discomfort. That way, there will be less risk of pains, muscle spasms or sprains. Always warm up first with gentle bends and stretches, and cool down afterwards by walking slowly for a few minutes.

Do it Regularly

It will take at least twenty or thirty minutes of exercise, three times a week, for you to get fit, and you will need to keep it up for the rest of your healthy life in order to stay fit. Regular exercise needs to be a lifelong pursuit, well-integrated into a person's overall life style. As you progress, your aerobic stamina will increase, and your ability to exercise will improve. The great incentive is that early on, within three or four weeks, the

211

measured maximum oxygen intake will rise to the level of people ten to twenty years younger.

Testing Your Fitness

Once you have started exercising regularly, you may find it encouraging to test your fitness to see how much you've improved. The best way is probably just to concentrate, in a focused way, on how your body feels. Ask yourself, can you exercise longer and more easily now than when you started? When you finish a session of exercise, do you feel that you could easily do a bit more? If you've been exercising regularly for at least six weeks, and want to start keeping a record of your progress, try this test:

Find a safe, reasonably flat route one mile long. It could be a path in the park, a running track, or a footpath in your neighbourhood. You can measure the distance using your car's odometer or with a map. Put on comfortable clothes and a pair of running shoes, and wear a watch. By walking or running, or a mixture of both, cover the mile as quickly as you can without getting uncomfortably breathless. A little out of breath is all right, but not to the point of panting. This distance is likely to take you anywhere from ten to twenty-five minutes to cover, so aim for a pace you can maintain. If you have any pain or discomfort, stop! If you are over fifty-five or have not exercised regularly until recently, and if it's the first time you've tried taking this test, it's best to walk all the way. Measure the time it takes you to cover the distance. If it takes you:

- 20 minutes or more to cover the mile, you are fairly unfit
- 15–20 minutes, you're still a little unfit
- 12–15 minutes, then you have a fair degree of fitness

- 10–12 minutes, then you are undoubtedly fit
- less than 10 minutes, then you are very fit

Repeat this test every month to monitor the progress you're making.

This test gives only a rough guide to how fit you are. Your chronological age and many other factors will also affect your initial results; many young people can cover a mile in less than ten minutes easily. So if you are under forty and your result is 'very fit', don't reduce or give up exercising; to stay fit, you have to keep it up. If you do interrupt your programme, you will slowly lose some of the gains in endurance you've made, but you can soon catch up once you've re-started, as long as you do so gradually. Stamina is only one aspect of fitness, though probably the most important one for most people. However, to get really fit, you must also develop your suppleness, strength and balance.

Exercising for Suppleness

Exercises for maintaining suppleness can be started at any time of life. They are the exercises best suited to warming up, and ought to precede any strenuous physical activity, particularly aerobic exercises or weight resistance training. People who exercise regularly in a gym know this, but those who are attempting to get into shape on their own may fail to prepare the muscles with some basic flexing, and thereby put themselves at risk of strains and possible injury.

You should make such exercises an integral part of your fitness routine. Many of the other exercises you may choose for aerobic training or strength building can also help to increase the suppleness of the muscles. The following activities give excellent opportunities for improving flexibility: dancing, aerobics, gymnastics, circuit training, swimming and calisthenics. Some well-designed physiological studies have demonstrated that an exercise or dance programme followed three times a week, for a period of twelve weeks, can produce an increase in the range of motion in all the major joints, and greatly relieve perceived stiffness.

A lifetime of walking upright gives our species continual stress on the tendons, the bands of fibrous tissue that fasten the large thoracic muscles to the vertebrae, and on ligaments, which connect bones or cartilage, and help to hold the vertebrae together. However, in old age, we can actually shrink, as the discs of the spinal column can become compressed. Stretching exercises help to relax and loosen up these natural shock absorbers. The most common complaints from back sufferers who don't exercise are low-back pain, stiff necks and aching shoulders – all symptoms that can be prevented with exercise.

Of course, it's always important to adopt good postural habits; the power of gravity seems to grow stronger as the years go by, making it even more important to stand up straight. By squaring your shoulders (and by practising the neck unwinding exercises below), you can unlearn any tendency you may have to hunch forward. When you're trying to straighten up, visualize yourself stretching upwards, the crown of your head pointing vertically to the ceiling while your eyes are still looking straight ahead. Keep your weight evenly distributed on both feet, knees slightly bent, and your hips level. Correct postural alignment will help you to use your body more efficiently and safely, and to have more confidence when you work out.

Exercising for Strength

Some postural problems arise from weakness in the muscles. For instance, the common habit of curving the lower spine forward can partly be caused by weak abdominal muscles, which can't hold the torso in vertical alignment. This type of spinal curvature pushes the abdomen forward, accentuating an overweight – and older – appearance. Other people develop a tendency to swing their torso and hips to gain momentum when their leg, back and abdominal muscles are weak, creating a 'hitch in the get-along', as they say out west.

Without exercise, muscles atrophy and shrink to minimal size and capacity. As you age, you can lose up to five or six pounds of muscle per decade. By living the easy life for too long, everything becomes more difficult, even tasks that were once carried out effortlessly. Yet your strength can be not only maintained as you grow older but also improved, even in extreme old age. One expert in this field, Dawn Skelton of the Imperial College School of Medicine at St Mary's Hospital, London, has said, based on her own work, 'The older the person exercising, the more noticeable the improvement physically.'

The value of exercise in reducing weight, and keeping it off, goes far beyond the burning of calories. After strenuous exercise, the body's metabolic rate is elevated for hours – according to some research, for as long as fifteen hours. Vigorous activity also releases small amounts of human growth hormone, which has the effect of laying down and retaining more lean muscle in place of fat. Moreover, aerobic activity actually suppresses the appetite, mildly and temporarily; a person who doesn't exercise needs more food just to feel mildly full.

Increasing strength throughout life is like taking out an insurance policy for fitness, in that it also reduces cardiovascular stress while carrying out tasks that might be too much for an out-of-shape person. Weight resistance training can build strength and vitality at any time of life. Moreover, what's good for the muscles is good for the bones: as few as two weight work-outs per week can prevent unnecessary bone loss in women past the menopause.

Exercising for Well-Being

The benefits of regular exercise extend to the mind: the New England Research Institute's Strong-for-Life programme found that the older participants in this carefully controlled regimen of vigorous exercise not only experienced muscular improvements and greater endurance, as expected, but also reaped a number of psychological effects: previously misdirected hostility was channelled into greater self-awareness, and futile forms of tension were converted into quiet physical calm. These results may be at least partly attributed to the social aspect of the programme: group sharing and participation deepens the commitment to stick with it, and sustains a positive, 'can-do' attitude throughout the sessions.

The full range of benefits to body and mind are available to anyone who's ready to get up and move. The most important thing is to get started!

The Exercises

The following exercises are based upon the latest physiological research, and are similar to those used by many participants in the superyoung project – indeed, some of them are taken directly from their own work-out programmes. However, there is a great deal of variability among beneficial programmes of physical activity. Any course of strenuous exercise should be planned in conjunction with a sound diet, and while it should be vigorous it should never risk injury. If you feel dizzy or utterly exhausted during an aerobic programme – stop. If you feel undue pain in a joint while stretching – ease back. Give yourself a few weeks on the programme before

The Superyoung Plan

attempting to gauge its results. Muscle weighs more than fat, so it's better to measure your improvement with a tape measure than with the bathroom scales.

217

Exercises for Improving
Visual Balance and Coordination

Exercise 1. Left–Right Coordination Exercise

To improve balance and coordination

1. Stand, as erectly as possible, with your feet about six to nine inches apart, with a chair to either side of you, or one close behind you. Let your arms hang down at your sides.
2. Cross your right leg over to the left side, across the vertical line of the body, while slowly and simultaneously, in one fluid movement, moving your left arm across to the right side.
3. Return to the starting position and repeat with the opposing limbs, drawing your left leg over to the right side while simultaneously moving your right arm to the left side.

This exercise should be repeated for no more than five minutes, at any time of the day. Monitor and record the number of times you perform this exercise, and the specific nature of any difficulties you may have while doing it. Do it at least once a week, and if you have persistent problems with your coordination, do it more often – up to several times a day, if necessary.

Exercise 2. Left–Right Coordination Exercise with Verbal Guidance

To further improve balance and coordination

Stand erect as for Exercise 1, with a chair to either side of you, or one close behind you. This exercise is composed of essentially the same movements as those in Exercise 1, but as you do the exercises, simultaneously vocalize what you are doing. For example, say out loud, 'Right leg to the left, left arm to the right', followed by 'Left leg to the right, right arm to the left'. This exercise should also be repeated for up to five minutes. My research has shown that people who have suffered from chronic coordination and balance problems find distinctly greater difficulty, at least initially, in performing this exercise fluently than in doing Exercise 1.

Exercise 3. Visual Tracking of One Hand

To improve hand–eye coordination

1. Point a finger in front of you at arm's length, and follow it with your eyes as you move your finger to the right and back again to the left. Use the left and right hands alternately. In the beginning, let your head and eyes move while tracking the moving finger. Repeat for up to three minutes at a time.
2. In the second part of this exercise, keep your head motionless, and only let your eyes track the moving finger. This, too, should be repeated for periods of up to three minutes.

Do this exercise about once a week, unless you have a particular problem with balance, coordination, or visual perception, in which case repeat it daily, noting your progress and any difficulties that you may have in doing it.

Exercise 4. Visual Tracking of Both Hands

To further improve hand–eye coordination and balance

1. Stand facing straight ahead, with both arms stretched out together in front of you. Move your arms slowly apart, your right arm to the right and your left arm to the left, parallel to the floor.
2. Keeping your head still, try to track the movements of both arms simultaneously with your eyes. Move your arms outwards until they're out of the range of vision.

This exercise should be conducted and repeated as in Exercise 3, above. For the first two weeks, confine yourself to Exercise 1, then stop doing Exercise 1 and go on to Exercise 2 for a period of three weeks. Next, move on to Exercise 3 for four weeks, followed by Exercise 4 for six weeks. Finally, practise all four exercises for about five minutes each day, for a period of eight weeks. Throughout this cycle, you should record how often you are able to do each of the exercises, rating how difficult it was, on a scale of zero to a hundred. However, don't feel that you need to complete all the exercises every time; just do as many as you can. People who have had chronic, persisting problems with balance and coordination may need to repeat the cycle for longer periods of time, or continue them on an ongoing basis. These exercises are also beneficial for awkward 'clumsy' children,

Deep Diaphragm Breathing Exercises

Much research has shown that diaphragm breathing is associated with good health and feeling relaxed. Most people breathe using only the upper half of their lungs. The diaphragm is a strong band of connected muscles, which forms the floor of the thorax, the chest cavity, separating it from the abdominal area below. It is formed in the shape of a dome, rising from the area around the lower ribs. The diaphragm is very flexible, and moves up and down as we breathe. The intercostal muscles, those which lie between the ribs, and the accessory muscles of respiration attached to the outer chest, are also involved, and can be better controlled with practice.

These exercises are most easily attempted at first by slumping back comfortably in an easy chair. In the learning stage, you should practise these exercises for at least ten to twenty minutes, twice a day. In fact, I always encourage people to *over*-learn them, to arrive at a point where they become second nature, and then to go even a little beyond that.

Moving the diaphragm upwards forces out used air, allowing a greater quantity of air to be exhaled. When the diaphragm moves downwards, the lungs fill easily. Deep breathing exchanges *all* the air inside your lungs rather than just the upper part of it, which means that the air is entirely fresh – and full of oxygen, which is picked up by the bloodstream and energizes all the organs, including the skin.

The aim of these diaphragm breathing exercises is to better balance your overall breathing pattern. Ideally, your breathing should be deep but gentle and silent, with very little upper chest movement. The first exercise towards achieving that goal is to draw in, and then slowly tense, the muscles of the abdomen lying just below the breastbone. When this movement is accomplished, the diaphragm moves up, pushing a greater

221

volume of air out of the lung. When these same muscle groups are relaxed, the abdomen can protrude a little, and then we can inhale. Practise doing this by breathing out through your mouth, then breathing in through your nose. There should be very little upper chest movement, because the normal rhythmical pattern for this is gentle. If the breathing is at all noisy, you are expending too much energy.

Try to breathe as deeply and slowly as possible when you are at rest. This is all about reducing unnecessary effort and giving you more, not less, energy. Aim for no more than six to nine complete breathing cycles per minute. Pause and relax before beginning the intake of your next breath. That's the goal, but don't worry about timing it too exactly at first.

Try to become more aware of the rate of your breathing by placing one hand on your upper chest and the other hand over your stomach, just an inch or two above the navel. Let your upper chest relax inwards, and with the next breath push out your stomach to swell it forward as you breathe in, then let it fall back gently as you breathe out.

Most people aren't very practised at intentionally slowing down their breathing rate, but once you get the knack of it, it becomes easier and easier. Some of my patients have gone to the length of learning this skill by timing themselves with a metronome. At first you may feel that you are not getting enough air in all at once, as you may have done before doing this exercise, but with fairly regular practice the slower rate soon feels natural and comfortable, producing a warm glow of new-found energy resources.

Many people, if anything, unconsciously *over*-breathe, inhaling more air than the body needs. When this happens, the breathing pattern is usually too rapid and too shallow, although most people are not aware of it at the time. Over-breathing can lead to a speeded-up heart rate, and sometimes palpitations. People who are anxious or acutely angry – especially those trying to suppress nasty, negative emotions, or experiencing difficult, frustrating situations – are more apt to suffer the effects of this. Their breathing becomes fast and erratic, sometimes noisy and strained, with most of the breathing action taking place within the upper part of the chest.

As over-breathing becomes chronic, there is a slow, unnoticed increase in the rate of breathing, but instead of inhaling deeply, the over-breather pants unevenly. This condition is more widespread than was once thought to be the case, affecting as much as 10 per cent of the population. Chronic over-breathing can be a covert and much misconstrued cause of ill health. Also called hyperventilation, it lowers the level of carbon dioxide (CO_2) in the bloodstream, even when the sufferer is at rest. As the rate of breathing increases, carbon dioxide in the blood then decreases. Carbon dioxide is one of those many substances which the body probably needs to keep in a state of balance, neither too much nor too little. Hyperventilation is a state in which there is an increased amount of air entering the lungs' alveoli (the alveoli are small sacs which look like tiny interconnected bubbles). Each bubble expands and contracts with air, just like miniature balloons; in them, oxygen and carbon dioxide are exchanged – this is the real reason for breathing. However, hyperventilation results in a more marked reduction of carbon dioxide tension and eventually leads in turn to alkalosis. Alkalosis is a pathological condition resulting from an accumulation of base, or from loss of acid without a comparable loss of base in the blood and other body fluids, and characterised by a decrease in hydrogen ion concentration (increase in pH, a measure of acidity).

Our blood normally picks up carbon dioxide from the body's cells and delivers it back to the lungs. The lungs act as gas exchangers, with carbon dioxide expelled from the blood solution, while oxygen dissolves in it, combining with molecules in the blood. Carbon dioxide increases the blood flow to the brain. But the automatic quality of breathing depends on the pH (degree of acidity) registered by the respiratory centre of the brain. A change in this factor quickens or slows the rate of breathing. For this reason, it has been postulated that sufferers may have a greater sensitivity of the 'suffocation alarm mechanism' to the initial rising levels of CO_2. Many sufferers complain that 'I can't take deep enough breaths' or 'I can't catch my breath'. However, as the condition worsens, and alveolar CO_2 diminishes, the adverse effects on the brain can be demonstrated by poorer learning ability on psychometric testing.

Because the blood circulates all around the body, a decreased CO_2 level can produce many other different symptoms, including shortness of breath, chest pain, sensations of tingling in the hands or feet, uncontrolled trembling, muscle tremors and cramps, headaches, dizziness with feelings of unreality, and excessive exhaustion. Many of these symptoms can mimic those of other illnesses, such as heart disease, epilepsy, intestinal disorders, and some chronic fatigue syndromes. For this reason, distressed sufferers become understandably preoccupied about the state of their health and may even come to question their sanity. By exerting a little self-control over your breathing, all this can be avoided.

Suppleness and Flexibility Exercises

These exercises begin gently but soon work up to a full range of motion. In addition to improving suppleness and flexibility, they also correct balance and left–right coordination problems. That's important: without preventative exercises such as these, the complex balance reactions can diminish by up to 40 per cent between the ages of twenty and seventy, increasing the likelihood of falling and injuring oneself.

Whenever doing prone floor or mat exercises, start by using a large, comfortable pillow for resting your head, so that the neck alignment can be maintained as straight as possible. You should be completely comfortable with these exercises; otherwise, you'll be less likely to pursue them long enough to reap the benefits. Unless otherwise stated, these exercises should be done slowly, at least to start with. For maximum advantage, concentrate on making controlled, sustained movements.

Exercise 1. Neck Unwinding

To relieve stiffness in the neck

The neck can easily become a focal point of excessive muscle tautness, located as it is at a crucial physical crossroads between the large muscle groups of the upper torso and the delicate muscles lying just under the scalp – the spatial interface between the body and the brain.

When you participate in weight-resistance training, the shoulders and neck muscles bear the brunt of the effort, becoming contracted and tightened, giving them a 'scrunched-up' feeling. However, these reactions can come on just as often when you are at work, sitting behind a desk and concentrating hard. Therefore it's important to be able to do an appropriate exercise to counteract such symptoms whenever they occur, especially in the workplace.

1. To unwind stiffness at the back of the neck, whether you are seated or standing, first align your head, neck and spine in as straight a vertical line as you can manage.
2. Drop your shoulders and then pull them back. Stretch your neck upwards, as if the top of your head were being pulled towards the ceiling, as hard as you can. Hold this stretch to a count of three, exhaling slowly as you complete the stretch. Do this several times, until you become aware of the difference between the taut feelings and the looser, relaxed ones.
3. The next part of this exercise can be done either sitting on an upright chair or standing up. Rotate your right shoulder gently in a forward, upward and backward pattern of motions, as if describing the arc of a circle.
4. Stretch your right arm as far downwards as you comfortably can, with the palm of your hand facing forwards. Try to feel each part of your arm stretching, right down to your fingertips. Visualize your fingers and hand being pulled down towards the floor. Hold this position for a count of three, exhaling slowly as you come to the third count. Repeat this part of the exercise using your left shoulder.
5. Rotate your right shoulder as before, but when you stretch your arm, have the back of your hand facing forward, and imagine your thumb stretching, being pulled towards the floor. As above, hold the stretch for a count of three, slowly exhaling.
6. Repeat with the left shoulder as the point of rotation.

These exercises can be done as often or as seldom as you like, at any odd minute throughout the day. Even if you don't do the entire series of shoulder rotations, whenever your neck or shoulders feel tense, pull your shoulders down and back, and stretch your neck straight upwards gently. The combination of rotational movement and stretching should help to loosen up and alleviate the tension in that tight triangle of neck and shoulders.

Exercise 2. Arm-Whirling Rotations

To relieve stiffness in the shoulders

1. From a standing or sitting position, stretch your arms outwards, and slowly rotate them forwards and backwards, tracing an initially small, tight arc from the shoulders.
2. Do this exercise for two minutes, at a rate of 60 to as many as 120 rotations per minute. As you improve, your arms will feel less heavy and tired after doing the exercise – and after carrying a heavy bag of groceries.

Exercise 3. Leg Lunges

To build strength in the leg muscles

1. While standing, take one large step forward on to the ball of your left foot. Ensure that your back is erect and vertical. Hold your arms outstretched or firmly on the side of your hips to maintain good control over your balance.
2. Bend both knees simultaneously, pressing your feet down, holding the downward pressure for a count of three, then relax, and rock softly but firmly on the ball of the left foot for another count of from three to ten.

3. Press your hips forward. Keep your leading knee bent over the line of your ankle, but never further forward. Don't allow the knee to bend beyond a ninety-degree angle.
4. Rising slowly, bring the left leg back to the starting position. Do at least ten and no more than thirty of these forward lunges.
5. After returning to the starting position, execute the same exercise on the right foot and leg, doing an equal number of repetitions.

These exercises can also be reversed by slowly lunging backward. Take a step back, landing again on the ball of the foot. Stay on it, bend both knees, keeping the knee at no more than a ninety-degree angle, and the rear knee just a few inches above the floor. Repeat and alternate as above. These exercises can also be slowed down and combined with Deep Diaphragm Breathing: before beginning, inhale deeply, as described above, and exhale slowly and steadily during the exertion phase. Repeat the slow breathing pattern while holding the exercise position, and again after releasing it.

Exercise 4. 'Tilting Teapots'

To increase the strength and flexibility of the lower back

1. Stand with your feet spread about eighteen inches or a little more than a hip-width apart. Hold the palms of your hands against the sides of your hips, squeezing firmly.
2. Gently lean to the left, and rock back and forth for a count of ten, bending your left shoulder down and to the side. You can lean your upper back slightly backward, but do not lean forward.
3. Slowly return to the upright position, and repeat.

The gentle force of this exercise strengthens the lower back, and, to a lesser extent, the shoulders and upper back. All these movements should be smooth, and definitely not the intermittent, stop-start jerking motion that is sometimes seen. Repeat all these movements, alternating sides, for three to six minutes. This exercise, once learned, can also be combined with Deep Diaphragm Breathing, as described in Exercise 3, above.

Exercise 5. Abdominal Crunches

To build the strength of the stomach muscles

These exercises are intended to firm and strengthen your abdominal muscles, and, secondarily, your lower back.

1. Lying on your back on a mat or large bed, stretch out, pointing your legs straight in front of you.
2. Sit up to about a forty-five degree angle, lifting your arms over your head, and then gradually move your torso forward, exhaling as you go.
3. Reach towards your toes with your fingers, even if you can't touch them; just go forward as far as you can without great discomfort (though a bit of stretching is good). Try to keep your back as straight as you can, and don't bend the knees.
4. Inhaling gently, return to the initial position.
5. Now bend your right leg up, so that your knee is above and to the right of your chest. Your right hand can rest on this knee, while your left hand supports your right heel and ankle.
6. Gently lift and pull your right heel inwards towards the centre of your abdomen, but not all the way. Exhale. At this point, keep your shoulder flat against the mat and your left leg in front of you for a few seconds.
7. Now make small, upward-pressing movements with your

head and upper torso, as you rhythmically move your right leg slowly further upwards towards the right shoulder, for a count of three. In this, you are opposing the upward lift of the head against the movement of the right leg.

8. Now return to the original position, with both legs and back flat on the mat. Inhale. In doing this exercise, move the leg as far as you can without undue stress, but no further; the object is to place a little extra tension on the abdominal muscles temporarily.

9. After each movement, slowly relax, then repeat the exercise on the opposite side. Repeat several times, but no more than five sets in the beginning, and increase by one repetition each week, if you feel your ability increasing.

Exercise 6. The Hamstring Stretch

To increase the flexibility of the lower body

1. While sitting on a mat on the floor, extend one of your legs straight out in front of you. Place the heel of your other foot against the thigh of the extended leg, as close in as you can.

2. Stretch first your right arm as far forward as possible, towards your toes, ensuring that the position isn't unduly painful. Inhale, count to three, and release.

3. Repeat, using your left arm.

4. Finally, reverse the whole exercise by extending the other leg forward, and pressing the foot of the just-stretched leg against it. Stretch both arms forward, as described above. Do up to ten sets of these stretches, alternating legs.

Progressive Relaxation Techniques

These exercises will teach you how to relax, so that you will be able to calm your body when you're feeling anxious. The training works by tensing and then relaxing muscles by groups. The exercises reduce the flow of adrenaline in your body, which is known to keep anxiety levels high. There are two reasons for relaxing in this more intensive way. First, when you are suffering from anxiety, tension becomes such a habit that you begin not to notice it. These exercises will make you aware of the differences between tension and relaxation. Second, by tensing a muscle, we also temporarily fatigue it and so make it easier to relax.

You will feel some physical sensations when you are doing these exercises: heaviness and warmth, changing to a feeling of lightness, as if floating. You may also notice a slight tingling in your fingers and toes. These sensations are an indication that you are doing the exercises correctly. The immediate goal of relaxation training is to reduce the muscle tension in your body to far below the level you have become accustomed to – and to do this any time you wish.

Learning these exercises involves:

- Doing them at least once a day for seven days. By the end of the first week, you can use them at the first sign of anxiety, or just before doing something that makes you feel anxious.
- After the first week, trying to relax in 'bursts' throughout the day. Do this by deep breathing, tensing your arms briefly, or just by thinking yourself into a relaxed state. You can relax like this in almost any situation: at work, while waiting in a queue at a shop, even while walking down the street.

Relaxation is a physical skill, just like learning to swim or to type; in order to stay good at it, you must practise regularly. Once you've learned this technique, you'll be able to control anxiety in stressful situations, by applying relaxation in bursts. Such rapid and more sudden releases of tension create a kind of momentum, which efficiently eases the muscles into a milder resting level.

Watch out for two common mistakes:

1. Make sure you *don't tense up too hard*. You should never cause pain with these exercises. If one of them hurts you – omit it.
2. *At first, don't release the tension slowly*. Relax suddenly, so that you emphasize the contrast between tension and relaxation.

Practise the exercises at least once a day. Choose a time when the house is quiet, when you feel relaxed and won't be rushed. Make sure that the room temperature is comfortable, and that you're not feeling any hunger pangs. It's best to have a regular time of day devoted to them, so that they become a part of your routine. If you work at an office job, early evening is a good time. Allow twenty to thirty minutes for them, when you know you won't be interrupted. Begin by lying on your back or sitting comfortably in an armchair, but don't cross your legs. Do each set of exercises in each muscle group at least five times, and no more than ten times, before proceeding to the next group.

1. Relaxing Hands and Arms

1. Try to keep the rest of your body relaxed, and clench your right fist. Notice the feeling of tension in your fingers, your thumb and the palm of your hand, your knuckles and the back of your hand. Keep your fist clenched and notice the tension in your wrist and up into your arm.

2. Still concentrating, let your hand relax *suddenly*. Let your fingers relax, and notice how warm they feel; also, your arms should feel heavy. Breathe slowly and continue concentrating on your right hand for a few moments.

3. Switch your attention to your left hand, going through all the same procedures you have just followed with your right. Let your breathing become slow and regular after each relaxation exercise. By the end, both arms should feel heavy.

2. Relaxing Shoulders, Neck and Face

Shoulders

1. Concentrate on your shoulders and the upper part of your arms, your chest and your back. Tense these muscles by hunching your shoulders. Hold them in that uncomfortable position, concentrating on the tension across the tops of your shoulders, in your neck, and in your upper chest, back and arms. Notice how your breathing is affected by tensing these muscles.

2. Quite suddenly, let go and relax. Let your arms become heavy and soft again, and slump your shoulders as low as you can. Your breathing will become slow and regular, and you will feel much more comfortable.

Neck

3. Now concentrate on your neck. Tense the muscles by pushing your head back. If you are lying on a bed or sitting in a chair, push your head back against a pillow or cushion. Be careful not to tense too hard; you should feel a zone of

tautness in the back of your neck, the back of your head, and across your shoulders, which pushes forward to the jaw and the lower face.

4. Bring your head forward, and let your neck muscles relax quickly. If you have been standing up or sitting up in a chair, your head should drop forward a little and feel floppy and pleasantly heavy; your breathing should become slow and regular.

Face

5. Begin by frowning and creasing your forehead emphatically, then add to the tension by closing your eyes as tightly as you can.
6. Make your face tenser yet by clenching your jaw, pursing your lips and pressing your tongue against the roof of your mouth.
7. Concentrate on the tension throughout your face, then suddenly relax all the muscles. When your breathing returns to normal, your arms will feel pleasantly heavy, your shoulders and jaw will sag, and your face will feel soft.

3. Relaxing the Back and Stomach

1. Concentrate on the feelings in your back, producing tension by arching it slightly. Hold the position, and try to notice which muscles in your back are working.
2. Relax your back suddenly, relishing the contrast and slowing your breathing.
3. Tense your stomach muscles by pulling them in, as if making yourself look as thin as possible. Hold it for a long count, concentrating on the tension.

4. Gently let your stomach return to normal, and notice how comfortable you feel. Now you're breathing slowly and regularly.

4. Relaxing Legs and Feet

1. Straighten your right leg (but if you're sitting on a chair, keep your heel on the floor) and point your toes down and away from you, curling them under your foot. Feel the tension in your toes, the sole of your foot, the arch and the ankle, as well as in your calf and behind your knees – right up the leg into the thigh muscles.
2. Suddenly relax your leg. Your foot will feel soft and floppy, your leg heavy and lazy. Again, your breathing slows.
3. Repeat this exercise with your left leg, concentrating intently as you tense and relax.

5. Visual Imagery

Some people find that despite feeling physically relaxed, worrisome thoughts still intrude occasionally, preventing the mind from feeling as relaxed as the body. To counteract this, not only when doing relaxation exercises but at any time, visualize a number of imaginary scenes, which you can associate with pleasure and enjoyment – such as lying on a tropical beach, or sitting in front of a blazing fire. Make these images as detailed as possible, then empty your mind of any remaining negative thoughts. Some people find it helpful to do this before beginning the physical parts of the relaxation exercises.

6. Finishing a Relaxation Session

Your breathing should be slow and gentle. Your arms, legs and head should be heavy. Your face, neck, shoulders and stomach should feel soft. Just lie there for a while, as if letting your body sink downwards. Now think 'CALM' each time you breathe out. Repeat ten to twenty times. Conclude the session gradually. Let your muscles get ready to move again, as you think 'Three, two, one, awake'.

CHAPTER TWELVE

NUTRITION AND THE SUPERYOUNG

Man and the animals are merely a passage and a channel for food.
Leonardo da Vinci

How well we age is only partly determined by genetic inheritance: much of it can be controlled by the way we eat, exercise, and our overall approach to life – factors under our direct control. One of the earliest findings of my research with the superyoung was that nutrition cannot be divorced from life style: it is an integral part of it. Food can and ought to be a pleasure, rather than a source of anxiety. As the data from the superyoung project have made clear, food is beneficial primarily when it creates a holistic state of good health, which allows people to fulfil their goals as individuals.

Most nutrition plans are based on a single, catchy idea which is presented with great emphasis, rather than giving top priority to sound guiding principles. Instead of enforcing sweeping prescriptions and prohibitions, which only invite cheating, it might be a better idea to build into the diet more choice, allowing for the natural variability in tastes and appetites that exists in the real world. Three square meals a day, including a good breakfast, is only one ideal among many. Some researchers now support the notion of eating several small, highly nutritious meals at regular intervals throughout the day, a strategy known as grazing. This approach prevents the metabolism from plunging up or down, while providing a constant supply of food energy.

If you take pleasure and enjoyment into account – as the

superyoung generally do – rather than simply basic energy requirements, variety and flexibility become prominent, positive values. You cannot eat the same foods all the time, and instructing people to do so is programming failure. One lesson we can all learn from the superyoung is that continually introducing novelty into the diet is the key to success.

The body 'knows' or 'feels' its basic needs, and it valiantly compensates for whatever bad behaviour its proprietor throws at it. It has regular rhythms, and strives for balance by a process called *homeostasis*. According to this process, a state of disequilibrium is set up in the body whenever the internal conditions deviate from a normal steady state. Thus, when the nutritional supply is depleted in the body, the person feels hunger, food is sought and eaten, and so equilibrium is restored. When the body receives too little food, it stores energy as fat and slams the brakes on the metabolism. Dieting itself can often make people feel miserable and add further stresses to life, and mild negative moods can increase food cravings, or make them erratic. The positive effects on mood created by indulging these short-term cravings are brief, lasting less than two hours, and are more likely to be psychological than biochemical in nature. This is soon followed, in about 40 per cent of cases, by feelings of guilt for having 'failed'.

Low-calorie diets can even be dangerous. There may be short-term weight loss, but at the expense of muscle wastage. Furthermore, the effect is often so short-lived as to be illusory. When you go off the diet, your body will temporarily need less energy, as there is less lean muscle to be serviced; then, if you revert to the previous dietary regime, whatever it was, even more weight will be piled on. The main reason people regain weight and then overshoot, gaining even more weight after boomerang dieting, is that they continue to eat the same over-large portions as before. When more food is consumed than is needed, the body stores it – in the form of fat.

Healthier living is not something to be endured as a prescriptive, pleasure-free regimen; it can and should bestow immediate, recognizable benefits, which require only modest adjustments in life style and quickly lead to further progress. Left to their own devices, people generally prefer to eat what is good for them. However, even as we become accustomed to the widely accepted notion that certain foods can cause or contribute to disease, while other foods may help prevent it, 'wellness' has always been more than the absence of illness, much more. And if a food substance has been implicated in a disease, such as excess sugar in the case of diabetes, then it is not unwarranted to suspect that the same food when used to excess may have long-term detrimental effects on the ageing process, even if it does not actually produce disease.

There are two current theories of ageing that pertain to nutrition. One influential body of evidence, called the oxidation thesis, claims that ageing results, at least in part, from the breakdown of certain toxic by-products of the body's normal biochemistry. Oxidation is one of the biochemical ways that energy is liberated for use. However, when the body uses oxygen it also sets loose elements called oxygen free radicals, which are highly reactive forms of oxygen. When they react with delicate blood fats, genes, DNA and proteins, they can damage them. It's particularly serious in the case of DNA, for it can create defects in the information that is stored in the molecules, or miniature breakages in the ways the coded information is retrieved; that, in turn, can cause the enzymes and membranes to function less effectively.

Unstable free radicals are not only created by the body's normal use of oxygen: many of the substances and pollutants encountered in everyday life, such as those in car exhaust gases, cigarette smoke and alcohol, have the effect of increasing both the number and the activity of these harmful substances in our bodies. These oxidants also appear in greater numbers when we are fighting off an infection; the immune response system uses some of these oxidants to kill off outside invaders. The sun's ultraviolet rays also stimulate the formation of free radicals, and have been shown to damage DNA molecules. The degree to which your skin wrinkles is almost directly proportional to how much exposure to sunlight has taken place over the course of a lifetime.

The cumulative damage thus provoked has been associated not only with ageing but also with several serious diseases, including heart and circulatory system ailments, strokes, diabetes, cataracts, arthritis and cancer. Lipo-fuscin, a brown pigment which produces the small brown patches on the face and the back of the hands known as 'age spots' or 'liver spots', has also been shown to be a marker of the adverse effects of oxygen free radicals.

The body has its own ways of controlling free radicals, but as we age, prolonged exposure to the factors that cause them to form eventually overwhelms these defence mechanisms. However, changes in diet and lifestyle can inhibit the production and reduce the toxic effects of free radicals – and may alleviate or postpone the symptoms of ageing and some of the diseases associated with it. Researchers at Edinburgh University's Cardiovascular Research Unit have discovered that the risk of angina is nearly three times higher in men who eat a diet low in vitamins C and E, which have powerful anti-oxidant functions, irrespective of other factors such as weight, blood pressure and cholesterol levels.

It is currently believed that such dietary deficiencies contribute as much as 35 per cent of the attributable risk of the major diseases associated with age – cancer, cardiovascular disease and mature-onset diabetes. In addition, in older people, mild inadequacies in these nutrients may contribute to complaints such as inexplicable, uncharacteristic feelings of lethargy, backaches, persistent headaches, and joint pains. Traditionally, the reduced food intake of older people has been regarded as a normal response to lower energy use; as a result, subclinical deficiencies are almost certainly much more prevalent than has sometimes been thought. For instance, the tissues of older people ordinarily contain lower concentrations of vitamin C than do those of younger people. We cannot synthesize vitamin C in our bodies, nor can we store it up to be used later for difficult, stressful conditions. Therefore, our daily diet needs to take in plenty of it, especially if we wish to slow down what has been accepted in the past as the normal ageing process.

Natural anti-oxidants are active compounds which inactivate the free radicals before they can do any damage, by becoming harmlessly oxidized themselves. They work together in different combinations, often synergetically, to absorb or neutralize the harmful parts of the molecules, making them safe while at the same time protecting intact body tissues. Vitamins A, C and E, and the minerals selenium, zinc and copper, are free-radical scavengers that can slow down or interrupt these destructive processes. These nutrients are found mainly in fresh fruit, vegetables and wholegrain cereals (see Table 1).

Table 1. Food Sources of Anti-Oxidants

Vitamin A

Carrots	Cod liver oil	Spinach	Liver	Red cabbage
Butter	Chicory	Cheese	Parsley	Egg yolk
Watercress	Herring	Cherries	Papaya	Cantaloupe melon
Sweet potatoes	Watermelon	Bananas	Turnips	Peaches
Pumpkin	Nectarines	Winter squashes	Chick peas	Avocados
Blackberries	Blackcurrants	Cranberries	Raspberries	Strawberries
Passion fruit	Pineapple	Plums	Kiwi fruit	Mangos
Broccoli	Brussels sprouts	Cauliflower	Lettuce	

Vitamin C

Citrus fruits	Green peppers	Strawberries	Raspberries	Kiwi fruit
Blackcurrants	Cranberries	Gooseberries	Mangos	Melon
Papayas	Peaches	Pineapple	Apricots	Nectarines
Watercress	Radishes	Potatoes	Cauliflower	Parsley
Asparagus	Broccoli	Cabbage	Kale	Spinach
Leeks	Bananas	Turnips	Sweetcorn	Onions
Brussels sprouts	Celery	Peas	Tomatoes	

Vitamin E

Wheat germ oil	Sunflower seed oil	Safflower oil
Rapeseed oil	Margarine	White vegetable fat
Wheat germ	Whole grains	Soya bean products
Almonds	Hazelnuts	Peanuts
Asparagus	Salmon	Mackerel
Dark leafy greens	Clams	Scallops
Prawns		

Zinc

Wheat germ	Whole grains	Brazil nuts
Mushrooms	Fish	Shellfish
Liver	Sunflower seeds	

Selenium

Brazil nuts	Celery	Sunflower seeds	Onions
Turkey (dark meat)	Radishes	Dairy products	Broccoli
Garlic	Crab meat	Lobsters	Oysters
Mushrooms	Tuna	Swordfish	Plaice or Sole
Beef	Rye	Barley	Oats

Other anti-oxidants obtained from our diets include a wide spectrum of substances classified as bioflavonoids, which are present in fruit, red wine, green tea and herbs. Melatonin, the natural biological component produced within the pineal gland, is also known to have powerful anti-oxidant effects, and is soluble both in water and the body's oils. Researchers in Scotland have also been examining the beneficial effects of free-radical scavengers found in extracts of common herbs and spices such as paprika, sage and thyme.

Another theory of how the ageing process can be accelerated (and, alternatively, retarded) by the diet, formulated in 1989 by British medical scientists Anna Furth and John Harding, focuses on some of the detrimental effects of excess sugar. Still controversial, their theory is based on the observation that if you put proteins into a concentrated solution of sugar, they undergo a striking change: through a process known as glycation, the sugars slowly bind themselves on to the proteins. The proteins turn brown as the sugar permanently alters their molecular structure, and, it is argued, the way they function from that point onward. This process leads to an irreversible cross-linking: amino-acid groups attach on to other proteins until they form large clumps composed of many molecules. These abnormal clumps are known by the fortuitous acronym AGE, meaning Advanced Glycation End-products. AGEs are believed to accumulate as we grow older. Moreover, the free-radical processes noted above also contribute to this damaging cross-linking process, though they may not be essential to it.

The body needs glucose as a fuel for the brain, red blood cells and kidneys. Of course, the need for it increases with exercise and stress. However, it is not merely coincidental that the older people become, the more pronounced and prolonged is the rise in blood glucose after they eat a sugary snack. This process may also have an impact on collagen, the fibrous, interwoven structural protein found in skin, tendons, the matrix of bones, and basement membrane (the permeable tissue lining the capillaries, the filtration units of the kidneys, and larger blood vessels). In fact, collagen, with its characteristic triple helix fibres, is the body's most abundant protein. The degree of collagen glycation is directly related to the amount of time it has been exposed to the action of sugars, a period that is obviously longer the older you are.

Collagen in the skin diminishes by about 1 per cent annually throughout normal adult life, and it becomes less elastic. If you could examine collagen by itself outside the body, you would see that it looks something like soft, flexible rubber, with tensile strength and the ability to be twisted into various shapes. Running through the skin's collagen are fine networks of elastic fibres. With increasing age, these tissues lose some of their elasticity and stiffen up. Sagging wrinkles occur when the skin loses its elastic recoil properties, and fails to snap back into its usual shape.

Maintaining collagen is one of the most important factors in retaining a youthful appearance of the face. The collagen fibres begin to break down around the age of twenty-five because the skin retains less water; it is at that point that the skin begins to appear drier. Vitamin C helps to form collagen, giving the skin a youthful elastic quality, and thus maintaining a healthy, plumped-up appearance.

Other important organic substances are also affected by sugar: for example, haemoglobin, the protein that carries oxygen in the blood, is glycated five times as rapidly with fructose as with glucose, and the common protein albumin, which contains a good proportion of the essential amino acids, can be cross-linked ten times as quickly. The accumulation of damage from eating sugary foods in excess of the body's needs eventually results in overpowering the repair and protective systems that maintain proteins.

While this theory is clinically credible, much of the evidence backing it up is based entirely upon chemical experiments carried out in laboratories, which involve the exposure of proteins to glucose under artificial conditions rather than by studying live subjects. However, long-term tests with human subjects would be costly and questionable for obvious ethical reasons.

Refined sugar is often described as containing 'empty calories' – providing energy, yes, but with no useful nutrients. As the British clinical scientist John Yudkin pointed out as long ago as 1964, sugar has the effect of displacing more nutritious foods. Refined white sugar is far from being a 'natural' product: juice from the sugar beet is treated with lime, carbon dioxide and soda ash, then passed through an ion exchanger, and finally treated with sulphur dioxide. Sugars of all types are nearly ubiquitous in prepared foodstuffs; unfortunately, they are often there only for their taste. Sweet foods tend to encourage overeating, by suppressing bitter tastes and emphasizing sweet tastes.

Some people are killing themselves with too much food. Once they get to be overweight, they feel less able to exercise, and soon they're trapped in a spiral of disastrous behaviour. The overeating thus encouraged raises the risk of heart disease and diabetes as a consequence of obesity. The pancreas, the organ that produces insulin, becomes overstimulated, and the balancing act of homeostasis is compromised. Nowhere in the course of human evolution has man ever adapted to such a constant bombardment of pure sugars for so long a time. And the more overweight a person becomes, the greater the risk of mature onset diabetes, which in turn raises blood cholesterol levels.

My research has convinced me that both the free-radical and excess sugar theories have a degree of truth. They need not necessarily be seen as mutually exclusive; in fact, I've concluded that they work together in a kind of synergy. Yet the two theories, as they now stand, do carry slightly differing implications for healthy eating advice and consequent behaviour. The anti-oxidant approach would highlight the value of including more fresh fruits and uncooked or lightly cooked vegetables in the diet. Vitamin E is a bit more problematic to obtain in large amounts from food alone, but reasonable levels can be obtained from wheatgerm, nuts, margarine and some cooking oils. For those who feel particularly at risk for having an inadequate diet while under stress, the careful use of vitamin and mineral supplements can be recommended.

The sugar glycation thesis would counsel against adding any extra sugars to the diet, particularly in the form of sweet snacks. Because sugars appear naturally in many foods, eating healthy amounts of complex carbohydrates, soluble fibre and high-protein foods could compensate for this. Soluble fibre is especially important, for it is only partially broken down during digestion, thereby slowing the uptake of sugar into the bloodstream.

A number of other dietary factors also contribute to our ability to cope with stress. Balanced blood chemistry is necessary for maintaining a sense of calmness. A person who consumes mainly acid–producing foods, such as sugars, massive quantities of proteins, overly processed foods made with white flour, and excess caffeine, may feel nervous and sometimes less able to cope with the pressures of life. Too much protein all at once can also deplete your supplies of vitamin B_6, which can lead to jitteriness, insomnia and vague feelings of anxiety.

Prolonged stress can be very ageing: the stomach produces more acidic compounds, and other symptoms are not only uncomfortable but demoralizing, such as fatigue, headaches, insomnia and indigestion. One reason put forward for this is that the individual's alkali reserves become low from having to balance the high-acid producing foods. This is a minor, but distracting, effect. In normal health, the blood is maintained within a narrow band of alkalinity, between pH 7.35 and 7.45. If you're already feeling the bad effects of too much stress, eating foods that produce excess acid sets you up to feel the bodily sensations accompanying anxiety, such as queasiness or edginess. A diet rich in raw vegetables and fruits is a good way to redress this acid–alkali balance. In this respect, frozen fruit and vegetables are just as healthy as fresh foods.

Given the enormous diversity among the participants in the superyoung project, I was surprised to find a broad consensus among them about what constitutes a good diet for positive health: fat levels should be controlled and cholesterol low, and it should include generous quantities of carbohydrates and good proteins from a variety of sources. As a group, the superyoung believe that the risks from excessive eating grow greater throughout life; they also feel attuned to their instincts, and trust them to help evaluate which foods are good for them, and in what amounts.

The superyoung eat an extraordinary variety of foods, even by the most generous American standards. Because they are good socializers, the superyoung dine out more often, and rise cheerfully to the challenge of trying new dishes. There's an element of rebellion in all this, too. Their omnivorous tastes help fulfil their wish to experiment and seek out novelty. They are truly inclusive, enriching their diets with all kinds of food types, from a great number of food sources.

By introducing a wider range of foods into their diet than most of the rest of us consume, the superyoung place themselves at a health advantage in several ways. An obvious point first: the greater the variety in the diet, the better the likelihood of attaining a good balance. (Under this rationale, even dining out, preferably at different places whenever possible, would also be encouraged, as that too could lead to increases in the variation factor.)

A wide variety of foods also helps to ensure a full supply of the amino acids needed to create proteins, which are essential for building and repairing muscles, fighting off disease, and helping to control the hormones that promote a well-regulated metabolism. However, most people in the developed world receive more than adequate intakes of protein. If you eat a reasonably varied diet and ingest sufficient calories, you will undoubtedly get all you need. As little as two to three ounces of protein daily may be more than enough for average needs. The Food and Nutrition Board of the US National Academy of Sciences has proposed that the ideal *minimum* daily intake of protein is 0.57 grams for every kilogram of body weight. This would mean that a person of 10½ stone would require a minimum of only 1.4 ounces of protein daily – roughly the amount in an average tuna or turkey sandwich. Other authorities have recommended as much as twice this amount, and people in special health circumstances, such as pregnant women, are advised to consume somewhat more. The diets of average American and British people usually provide two to three times this minimum amount, about half of which is derived from animal protein sources (see Table 2).

Table 2. Proportions of Calories from Protein Sources

Protein foods	% protein calories
Fish meat and dairy	
Oily fish, e.g. tuna, salmon, trout	45
Milk (skimmed)	40
Lean beef	38
Milk (semi–skimmed)	22
Pulses	
Soyabeans	35
Lentils	29
Split peas	28
Beans	26
Vegetables	
Spinach	49
Watercress	46
Kale	45
Broccoli	45
Cauliflower	40
Brussels sprouts	44
Mushrooms	38
Lettuce	34
Peas	30
Green pepper	22
Cabbage	22
Tomatoes	18
Onions	16
Beetroot	15
Potatoes	11
Grains	
Wheat germ	31
Rye	20
Wheat	17
Wild rice	16

Oatmeal	15
Buckwheat	15
Millet	12
Barley	11
Brown rice	8

Fruits

Lemons	16
Melons	10
Cantaloupe melons	9
Strawberries	8
Oranges	8
Grapes	8
Tangerines	8
Papayas	6
Peaches	6
Pears	5
Bananas	5
Grapefruit	5
Pineapple	3
Apples	1

Nuts and seeds

Pumpkin seeds	21
Sunflower seeds	21
Peanuts	18
Walnuts	13
Sesame seeds	13
Almonds	12
Cashews	12
Hazelnuts	8

However, for the body, all proteins are not equal. Different combinations of the twenty known amino acids are used to create about 150 intermediate compounds and the more than

40,000 proteins known so far to science. This process might be compared to the way the twenty-six letters of the alphabet can form millions of words. While most of the twenty amino acids can be manufactured within the human body, eight cannot: isoleucine, leucine, lysine, methionine, phenylalanine, threonine, tryptophan and valine must be provided by the diet (see Table 3).

Table 3. The Essential Amino Acids

Amino acid	Main functions	Best nutritional sources
Isoleucine	Important in the construction of muscles, and structure of the body	Yogurt, milk, eggs, hazelnuts, yeast, beef, wheat flour
Leucine	Building enzymes and general body proteins	Walnuts, spinach, milk, eggs, beef, wheat flour
Lysine	Growth; tissue repair; calcium absorption; production of antibodies; used to form collagen	Fish, poultry, lamb, beef, milk, eggs, wheat flour
Methionine	Anti-oxidant; helps to break down fats; formation of blood proteins	Yogurt, beans, lentils, liver, fish, beef, eggs, milk, wheat flour
Phenylalanine	Mental processes; appetite reduction; hormones; pigments	Egg white, spinach, beans, peas, milk, beef, wheat flour, chocolate
Threonine	Essential part of many body proteins; recovery	Fish, meat, eggs, milk, wheat flour
Tryptophan	Helps body make niacin; mental processes; mood; sleep	Soya, brown rice, fish, dates, lamb, chocolate, beer, milk, beef, eggs, wheat flour
Valine	Works with isoleucine and leucine	Fish, yeast, milk, chocolate, eggs, beef, wheat flour

The proteins of different foods are composed of different proportions of amino acids. A low concentration of a particular amino acid in any one protein can be compensated for by eating a widely diversified mixture of protein-bearing foods. The wider the variety, the more likely it is that the diet will contain the necessary amounts of each of the essential amino acids. Another important factor is turnover – whether or not all the amino acids need to be consumed every single day for best effect, or only on a fairly regular basis. Proteins which turn over at slower rates, or are renewed more slowly, may be just as important to our long-range well-being as those that are in constant demand. Unfortunately, most scientific studies of nutrition have been of brief duration, and therefore cannot detect such long-term needs.

The issue of programming the best proportions of protein, carbohydrate and fat in the diet is a complex one. Over the years, many experts have attempted to resolve this question with widely varying methods – which, predictably, have arrived at quite different prescriptions. The four main schools of thought are as follows:

1. Decreasing overall intake, while maintaining good nutrition in other respects;
2. Decreasing the amount of protein intake;
3. Decreasing cholesterol and 'bad' fats (saturated fats such as those in egg yolks, butter and red meat), and/or increasing 'good' fats (mostly polyunsaturated fats, such as sunflower oil and margarine); and
4. Increasing carbohydrate intake, especially fruit, vegetables and fibre.

The first approach, that of lowering overall intake, dates back to the pioneering work of the sixteenth-century Venetian nobleman Luigi Cornaro (see page 92). In his book *The Temperate Life (Discorsi della Vita Sobria)*, Cornaro outlined his dietary habits. He had the conviction, based upon assiduous experimentation upon himself, that less was best. Cornaro managed to reduce his daily total food allowance to just 12 ounces (340 grams), washed down with an additional 14 fluid ounces (398 millilitres) of light wine. In terms of calories, this has been estimated to be no more than 2,050 calories a day. For a sedentary man of average weight, that is about 15 per cent less than the daily requirements estimated by modern nutritionists. Cornaro was a pioneer of the grazing strategy: he ate a great variety of foods, though always in small quantities, partaking of four light meals each day. His alcohol intake also moderated further as the years went by. He followed this diet for the last fifty-five years of an active, vigorous life, until his death at the age of ninety-six.

In recent years, the concept that restricting total daily calorie intake prolongs life has become widely accepted by science – with the single caveat that the experiments to date have been conducted on mice, rats and other small mammals. These experiments usually restrict food intake by 20–40 per cent, compared with the normal diet of the control groups. The pay-off has been a 10–20 per cent increase in average lifespans. If extrapolated to human beings, such a strategy could represent an additional fifteen years of life. A perfect laboratory for this approach has existed for centuries on the island of Okinawa, where the people have traditionally eaten a widely varied diet in much smaller quantities than elsewhere in Japan. Researchers have found that the Okinawans actually prefer to eat small meals – on average 20 per cent less than other Japanese people. At least partly as a result of their dietary tradition, the island's male inhabitants live 1.4 years longer than the Japanese average, and the women add three years – a very significant figure for such a large population. Moreover, the rates of death from age-related illnesses on Okinawa are 60 per cent lower than the Japanese average. Other benefits claimed for the reduced-calorie diet include lower blood pressure, improved psychological functioning, and better mobility in later life.

The key to such a dietary scheme is to reduce calories overall, while maintaining the proper proportions of vital nutrients – which, of course, begs the question of what exactly *are* the optimal proportions in a healthy diet. The self-experimenter runs grave risks, needing to navigate between the Scylla of malnutrition and the Charybdis of specific deficiency-induced illnesses. Not enough is known as yet about the long-term effects of the low-calorie regime in human populations. The prudent clinical advice remains the Hippocratic admonition, 'Do no harm.'

The second approach, that of reducing protein intake, goes back to the nearly forgotten achievements of the American physiologist Robert Chittenden, in the early years of the twentieth century. He was trying to answer the difficult question of what amount of protein is sufficient for human needs. What happens if you reduce your protein intake – or, indeed, if you increase it? Chittenden followed Cornaro's example: he experimented on himself. He restricted himself and other healthy male volunteers to a daily limit of forty grams (a mere 1.4 ounces) of protein. He believed that this low-protein regimen was not only safe but also improved intellectual power and physical vigour. He theorized that these benefits accrued because the body was doing less work to rid itself of the excess nitrogen-related products commonly found when protein intake is high. In his view, high levels of protein placed additional stress on the kidneys; therefore, he reasoned, lowering protein intake might lessen the chances of contracting a variety of kidney, heart and circulatory ailments.

Though his pioneering work marked out the lower threshold of protein requirements for healthy young men, Chittenden's beliefs may have been too subjective. The superyoung subjects in my project consumed substantially higher amounts of protein than the Chittenden levels, and they greatly varied their sources of protein. Cross-cultural comparisons and research have shown that no particular harm befalls people who have high protein intakes. (The classic case is that of the South American gauchos, who until recently thrived robustly on a diet composed almost entirely of fresh beef, much to the amazement of Charles Darwin, when he visited the continent.) Of course, if overall food intake continually outstrips a person's energy needs, it will result in obesity.

People who have weight-related problems have been encouraged to try the third approach, that of pursuing a low-fat strategy. In terms of ageing research, the theory goes that what's good for the heart is good for the whole body. Many variations on this theme have been promulgated over the years, usually with the goal of reducing cholesterol (see Table 4), or of reducing the amount of saturated fats in the diet. Some cholesterol is absorbed directly into the bloodstream when the body tries to digest cholesterol-rich foods, and the levels of cholesterol in the blood surge after eating too much saturated fat. Other factors which push it higher are smoking, uncontrollable anxiety levels, and drinking too much coffee (more than five cups a day).

Table 4. Cholesterol in Foods (in milligrams per 100 grams)

Food	mg	Food	mg
Egg yolks	1,260	Canned salmon	90
Boiled eggs	450	Beef	82
Butter	230	Bacon	80
Prawns	200	Haddock	75
Duck	160	Chicken (white meat)	74
Lobster	150	Camembert	72
Double cream	140	Cheddar	70
Stilton	120	Hamburger	68
Chicken (dark meat)	120	Single cream	66
Lamb	110	Pork sausage	53
Pork	110	Fish	50
Clotted cream	100	Ham	33
Sardines	100	Beef stew	30
Turkey (dark meat)	100	Cottage cheese	13
Cream cheese	94	Low-fat yogurt	7
Parmesan	90		

Cholesterol shouldn't be considered in any way an abnormal substance, nor is it something to be feared *per se*. In fact, it is an essential part of every cell in our bodies. It is used to create membranes, including those vital to the brain and nervous system; it's also necessary for the synthesis of oestrogen, the female sex hormone, and testosterone, the male sex hormone. Without following any special diet plan, the body can absorb some of the extra cholesterol coming from the foods we eat. Exactly how much it can cope with depends upon genetic factors, whether a person exercises or not, and other components of the diet, such as soluble fibre (which scavenges cholesterol) and vitamin E (which prevents it from furring up our arteries, causing heart and circulation problems). The best evidence shows that good doses of vitamin E (between 400 and 800 international units daily) can lead to a risk reduction of as much as 47 per cent for non-fatal heart attacks.

There is also strong evidence that a sound diet can reduce the risk of cancer. An excellent report from the US National Academy of Sciences on this subject, released in 1982, surveyed 10,000 previous studies and came to the conclusion that 'the evidence is increasingly impressive that the cancers of most major common sites are influenced by dietary patterns.' Their main recommendation, which has been buttressed and confirmed by subsequent research, was two-pronged: reduce fat intake and increase foods rich in vitamins A, C and E, mostly fruits and vegetables.

In 1997 the US Food and Drug Administration, for the first time in its history, approved a food-specific health claim. Millions of packets of porridge oats now feature a blurb which reads 'Soluble fibre from oatmeal, as part of a low saturated fat, low cholesterol diet, may reduce the risk of heart disease.' To qualify for the FDA claim, a product must contain at least 0.75 grams of soluble fibre from oats per serving. Oats are digested more slowly than many other foods, so their goodness is released over an extended period of time, providing sustained energy as and when it is needed. Humble barley performs similarly; it contains a helpful oil compound called tocotrienol, which gently slows the rate at which cholesterol is produced.

Vegetarianism increased in popularity over the ten years of the superyoung project, particularly in the UK; about a quarter of the subjects in my study pursued vegetarian diets of one sort or another. Yet despite their best intentions, some of them frequently 'lapsed' by including fish or lean meat dishes in their diets, particularly when dining out. Of those subjects who described themselves as either omnivorous or carnivorous, the reasons cited for rejecting vegetarianism revolved around taste preferences, concerns that they would not be satisfied or even feel full after a vegetarian meal, and the fear of becoming anaemic. In general, the superyoung tended to avoid extravagant pastries and cream concoctions, but they did allow themselves the occasional sweet treat. They understood that having an outrageous, sinful dish, if done only rarely, wouldn't do them any harm.

The overall attitudes of the superyoung concerning food and diet were positive. Even among the carnivores, a majority of 60 per cent said that they had increased their consumption of fruits and vegetables. They didn't perceive themselves as being unduly influenced by friends, family members, or health professionals to conform to any particular model or pattern of eating. However, they rightly regarded their own nutritional habits to be within the scope of a healthy life style, based on the latest science. To this degree, they had been positively influenced by new studies and public health education.

Just over 85 per cent of the subjects in my study said that they knew that a healthy diet should be low in fat and high in fibre. To some extent, the superyoung were ahead of these trends, and more apt to put this knowledge into practice: 53 per cent said that they had reduced the quantities of red meat they ate; 60 per cent had increased how often they ate fish; 70 per cent had cut down on between-meal snacks; 75 per cent had reduced the amount of junk food and fast food they ate; and 90 per cent had increased their fruit and vegetable intakes.

The superyoung were also aware of their own occasional, unhealthy eating habits, and said that they regretted them – but not too much. Although they characterized themselves as 'healthy' or 'very healthy', about 75 per cent nonetheless felt that their diet could be further improved. In particular, they worried that their fat intake, although reduced, might still be too high. The vast majority reported that when they were children, and later in their own homes, food had never been an issue of stress or disagreement – not surprising, considering the overall positivism of these people.

The Superyoung Diet

The following recommendations are derived directly from my observations of the subjects in the superyoung study, most of whom devote a great deal of time and energy to the pursuit of personal health. By inviting them to describe their dietary principles and practices in detail, I was able to obtain a wealth of information for analysis and interpretation. These recommendations are based upon the experiences of real people who have found creative ways of eating well and living a healthy, creative life.

At-a-Glance Summary of the Superyoung Diet

1. Five portions of fresh fruits and vegetables a day should be a fundamental target.
2. In preparing fruit and vegetable portions, to benefit from a broad spectrum of nutrients, try to use as many different colours as you can, both on a daily basis and from one day to the next: green and yellow vegetables could be balanced by

red (beetroot, aubergine) and white (turnips, cauliflower). This strategy will provide you with a variety of helpful carotenoids and bioflavonoids. There are around 600 different types of carotenoids in nature, and about fifty of them can be transformed into vitamin A by the body.

3. Experiment with international cuisines, especially those that carry little or no risks to health, such as the southern Mediterranean, Japanese and California-style vegetarian diets. (The California vegetarian diet is a combination of the Mediterranean diet and an organic vegetarian diet with a little more emphasis on exotic mixed fruit drinks.) Try different dishes from different ethnic origins throughout the week, to further increase choice and variety. Simple, savoury recipes, which make ample use of fresh herbs, aromatic vegetables, pungent spices and unusual condiments, create delectable new flavours. (See, for instance, the *High-Flavor, Low-Fat* cookbook series by Steven Raichlen, or *The New Living Heart Diet* by Michael DeBakey and others.)

4. Foods low in saturated fat and cholesterol are best whenever possible. Eat low-fat rather than full-fat cheese. Also try to rotate the use of different fat sources, but always keep them to a minimum. Removing saturated fat from your diet is extremely important. You can get an additional 10 per cent decrease in your cholesterol levels if you replace saturated fat with fruit and vegetables.

5. Exercise personalized portion control – i.e. smaller quantities but sufficient to satisfy your appetite. Find your own minimum effective amounts of your favourite high-protein foods.

6. Ideally, added sugar should be reduced to nil.

7. Reduce added salt, particularly in the form of salt-pickled, smoked and salt-preserved foods.

8. Include a salad in at least one meal every day.

9. Use fresh herbs generously.

10. Use a wide variety of spices.

11. Every now and then, if you have successfully attained some of the objectives described above, reward yourself with a favourite treat – but don't go crazy! Once a week is enough.

12. If for any reason you cannot obtain sufficient anti-oxidant vitamins and minerals in your diet, take supplements as an interim measure. However, these supplements probably cannot correct the deficiencies of a bad diet.

13. It might also be advisable to use anti-oxidant supplements during periods of great stress, particularly if you are experiencing apparently unresolvable feelings of anger or anxiety, or somatic symptoms such as poor sleep, palpitations or headaches.

14. Learn to eat at regular times.

15. Never eat when not hungry, and stop eating the moment you reach the point of satiety.

16. Do not exceed four cups of coffee in a single day, or drink anything with caffeine in it within four hours of the time you wish to go to sleep.

17. Opt for low-calorie desserts whenever possible – fruit is always the better choice.

18. You may find that some organic food staples, though more expensive, are better value for money in terms of taste and nutritional quality. Organic produce is grown without the use of polluting artificial fertilizers, organophosphates and synthetic pesticides.

19. Try not to overcook fresh vegetables. The vitamins and other nutrients in them are better preserved by cooking them quickly or by using a microwave oven well.

20. Have at least one eight fluid ounce (230 ml) glass each of fruit juice and vegetable juice every day. Pure fruit juices are healthier than sweetened beverages such as lemonade.

21. For those who are mathematically minded, I recommend eating from 60 to 70 per cent of your food in the form of complex carbohydrates, including fruit, vegetables, beans

and grains. Protein sources, varied greatly, should contribute from 15 to 20 per cent of calories daily. (Good alternative sources of protein include beans, lentils, seeds and nuts; see Table 2, page 248). The remainder, ranging from 15 to 20 per cent, can be from fatty substances, but never more than about 5–10 per cent from saturated, animal-sourced fats.

22. Chew your food thoroughly and slowly. Sip drinks, whether soft or alcoholic, slowly, rather than gulping them down.

23. Look for new substitutes to make your nutrition plan easier and more enjoyable. For example, carob sweets and carob-chip biscuits may be good replacements for those who find chocolate irresistible.

24. Remember that there are a number of substances which deplete the body's vitamin levels. The worst culprits are alcohol, cigarettes and coffee, all of which diminish the levels of practically every vitamin group.

SUGGESTED READING

Argyle, Michaèl, The Social Psychology of Leisure. London: Penguin (1996).

Banner, Lois, In Full Flower: Aging Women, Power, and Sexuality. New York: Alfred A. Knopf (1992).

Breytspaak, L. M., The Development of Self in Later Life. Boston: Little Brown (1984).

Cherlin, A. and F. Furstenberg, The New American Grandparent. New York: Basic Books (1986).

Cusinato, Mario, Parenting Over the Family Life Cycle. New York: John Wiley & Sons (1994).

DeBakey, Michael, Antonio M. Gotto and Lynne W. Scott, The New Living Heart Diet. New York: Simon and Schuster (1996).

Department of Health, The Health of the Nation: A Strategy for Health in England. London: Her Majesty's Stationery Office (1992).

Dorfman, Rachelle A., Aging into the 21st Century: The Exploration of Aspirations and Values. New York: Brunner/Mazel (1994).

Dowling, Colette, Red Hot Mamas: Coming into Our Own at 50. London: HarperCollins (1996).

Fentem, P. H. (ed), Good Health – Is There a Choice? London: Macmillan (1981).

Friedan, Betty, The Fountain of Age. London: Cape (1993).

Gibson, Hamilton, The Emotional and Sexual Lives of Older People. London: Chapman and Hall (1991).

Hayflick, Leonard, How and Why we Age. New York: Ballantine Books (1994).

Hess, Thomas M. (ed), Aging and Cognition: Knowledge Organization and Utilization. Amsterdam: North Holland (1990).

Honess, Terry and Krysia Yardley (eds), Self and Identity: Perspectives Across the Lifespan. Boston: Routledge & Kegan Paul (1987).

Jong, Erica, Fear of Fifty. London: Chatto & Windus (1994).

Ludwig, Frederick C. (ed), Life Span Extension: Consequences and Open Questions. New York: Springer (1991).

McGreat, Cathleen E., The Family Across Generations: Grand-parenthood. New York: John Wiley & Sons (1994).

Nemiroff, Robert R. and Calvin A. Colarusso (eds), New Dimensions in Adult Development. New York: Basic Books (1990).

Neustatter, Angela, Look the Demon in the Eye. London: Michael Joseph (1996).

Pillemer, Karl R. and Kathleen McCartney (eds), Parent–Child Relations Throughout Life. Hillsdale, New Jersey: Lawrence Erlbaum Associates (1991).

Raichlen, Steven, High-Flavor, Low-Fat cookbook series. New York: Viking (1995).

Ridgway, Judy with Jane Griffin, Food for Sport. London: Boxtree (1994).

Robbins, John, Diet for a New America. Walpole, New Hampshire: Stillpoint Publishing (1992).

Rowe, Dorothy, Time On Our Side: Growing in Wisdom, Not Growing Old. London: HarperCollins (1994).

Russell, Charles H., Anthony P. Russell and Inger Megaard, Good News about Aging. New York: John Wiley & Sons (1989).

Schaie, K. Warner and J. Geiwitz, Adult Development and Ageing. Boston: Little Brown (1982).

Seraganian, P. (ed), Exercise Psychology: The Influence of Physical Exercise on Psychological Processes. New York: John Wiley & Sons (1993).

Sheehy, Gail, New Passages: Mapping Your Life Across Time. London: HarperCollins (1996).

Smolak, Linda, Adult Development. Englewood Cliffs, New Jersey: Prentice-Hall (1993).

Steinem, Gloria, Moving Beyond Words. London: Bloomsbury (1994).

Van Hasselt, Vincent B. and Michel Hersen (eds), Handbook of
   Social Development: A lifespan Perspective. New York:
   Plenum Press (1992).
Young, Michael and Tom Schuller, Life After Work: The
   Arrival of the Ageless Society. London: HarperCollins (1990).

INDEX

Figures in italics refer to tables.